FINDING GLOBAL PEACE AND THE NEW WORLD ORDER

EDITOR

Emmanuel Orihentare Eregare, PhD

First Edition, August, 2021

Published By
Babcock University General Education Studies Unit,
Nigeria, West Africa.

Printed in Lagos, Nigeria By
FN Print Venture/Christ Coming Books
+234-70305088, 08023602885

FINDING
GLOBAL
PEACE
AND THE NEW
WORLD
ORDER
EDITOR
Emmanuel Orihentare Eregare, PhD

The Editorial Committee Members

1. Professor Philemon O. Amanze,
   Babcock University, Nigeria, West Africa

2. Professor Ante Jeroncic,
   Andrews University, Michigan, United States of America

3. Professor Nehemiah M. Nyaundi,
   University of Eastern Africa, Kenya, East Africa

4. Professor Nkosiyabo Zvandasara Zhou,
   Solusi University, Zimbabwe, South Africa

5. Professor Robert Osei-Bonsu,
   Adventist University of Africa, Kenya, East Africa

6. Marci S. Andersen,
   Loma Linda University, United States of America

General Editor
Emmanuel Orihentare Eregare
M.A (Religion), MA (History), PhD. (Church History)
Babcock University, Nigeria, West Africa
eregare@babcock.edu.ng/dr.eregare@gmail.com
+2348067676676, +2348084737771, +2348127854405

Table of Contents

Preface

The reason for writing this book is quite simple. It seeks to redress on what everyone should expect or live by as the globe moves and raises higher, the banner of ecumenical movements towards finding peace, health and the one world system of governance before the Second Coming of Jesus Christ. The seeming shifts in the biblical definitions on finding peace, securing health and safety and the establishment of the New World Order have uniquely been redefined through the historical, scientific and especially the biblical definitions. Nonetheless, I have been inspired to employ this study through some inter-disciplinary scholars from the fields of History and International Studies, Theology and Religious Studies, Public Health and Basic Sciences; yet using descriptive and analytical methods. May you find and experience timeless primitive godliness as you read through the pages of this book.

-Emmanuel Orihentare Eregare, PhD.
Babcock University, Nigeria, West Africa

Foreword

It is an incontrovertible fact that the common global human needs on earth are peace, health, and security. The nation-states and international organizations have failed to completely redress these human needs. Many anticipated that a state of utopia will be ushered into the world through the New World Order which is a highly organized movement, made up of the United Nations, Ecumenical movements and Elite Clubs.

Unfortunately, none of these institutions have been able to address the growing wave of insecurity, climate change, wars, pandemic effects, economic, political and religious crises. The advent of COVID-19 has brought to the fore conflicting philosophical, scientific, and biblical discourses on the probable media through which the New World Order will be established. This has left humans with various unresolved speculations that need clarifications.

The New World Order is a movement that many believe will rise to bring about the end of human crisis on earth. Nonetheless, the ultimate goal of establishing the New World Order is to identify, understand and redress the common global challenges. This will, in turn, provide peace and safety on earth before the coming of our Lord and Saviour, Jesus Christ.

From this study, scholars have been able to establish facts from the fields of History and International Studies, Basic Sciences, Religious and Theological Studies, that the potential of this movement has the capacity of turning humanity against God. No wonder, various scholars in this study attest to the fact that the New World Order shall be orchestrated through a secret conspiracy.

This work therefore, through a systematic and interdisciplinary study attempts to examine various philosophical concepts in order to unravel the complexity on the thoughts and understanding surrounding not just the claimed manipulations on the secrete conspiracy of either the Papacy or elite groups in a bid to achieve the one system of governance but as well as the COVID-19, a non-military war and saga and the implications in relations to human salvation in Christ Jesus. This book also unveils that the Bible, most especially, is not completely silent about this secret end time conspiracy for global peace and safety.

This edited work by Dr. Eregare and the other distinguished authors, who have contributed chapters in this work, aptly address the issues in a lucid manner. This edition tries to also identify and answer questions like: to what extent has the biblical prophecy connected with the global moves by the secret institutions and the development of the New World Order for global peace, health and safety? What is the role of COVID-19 pandemic in connection with the mark or number of the Beast? How has America come into the big picture?

I recommend this book to scholars, professionals, political and religious leaders, and the general public without any reservations as they will find this research illuminating. This study has, through a unique perspective given a clear direction or form through which global peace and safety particularly will be established and operated. I therefore unequivocally recommend this book to the reading public.

Professor Ademola S. Tayo
President/Vice Chancellor, Babcock University,
Nigeria, West Africa

Acknowledgments

Special thanks to the Almighty who gave me the vision, wisdom and strength to embark on these contentious yet germane contemporary issues that is worth assessing critically.

I appreciate the efforts of Professor Philemon O. Amanze, who is the Deputy Vice-Chancellor Academics at Babcock University, for his counsel during the conception, writing and challenges encountered in reaching out to the distinguished authors who contributed chapters on this project. Though, I have not met some of them physically at the moment, yet, they accepted to actualize the dream with me. This, no doubt shows that God led me through the conception of the idea, the selection of the authors, writing, organization and the production of this special edition. Special thanks go to Professor Ademola Stephen Tayo, the Vice-Chancellor/ President of Babcock University who has been supportive of my book ministry for over a decade now and for accepting to write the foreword of this book despite his demanding schedule.

Nonetheless, special appreciation goes to my distinguished editorial team members who have painstakingly, thoroughly and critically peer reviewed each chapter in this book. It is worthy of note to express their sense of humility to accept this project without queries but faith. They are: Professor Ante Jeroncic, a Professor of Ethics and Theology at Andrews University in the United States of America; Professor Nehemiah Nyaundi, a Professor of Religion at the Department of Theology and Religious Studies, University of

Eastern Africa, Kenya, East Africa; Professor Nkosiyabo Zvandasara Zhou, the Dean of the Faculty of Theology and Religious Studies, Solusi University, Bulawayo, Zimbabwe, South Africa; Professor Robert Osei-Bonsu, the Doctor of Philosophy Degree Leader of Biblical-Theological Studies for the Adventist University of Africa, Kenya, East Africa; Marci S. Andersen, who is an Assistant Professor and Practicum Director at the School of Public Health, Loma Linda University, Los Angeles, California in the United States of America.

I appreciate the support of the administrative staff in the Division of the General Studies, Babcock University, Adedamola Odugbemi and Mrs. Oluchi Onuoha. Special thanks go to Drs. Mercy Elegbede, Theodore U. Dickson and Gabriel Masfar and Ezinwanyi Adam for playing special editorial roles in this project. God bless them.

I remember my late father, James Onorakpene Eregare, he was a devoted Seventh-day Adventist minister, who dedicated over four decades of his life into Gospel ministry before his retirement. I appreciate his mentorship when he was still alive to ensure that I followed God's purpose for my life. To my mum, Comfort Eregare, I thank her for always being there to ensure, by the grace of God, that I 'stand tall' as a minister of the Gospel.

I specially thank my wife, Bolanle Eregare (sugar-spice) and our sons, Oghenemine, Oghenemaro and Oghenerukevwe, who have allowed me to sacrifice time and means to ensure the completion of this project.

To God be the glory for the great things He has done. God bless them all for believing in the production of this book.

Dedication

This book is dedicated to God,
the Creator and Sustainer of the universe.

Striving for Peace where there is no Peace

LOVEDAY C. ONYEZOWNU

It is incontrovertibly true that peace is one of the most essential needs of mankind. Without peace a society will be in a state of anarchy, tumult and commotion. In fact, as Youssef puts it, "There is no peace in the world around us, and no peace within us" (2015:138). According to Rummel (n.d.: para. 1) peace has always been among humanity's highest and supreme values. In the absence of peace, sophisticated civilizations with world's most renowned technological and infrastructural development can be destroyed in a twinkle of an eye through war. Thus, peace is necessary for the maintenance and sustenance of the world. Every person in the world, every society and civilization needs peace. No society or civilization can thrive in the absence of peace. In fact, one of the factors that led to the decline of many great civilizations of the world is the absence of peace.

Loveday Chigozie Onyezonwu holds a Doctor of Philosophy in Religious Studies from the University of Ibadan (2014) where he was also a Teaching/Research Assistant for three years. He has lectured at the Religious and Cultural Studies Department, Akwa Ibom State University and the Religious Studies Department, Federal University of Kashere, Gombe State. Currently, he is a lecturer in the Department of Christian Religious Studies, Federal University of Lafia, Nasarawa State, Nigeria. His Area of Specialization is Religious Ethics and his research interests are basically Environmental Ethics and African Ethics. Dr. Onyezonwu is a proud recipient of awards and prizes; author/co-author of several academic papers.

Despite the high level of enlightenment through education and the high sophistication in science together with technological advancement, the world has still been greatly starved of peace. There are many current global situations which have made peace to be wrestled out of the reach of individuals and nations. For many, peace obviously is reducing violence and avoiding violence (Galtung: 1996: 1). But a critical assessment of the happenstances in the world currently would make obvious that there is more to peace than just the absence or drastic reduction at the occurrence of violence. For instance, in some developed countries like the United States of America and the United Kingdom where o-ne would have envisaged a possible availability of peace considering their perceived political and economic stability, still lack peace. For example, a commissioned paper by Hourglass (formerly Action on Elder Abuse) reported that as many as 1 in 5 people in the United Kingdom over the age of 65 have been abused. This suggests a staggering number of 2.7 million victims across the U.K. (Jamie Doward, The Guardian, 29 November, 2020). In the U.S., an estimated 1,203, 808 violent crimes were reported in 2019 according to the FBI National Press Office. Also, in some highly religious nations, like Nigeria, India, etc., where one would have expected that the knowledge of religious truths would birth peaceful individuals who would then make a peaceful society, still experience lack of peace.

From the above viewpoint, it is evident that humanity is so constrained of peace, even in the face of ostensibly 'absence of war'. In fact, it will not be incoherent to aver that peace has seemingly become an endangered species of value. The world is filled with chaos; homes are in peril; there is high divorce rate; there is high rate of promiscuity ranging from adultery, fornication, rape, child pornography, and incest evident in family members sexually defiling fellow members; high rate of single parenthood with single parents traumatically raising emotionally deprived children; transgender controversies; political instability with different corrupt and irresponsible governments succession; starvation which is as a result of the high level of unemployment which has resulted in high crime rates; as well as lots of other moral decadence including cultism, fraud, child trafficking, drug addiction, etc. Also, the world has been witnessing diverse deadly diseases, such as Polio, Spanish flu, Asian flu, Acquired Immunodeficiency Syndrome, Zika Virus, Ebola, Corona virus, etc. surfacing in turns in recent years which have upset global peace. Also, terrorist activities have been reported by the media on daily basis with thousands of lives lost to such attacks. All the aforementioned events and conditions, among others, have deprived global peace.

Thus, this chapter is premised on the possibility of creating an environment of peace even in the midst of a chaotic and violence-ridden world. The enterprise of creating an environment for peace is necessitated by the desire for peace. The desire for peace, the need to create a society in which war plays little or no part has fired human imagination throughout history (Cortright: 2008:25). Despite the continuous advocacy and campaign for peace by peace-loving individuals and peace movements globally, peace tends to be lacking. The world and its governments who define peace merely as 'the absence of war' have tried to offer peace to the world through the prevention of war. But such efforts have yielded unsustainable outcomes. The preoccupation of this chapter will be to advance contributions to the discourse on creating a society where peace wholly thrives. Against this premise, this chapter endeavours to deepen discussions on the quest for sustainable peace from the biblical and ethical perspectives. This study employs qualitative method of research.

Contentions in the Notion of Peace:

The contention in the notion of peace arises from humans' inability to come to a consensus definition of peace. In other words, the contending ideas and opinions of people as regards to the notion of peace have become problematic. According to Youssef, the core of the problem lies in our definition of peace. According to him, the problem is not with God's promise of peace but with human perception; it is a semantic and a comprehension problem stemming from our inability to understand and define what it means to have peace on earth (2015:138). Also, many authors most at times, define peace within a framework which makes it difficult to arrive at an all acceptable or less problematic definition. As Rummel (n.d. para. 4) averred:

> The problem is, of course, that peace derives its meaning and qualities within a theory or framework. Christian, Hindu, or Buddhist will see peace differently, as will pacifist or internationalist. Socialist, fascist, and libertarian have different perspectives, as do power or idealistic theorists of international relations. In this diversity of meanings, peace is no different from such concepts as justice, freedom, equality, power, conflict, class, and, indeed, any other concept.

Another problematic issue to the notion of peace is based on the exclusive focus of literature on the legal and juristic aspects of peace and violence. For instance, Kalin notes that the use of violence, conduct of war, treatment of combatants and prisoners of war, among others, are discussed within a strictly legal context. Though that is necessary, it falls short of addressing deeper philosophical and spiritual issues that must be included in any discussion about religion and peace. Also, "relegating the discourse of peace to social conflict and its prevention runs the risk of neglecting the individual, who is the sine qua non of collective and communal peace" (2013: 220, 223).

The Concept of Peace

As simple as the concept of "peace" may seem, providing a clear-cut definition of it seems more demanding as historic events, ideologies and circumstances have hugely shaped the meaning of it (Olanrewaju, 2013:6). Peace is often a contested concept that has no fixed attribute due to its broad, elusive, subjective or inter-subjective nature since different individuals or groups have defined it in distinctive ways (Tanabe, 2016: 633). Thus, there is little or no agreement on what peace really denotes, though the most popular view of it implies 'an absence of dissension, violence, or war' (Rummel, n.d. para.2).

Accordingly, Hornsby defines peace as the situation or a period of time in which there is no a war or violence in a country or an area (2006:1071). In the article *"Definition of Peace"*, Ojumu (n.d: para.1) gives a detailed elucidation of the concept and submits that peace entails: a state of being calm and quite; a state or quality of living in friendship with somebody devoid of argument; the state in which one restrains him/herself from causing argument or violence; the freedom from war; the ability of one to unite with other people's behaviour or opinion and still be able to tolerate their attitude without complaining. In metaphysical-spiritual conception of peace, Kalin views peace as one of the names of God and an essential part of God's creation which is assigned a substantive value. For Kalin, peace denotes the presence of certain conditions birth an enduring state of harmony, integrity, contentment, equilibrium, repose, and moderation. As a substantive value, peace extends to the domain of both ethics and aesthetics, and it is one of the conditions that produces tranquility in the soul; resisting the temptations of discord, restlessness, ugliness, pettiness, and vulgarity (2013: 221, 223).

According to Cortright, many writers have distinguished between negative peace, which is simply the absence of war, and positive peace, which is the presence of justice (2008:6). In other words, the idea of peace as absence of mutually agreed hostility summarizes the notion of negative peace. Whereas, positive peace is best described by a social condition where multi-culture is respected; multi-ethnic group is loved; multi-idea is welcomed;

multi-religion is embraced; minorities are protected; equality of rights, equity, fairness, guided liberty and freedom are guaranteed (Olanrewaju, 2013:6). Elsewhere, Webel (2007:6) describes 'positive peace' as denoting the simultaneous presence of many desirable states of mind characterized by harmony, justice, equity, etc., while 'negative' peace has historically been denoted as the 'absence of war' and other forms of wide scale violence and human conflict.

Peace Movements

Peace is an old-time concept, dating back to the beginnings of organized society or human civilizations (say around 3000BC) and perhaps even earlier. But until the Renaissance, the conception of peace had not passed beyond the stage of individual thought. In other words, communal conception of peace, as it is today, was birthed during the renaissance. However, it is due to this collective conception of peace that led to the formation of peace movements with many individuals coming together for a singular aim of promoting peace. The origin of peace movement in the real sense of it can be traced to the Dutch merchant, Hugo Grotius and his supporters, who originally distinguished peace from war (Ferrell, n.d: para. 1, 2).

In the opinion of Cortright, peace societies first arose in the United States and Britain in the early part of the nineteenth century and later extended to Europe and beyond, but acquired their present form in the twentieth century. Pre and post-World War 1 years as well as the 1930s were characterized by widespread calls and alliances against wars. These anti-war campaigns were also heard during the Vietnam and Iraq wars. These movements challenged government policy, particularly that of the United States, and were generally anti-imperialist in outlook (2008:3, 16). Peace movements, in historical context and in terms of their contributions as well as in their actions and ideas, are concerned with fostering global peace. Peace movements are social movements that are preoccupied with the sole aim of ending wars, minimizing violence, and ultimately achieving world peace (Young, 1987:331). Some of the tactics employed by peace movements to achieve their goals includes: non-violent resistance, pacifism, demonstrations, boycotts, ethical consumerism, and supporting anti-war candidates (Gill, 2016: para. 1). From the above assertion, it can be said that peace movements are social movements whose underlying motivation is to promote and ensure the reign of peace in a society.

Old Testament Perspective on Peace

The subject matter of divine peace runs through the Old and New Testaments like a mighty river of water (Youssef, 2015:137). The Hebrew word *shalom* is translated as 'peace' in the Old Testament. The concept of peace in the Old Testament is basically referred to as the wholeness of being, total health, total welfare; it covers the sum total of God's blessing to a person who belongs to the covenant community (Arichea, 1987:201). Accordingly, God is known as a God of Peace – *Jehovah Shalom*. In fact, peace is one of the names of God. As Youssef notes, when Gideon, for instance, in Judges 6:24 built an altar to the Lord, he called the altar *Jehovah-Shalom*, "The LORD is Peace" (2015:137). While there are other words which are translated as peace, the principal word used to express the notion of peace in the Hebrew Bible is *shalom*. Since the notion of peace in the Old Testament implies wholeness, health, and completeness, peace is then not simply a negative notion, 'the absence of war'. It is a positive notion, a notion with its own content (Healey, 1992:206). More so, the concept of peace in the Old Testament is also conceptualized in the negative sense: "the absence of war" as Solomon averred in one of his poetic writings that there is "a time of war, and a time of peace" (Ecclesiastes 3:8). In this sense, peace is seen as a period of time that is devoid of war (and this corroborates with Hornsby's definition of peace as mentioned above).

Peace in the Old Testament embodies the calmness of mind, refrain from anger, a state of worriless-ness and tranquillity. This is often expressed with the phrase 'hold thy peace' which is employed as a form of admonition or encouragement, as dominant especially in the King James Version of the Bible.

More so, the Old Testament notion of peace is in the form of promise. The Old Testament is full of God's declaration and promise of peace to His people (Israel) which will be fulfilled in the future. In this context, the Old Testament's conception of peace is futuristic and points to the Messiah Jesus as He is called "the Prince of Peace" (Youssef, 2015:137). In Haggai 2:9 (NIV), God said, "…And in this place I will grant peace'…" Notice the transitive verb "will" in the passage; it is apparent that God's promise of peace in the Old Testament was more or less a promise in futurity which will be actualized at the birth of the Messiah. Accordingly, Miller (2015:4) is of the opinion that the covenant of peace promised by God in the Old Testament will be established through the promised "Prince of Peace" after which God will dwell among the children of peace for eternity.

Even though in futuristic sense, the peace in the Old Testament was attained temporarily through the offering of sacrifice, and this fact is evident, especially, throughout most of the Mosaic books: "An altar of earth you shall make to me and sacrifice on it your burnt offerings and peace offerings…" (Exo. 20:24 Amplified Version); "And if his offering for a sacrifice of peace offering unto the LORD be of the flock…he shall offer it without blemish" (Lev. 3:6). From the above passages, it can be deduced that peace was a product of one's efforts through burnt sacrifices.

The New Testament Perspective on Peace

The Greek word *eirene* and its derivative verbs which means "to reconcile", "to be at peace" and "to make peace" is often translated as peace in the New Testament. And the concept of peace in the New Testament is implied in, at least, five different ways: (1) peace as absence of war, (2) peace as a right relationship with God or with Christ, (3) peace as a good relationship among people; (4) peace as an individual virtue or state; and (5) peace as a part of a greeting formula (Arichea, 1987:201). The first significant mention of peace in the New Testament is seen in the announcement of the birth of Jesus to the shepherds by the angel:

> Don't be afraid! I am here with good news for you, which will bring great joy to all the people. This very day in David's town your Saviour was born – Christ the Lord! ... Glory to God in the highest and peace on earth to those with whom he is pleased (Luke 2:10-11)

According to the passage, the declaration of peace by the angel is attached to the birth of Christ. Recall that Isaiah in the Old Testament had earlier predicted Jesus to be the Prince of Peace (Isaiah 9:6). Thus, the angel's announcement was to inform the commoners (the shepherds) that the 'Prince of Prince' who would give the world peace was born. As Webber averred:

> The Prince of Peace is the one whose dominion brings this quality of life. In the New Testament, the peace of the covenant is extended beyond Israel to all people; in Christ, both Jew and Gentile have been united. Thus, Paul states, "He himself is our peace" (Eph. 2:14), having broken the dividing wall between cultural groups (1993:35).

The birth of Jesus Christ was an historic event that ushered the world with a special type of peace. This brand of peace is only experienced by one's relationship with God. Before the birth of Christ, many people did not have that wonderful relationship with God and they could not afford the peace that accompanied it. The one purpose of Christ's mission was to mend the broken relationship of man with God so that man could experience divine peace. As Jesus posited: "Peace is what I leave with you; it is my own peace that I give you, I do not give it as the world does. Do not be worried and upset; do not be afraid" (John 14:27). Here, Jesus was making a distinction between the peace that is available for the believers through a perfect relationship with God and the peace promised by the world which is just limited to an absence of hostility. For Richie "The peace of the world is a precarious thing" (undated: para. 3). On the contrary, Youssef argues that:

> The peace that Jesus brings is divine peace, the peace of God, the only peace worthy of the name. Divine peace is the only permanent peace. Divine peace is that kind of peace you feel inside even when the world is falling apart all around you. Divine peace is peace of mind, peace in your conscience, peace with your Christian brothers and sisters, peace with your boss and co-workers, peace with your environment, peace with your world (2015:141).

More so, Jesus enlightened his disciples that they should not expect Him to offer them the world's kind of peace. He said that His mission is not to end war but to even instigate it if that would lead to the distinction of good from evil: "Do not think that I have come to bring peace to the world. No, I did not come to bring peace, but a sword." (Matthew 10:34, Good News Bible). This statement, if not well understood, would seem as though Jesus was debunking His designation as being the Messiah of peace. According to Wikner (2013:1), though Jesus came to bring peace between God and people through His life, death, and resurrection, this passage explains that He also came to bring a sword, which means that He came to separate those who follow Him from those who do not. Also, the passage points to the pending judgment that is meant for those who do not accept His peace.

Christ went on to advise His followers to be peacemakers. He enunciated a state of blessedness to those who would lead peaceful lives: "Blessed are the peacemakers: for they shall be called the children of God." (Matt. 5:9). From the passage, it can be seen that for a Christian to be deserving of being called a 'child of God', he/she must be a peacemaker. Jesus taught the radical notion that the God of peace expects God's children also to act in peaceful ways. God's children are to love God; to love God is to love others as well, and this requires renouncing violence and adopting peaceable means to achieve individual and corporate goals (Anderson, 1994:110).

So, the futuristic element in the Old Testament notion of peace finds fulfilment in the person of Christ, the Prince of Peace who reconciled and still reconciles humanity with *Jehovah Shalom*. Those who accept Christ's offer of reconciliation are separated from those who refuse it. This reconciled community are continually discipled and empowered as divine agents/instruments of peace to continue with the mission of reconciling with God, those who are yet to accept Christ.

Having presented the Old and New Testaments' conception of peace, respectively, we shall also discuss how the above conceptions relate with the activities of peace movements.

Ethical Evaluation of Peace Movements

Before engaging in the ethical evaluation of peace movements, it would be pertinent to first of all attempt a brief explanation of the concept of 'ethics' which is the root word of the derivative 'ethical'. Ethics is focused with the judgment of rightness or wrongness, virtuous or vicious, desirability or undesirability, approval or disapproval of human actions (Ozumba, 2008:16). Also, as Omoregbe averred: "ethics is concerned with the question of right and wrong in human behaviour; how men ought to behave and why it is wrong to behave in certain ways and right to behave in certain ways." (1990: ix). However, this section succinctly deduces what is right and wrong about peace movements. Here, we shall ethically evaluate the campaigns of peace movements in the light of two major ethical theories: consequentialism and deontologism.

Consequentialism: This is the ethical theory that is based on the idea that the rightness of an act depends solely on its consequences. It involves the claim that the rightness of acts depends on whether their consequences are good enough together with the particular view that only the best possible is good enough (Slote and Pettit, 2008:140). From this viewpoint, the actions of peace movements can only be considered ethically good if the result of their peaceful agitations bring favourable outcomes. Yes, it is true that no nation prays for war, but in a situation where another nation is consistently terrorizing the citizens of another and all attempts for a peaceful dialogue have been exhausted, then war is inevitable as a means of self-defense. And an attempt to discourage an act of self-defense would be counterproductive. For instance, Banda (2005:32) sees the actions of peace protesters on the eve of the US' planned invasion of Iraq as counterproductive. According to him, the disdain of peace movements for violence and their yearning for peace is commendable until it begins to threaten the safety of the nation. He argued that the president would not be fulfilling his constitutional obligations to provide for the common defense if he heeded their advice and did nothing allowing Saddam's quest for WMD (Weapons of Mass Destruction) to take its course. Even as recent as 2020, more than 80 demonstrations were organized in cities and towns across the United States to oppose the killing of Iran's top security and intelligence commander, Qassim Suleimani, and the Trump administration's decision to send thousands more troops to the Middle East. The protests were spearheaded by Act Now to Stop War and End Racism, an anti-war coalition, and Code Pink, a women-led anti-war organization (Mariel Padilla, New York Times, Jan. 4, 2020).

Deontologism: In deontological ethics, actions are intrinsically good (right) or bad (wrong) in themselves notwithstanding the consequences of such action (Ekpoudom, 2011:31). In this sense, the actions of peace movements can be said to be ethically right, notwithstanding the consequence, since they agitate for a noble course of 'no war' mantra. Whether the avoidance of war brings peace or not, the agitation of peace movements will be good in itself. The peace movements will still be right even if their pacifist stance leads to the promotion of a temporary peace in detriment of permanent peace and justice which is sometimes established by war against an enemy nation. The peace movements will still be right for advocating for peace even when the call for 'Just War' is necessary for the opposition of injustice and self-defense in the face of the persistent enemy's perpetration of violence. Also, even if the peaceful demonstration of the peace movements turned out to be violent at last, the peace movements' actions would still be intrinsically right. For instance, the Vietnam anti-war movement which was supposed to oppose the Cold War and American intervention abroad later escalated into widespread civil disobedience, rejection of mainstream lifestyles, violent clashes with police and militant opposition to the government. Their strategy, less coherent than in earlier stages, was intended to force an end to the war by creating instability, chaos and disruption at home (Zimmerman, n.d: Para. 9). In Africa, precisely Liberia, there were non-violent anti-war movements championed by women. The women peace movement began in early 1994 with the formation of the Liberian Women Initiative (LWI) led by Mary Brownell. The LWI pushed for elections, full disarmament and an end to the war in Liberia. It was largely supported by African Women and Peace Support Groups. The LWI adopted different non-violent measures in its advocacy: it organized mass marches or vigils with the women wearing white to symbolize peace; published statements on the state of the war; lobbied rebel leaders and heads of state; attended peace conferences, as well as observing 'stay home' strikes which paralyzed markets, government buildings, transport and businesses. Later, other groups such as Mano River Union Women's Peace Network (MARWOPNET) were formed in 2000 and Women in Peace Building Network (WIPNET) was formed in March 2003 led by Leymah Gbowee. These women groups engaged in advocacy, at some point, blocked the doors of halls where rebel leaders were holding peace talks in a bid to force the rebel leaders to sign a peace agreement thus, sending a message that the women were fed up with the war. These efforts, among others, brought an end to the war in 2003. (Press, 2015:19-23). There were also anti-war protests by student groups in Myanmar, Asia against the armed conflict between Myanmar forces and the rebel Arakan Army in the western state of Rakhine (Sebastian Strangio: 2020). Radio Free Asia also reported that some activists protested in May 2018 in the commercial capital Yangon, Myingyan in the Mandalay region, and in Pyay in Bago region of Myanmar against the civil war in the northern state of Kachin of the country. The war was fought between Myanmar army and the Kachin Independence Army [KIA]. The protest devolved into fist fights between organizers and baton-wielding police. (Radio Free Asia: 2018). Thus, the intention of an act presupposes the rightness or wrongness of such action regardless of the outcome.

Biblical Evaluation of Peace Movements

Under this subsection, we shall explore the position of the Bible, both the Old and New Testaments on peace movements. In other words, we shall discover the Bible's stance on the activities of peace movements. One of the questions to be asked would be: are there records of peace movement in the Bible; and if there are, what were their aim? Also, would it have been possible for the existence of peace movements in the Old Testament era that was characterized by so many wars? Horst corroborates this fact by asserting that the Old Testament has been a problem and a stumbling block to the question of whether Christians should go to war. He also questions how we would reconcile the teachings of Jesus in the New Testament with all the wars in the Old Testament (2011: para. 2).

In response to the above question, it is pertinent categorically state that the Bible is a peace movement manual in its entirety. This claim may seem controversial and incoherent, especially, when considering the many wars in the Old Testament, where freedom and justice were mostly attained through the art of war and violence. However, we shall biblically evaluate the activities of peace movements by analyzing them based on the two main Christian traditions on peace and war: Pacifism and Just War.

Pacifism: Pacifism is rooted in religious traditions and most religions practice the concept of pacifism which resists violent acts. But pacifism itself has been particularly rooted in Christian traditions and scriptures. Early Christians were committed to the pacifist stance; they believed that it is a sin to participate in bloody and violent acts such as war (Farneubun, 2013:110). Pacifism as a personal and social philosophy seeks to convert enemies through love and non-violent actions. While there is support for peace in the Old Testament, pacifists believe that there is a stronger support for their position in the New Testament (Fahey, 2013:7). Some pacifist scriptures in the Old Testament are: "Depart from evil, and do good; seek peace, and pursue it (Psalms 34:14); "And the work of righteousness shall be peace; and the effect of righteousness quietness and assurance forever." (Isaiah 32:17). For pacifists, the hardcore of the "good news of the kingdom" (Matthew 4:23) that Jesus preached was that of peacemaking; and the Beatitudes in the Sermon on the Mount, "Blessed are the peacemakers..." (Matt. 5:9) corroborates this fact (Fahey, 2013:8). Jesus even took His non-violence campaign to another level when He admonished His followers not to retaliate at the face of violence: "You have heard that it was said, 'An eye for an eye, and a tooth for a tooth'. But now I tell you: do not revenge on someone who wrongs you. If anyone slaps you on the right cheek, let him slap your left cheek too." (Matthew 5:38:39). In order to be a good peacemaker, Jesus also admonished His followers to love their enemies: "You have heard that it was said, 'You shall love your neighbor and hate your enemy.' But I say to you, Love your enemies and pray for those who persecute you, so that you may be children of your father in heaven" (Matthew 5:43-44).

Most Christian pacifists also hold that St. Paul's counsel in Ephesians 6:10-17 that Christians should "put on the whole armor of God" demonstrates the centrality of non-violent resistance in Christian life. Paul urges Christians to use spiritual weapons, "the sword of the spirit" against their adversaries. Hence, pacifists contend that Christians are called to noble life of dealing with human conflict based on love and forgiveness (Fahey, 2013:8). Also, Paul in Romans 14:19 admonishes Christians to go for peace for their spiritual edification: "Let us therefore follow after the things which make for peace, and the things wherewith one may edify."

Just War: The idea of just war has actually been developed by Plato, Aristotle and Cicero but later reformulated and popularized by St Augustine. Just war doctrine permits war under certain circumstance, of which the key word here is "just" added to the war (Farneubun, 2013:112). For something to be just, it means that that thing is considered "to be morally fair and reasonable" or "appropriate in a particular situation" (Hornsby, 2006:807). Thus, a just war is established on two principles: "*Jus ad Bellum* (Justness of War, dealing with it when it is just to go to war) and *Jus in Bello* (Justice in War dealing with how it is just to behave in the course of a war)" (Farneubun, 2013:112). A Just War is a "war as a last resort" (Fahey, 2013:10). On this note, Catholic tradition affirms the necessity of Just War:

> Catholic teaching begins in every case with a presumption against war and for peaceful settlement

of disputes. In exceptional cases, determined by the moral principles of the just-war tradition, some uses of force are permitted. Every nation has a right and duty to defend itself against unjust aggression (See National Conference of Catholic Bishops: 1983:2).

The Old Testament offers bases for the conclusion on Just War. Many of the Old Testament passages can be used to support the 'Just War' theory:

> He is going to punish the people of Amalek because their ancestors opposed the Israelites when they were coming from Egypt. Go and attack the Amalekites and completely destroy everything they have. Don't leave a thing; kill all the men, women, children, and babies; the cattle, sheep, camels and donkeys (I Sam. 15:2-3, Good News Bible -GNB).

The reason for war, according to this passage, is because the Amalekites had opposed the Israelites on their way out from Egypt.

> When you are at war in your land, defending yourselves against an enemy who has attacked you, sound the signal for battle. I, the Lord your God, will help you from your enemies (Numbers 10:9, GNB).

The rationale for war here is on the event of the attack of an enemy. Here, war is necessary for self-defense.

In the New Testament, Fahey avers that those who advocate for 'Just War' in Christianity cite the following texts to support their belief that Jesus would support Just War:

> Mark 12:17: "Give to the emperor the things that are the emperor's, and to God the things that are God's." This is interpreted to mean that Jesus was telling his

followers to follow Caesar's laws and that included military service.

Matthew 21:12: "And Jesus entered the temple of God and drove out all who bought and sold in the temple, and he overturned the tables of the money changers and the seats of those who sold pigeons."

This is interpreted to mean that Jesus Himself used violence in driving out the money changers.

Matthew 10:34: "Do not think that I have come to bring peace to the earth. I have not come to bring peace, but a sword."

This is interpreted to mean that Jesus accepted participation in war for His followers.

Luke 22:36: "And let him who has no sword sell his mantle and buy one."

This is interpreted to mean that Jesus mandated the use of swords for self-defense while on a journey (Fahey, 2013:10).

From the above, we can deduce that peace movements are not always right in advocating for peace. They ignore the principle of self-defense and justice and still campaign for peace when 'Just War' would have been necessary. As Lysaught (2003:52) observes: "A just war must be fought to overcome injustice, but always with an eye to restoring peace... the just war tradition helps to clarify and limit when force may be used and to minimize the violence of war itself." Be that as it may, peace is a necessary factor for the non-violent co-existence of members of a society.

Peace as a Necessary Factor for Societal Co-existence and Sustainability

Peace is very vital for commotion-free co-existence of human beings in a society. In fact, peace keeps and sustains the human race. Though there is too much of tumult in the world today, it is still possible to restore peace back to the world if people would earnestly engage in the art of peace making. Accordingly, Taheri & Dehghan categorize peace-making into four basic ways: peace with God, peace with the universe, peace with one's self, and peace with others. And among the above mentioned, making peace with God is the easiest whereas making peace with the others is the hardest (2014:57). In other words, for one to be able to achieve the other categories of peace-making – making peace with the universe, making peace with oneself, as well as making peace with others - one must first make peace with God who is the Author of peace. In the words of Miller (2015:13):

> All mankind seeks peace in some way, but without God this goal cannot be reached. Through Jesus, the Prophet of Peace, the goal can be attained. Through Jesus, the believer undergoes an ontological transformation that brings them into both a covenant relationship with God and empowers them to practice peace.

More so, striving for peace is not a work of an individual person; it is a collective endeavour. The peace process must be driven by shared determination in order to arrive at a viable and durable peace formula (Bose, 2003:218). Building peace within and among nations is the work of many individuals and institutions; it is the fruit of ideas and decisions taken in the political, cultural, economic, religious, or social domains. And the Church, as a community of faith and social institution, has a proper, necessary, and distinctive part to play in the pursuit of peace (National Conference of Catholic Bishops, 1983:7). Christians, most especially, being those who follow the teachings of Christ on peace, have a great role to play in this regard. In this sense, Anderson decries that Christians, unfortunately, have often found it too easy to embrace some of Jesus' teachings without heeding to the most principal ones, one of which is 'peace'. He went on to opine that those who seek to model the lifestyle of Jesus must come to grips with His teachings on peace (1994:109). In other words, Christians are the ones to live as peaceful models in the world today as followers of the greatest Teacher of peace in history.

Furthermore, for there to be continuous and sustained peace in the world, the people of the world from all spheres and backgrounds of life must involve in peaceful acts. If, at least, half of the world's population indulge in acts of peace, the peaceful act will then define what peace entails. Though, the notion is always well understood by most people, the 'peaceful act' and 'peaceful individual' can be differently interpreted. Peaceful act is an act that brings humans closer to peace while a peaceful individual is a person who is at peace. Such an individual has overcome his internal conflicts and has freed himself from other conflicts. Accordingly, the status of a peaceful person is the highest status that the individual can ever acquire (Taheri & Dehghan, 2014:56-57). Sequel to the above, every individual should be encouraged to be a peaceful person by indulging in peaceful acts. It was in this sense that Jesus pronounced blessings on His followers who are peace makers (Matt. 5:9). For there to be genuine peace in a society, there must be justice.

Justice and Quest for Peace

The word justice in Arabic implies being 'straight' and 'equitable' and it denotes straightforwardness, trustworthiness, and fairness in one's dealings with others; this goes beyond the limits of formal justice dispensed by the juridical system due to the presence of attitude which brings about a state of balance, accord, and trust (Kalin, 2013:224). According to Blackburn, justice is a common basis that persons should be treated equally unless reasons for inequality exist (1994:203). Justice is "a set of propositions that tells us who ought to do what, to whom, for whom, and on behalf of whom and the reasons why" (Philpott, 2012:5).

The presence of justice is what positive peace entails (Cortright, 2008:6). Justice and peace are realities that need to be realized at various levels of development beginning with family, intermediate communities, the religious bodies, up to the nations and groups of nations (Opoku, *et al*, 2017:6). Peace is synonymous to a state of justice or goodness, a balance or equilibrium of powers (Rummel, para.3). Elsewhere, *Catholic Pastoral Constitution* states that the notion of peace transcends beyond the mere absence of war and it cannot be reduced solely to the maintenance of a balance of power between enemies. Rather, it is richly and appropriately called "an enterprise of justice". It originates from that harmonious existence built into the human society by its divine founder (God) and actualized by men who thirst after 'ever greater justice' (quoted in The National Conference of Catholic Bishops, 1983: 15). As a substantive concept, peace is based on justice since it is predicated upon the availability of equal rights and opportunities for all to realize their goals and potentials. It is an enduring state of harmony, trust, and coexistence only when coupled and supported with justice (Kalin, 2013:224).

In a deeper sense, we can say that peace is a criterion for a just society. Thus, peace is noted by Howard as "the maintenance of an orderly and just society" (1971:225). For there to be a just society for people to experience peace, certain domestic and international practices are to be embraced by all, and for this to happen, socio-economic justice and respect for the rights of the individuals must be ensured. For the Marxists, peace is not feasible unless there is justice and equality in the distribution of resources (Olanrewaju,

2013:9). In this sense, any peace discourse or theory that does not make room for the inclusion of justice is incomplete and lacking. Thus, such theory lacks merit and credibility as far as the notion of positive peace is concerned.

Moreover, the mere proclamation of peace is not enough. One who claims to lead the peaceful lifestyle must also act accordingly with good works that build peace since these good works encompass the call to bring justice (Miller, 2015:18). Though peace might seem unachievable, at least, for a sustained period of time, that does not invalidate the struggle to achieve a world with greater justice and equity, or at least with significantly less violence, injustice and inequity (Webel, 2007:8). The pursuance of peace does not call for one to keep quiet in the face of injustice. The proclamation and pursuance of peace is a call for a combat against any form of injustice, be it social, economic, religious or political. For instance, Philpott (2012:24) sees political injustices to be: the unjust deeds that people commit, the unjust regimes, the unjust laws or constitutions that people (in power) sustain in the name of a political ideal. Striving for peace entails the fight against such injustices. Most times, striving for peace can lead to a situation of protests and can even escalate to violence and full-blown war. Christians are however encouraged, even though they are against warfare, to go all out for their justice in order to enjoy a guaranteed peace. Thus, peace is not a mere state of passivity; it is a condition where one is fully active against the menace of evil, destruction, and turmoil that may come from within or from without (Kalin 2013:223). As Pope John Paul II puts it:

> ...Christians, even as they strive to resist and prevent every form of warfare, have no hesitation in recalling that, in the name of an elementary requirement of justice, peoples have a right and even a duty to protect their existence and freedom by proportionate means against an unjust aggressor. (See National Conference

of Catholic Bishops, 1983: 17)

More so, it is noted that an individual can achieve a peaceful state by putting an end to inner conflicts with anyone and anything, though this does not prevent one from defending the right and opposing the wrong. In fact, peace loving individuals are to dutifully stand against oppression and are to defend justice at all times without any hatred and detestation (Taheri & Dehghan, 2014:57).

From the above adumbration, it is clear that the world is in lack of genuine peace. The peace of the world is temporal because it is based on the systems of this world which are controlled by human beings; thus, it is bound to failures. Thus, no government, individual or group of individuals (peace movements) can offer peace with his/her/its power, affluence or wisdom. The 'Prince of Peace' is the only giver of peace. And one can only have access to His peace when one would have accepted Him as Lord and personal Savior. As Youssef (2015:148) puts it, divine peace cannot be received only by church membership, or intellectually assenting to Christian doctrines or even by admiring Jesus as a great prophet and teacher. It is only when we surrender our lives to Jesus. Also, one who enjoys the peace offered by Christ should affect the lives of others positively by peaceful acts. The world today does not only need people who talk about peace, but people who are peaceful themselves. This chapter concludes that God is the author of genuine peace and one can only achieve this peace by having a good relationship with His Son, Jesus Christ who is the 'Prince of Peace'. Also, Christians are admonished to be good ambassadors of peace in line with the pacifist disposition of Jesus. The peace of God promised in the Old Testament found fulfillment in Christ as recorded in the New Testament. With Christ's ascension and the outpouring of the Holy Spirit upon Believers, the peace of God finds expression in and through them (Christians/Believers) in very practical and enduring ways.

The acts of peace should be strictly emphasized in the curriculum of schools at all levels, in the sermons of church denominations as well as in the rules and regulations that guide the conducts of people in a society. Leaders should be good ambassadors of peace in their body languages and utterances. Everyone, whether young or old, poor or rich, educated or uneducated, ruler or ruled, should be encouraged to indulge in peaceful acts at all times even at the face of provocation. However, those (Christians) who truly follow the footsteps of Christ must model His peace to others. Christians are those bestowed with the responsibility of restoring peace back to the world. As Woodley (2009:8) avers, the call from Jesus to be a peacemaker is incredibly hopeful. God does not call the perfect and unbroken to be His peacemakers; instead, He chooses the lame and outcast (Isaiah 4:6–7). The Prince of Peace who brings peace to the world calls us to partner with Him.

CHAPTER TWO

Emergent Jaw-dropping Peace Movements

Emmanuel G. M. Kollie

We are in a world where superpower nations hope to continue as the voice of poorer nations. These superpower nations are determined to serve as decision makers for the nations considered as poor and underdeveloped. They even desire to regulate how these underdeveloped nations would be administered and governed. Consequently, there are conflicts and wars such as internal violence and instabilities within the poor and underdeveloped nations as well as within some other developed nations of the world. The lack of real peace has further resulted in terrorism which is now a global concern. There is a growing concern that ethnic minorities protesters especially among women and youth are increasing in many nations of the world. The desire for peace has encouraged the emergence of national and international liberation movements in many nations. Carter (2014: n.p) asserts that the desire for peace has turn into a world-wide scope of peace movements that have gained the attention of the public, especially religious leaders, politicians, and other activists

Emmanuel G. M. Kollie, PhD, M. A, M. Ed (kollieegm@auwa.edu.lr) is currently the President/ Vice-Chancellor of the Adventist University of West Africa (AUWA) in Liberia. He is a Professor of Systemic Theology. He is an ordained minister of the Gospel in the Seventh-day Adventist Church.

across the globe. From the author's perspective, this chapter calls for a reflection on the world's quest for peace and the anticipation of the emergent jaw-dropping peace movement. It focuses on redirecting minds from the mundane to the celestial form of peace finding movements.

The Global Quest for Peace among Nations

The quest for peace is a delight to the inhabitants of the world based on the protests and peace movements across the globe. According to Pilisuk and Nagler (2011: 314), there are many known peace organizations in North America alone. Furthermore, it is estimated that there are 1,538 United Nations's organizations that are involved with mission initiatives and global communications around the world (un.org). Yet, the more the increment in the number of peace organizations, the more there is instability around the world. The numbers of these organizations have been growing geometrically especially after the World War II. Nations within the poorer continents like Asia and Africa depend on either the United States or the Communists powers of Europe and other superpowers in Europe to keep the peace that is so desire. Consequently, instead of experiencing global peace, there have been rather escalations of instability and conflicts and violence. For example, in Asia, Pilisuk and Nagler (2011:314) declare that "wealth inequalities, chronic poverty, political, and social inequality created more sources of Asian structural violence". Pilisuk and Nagler (2011:314) postulate that the "widespread religions in Asia such as Islam, Buddhism, Hinduism together with the intra-country language variations did not instill peace as a result of the relative views of these sub-groups and the political incongruent views of the various nations of Asia. Thus, Asian peace movements are deeply aware that their struggle is in the facts of a larger provisional activity. The situation of Africa is not quite different from that of Asia. It is thus, appropriate to state some few aspects of peace from the viewpoints of political, anthropology, linguistic and medical.

Some Views about Peace

The political quest of peace calls for nations to observe the senselessness and destructiveness of wars and conflicts. Yet, the quest for supremacy of one nation over the other among the superpowers has created a high level of antagonisms. There is production of weapons that are capable of destroying the world and the people who develop those weapons. In the political sense, to experience peace is to prepare for war. Goedde (2019:1) in his book the *Politics of Peace: A Global Cold War History*, postulates that nations are aware that "excessive concern for peace on the part of any nation impedes or prevents adequate defense preparation and hinders effective diplomacy in the national interest. Hence, it undermines the will to resist, and saps national strength." In the writer's view, such political strive for peace enormously suppresses the views of the weaker nations and install the fear of victimization in the already suppressed underdeveloped nations. In this way, relative human peace is restored on a surface perspective.

From the anthropology perspective, the difficulty in understanding the ethnographic description of human social behavior makes it almost impossible to find a general conclusive definition of peace. Foster (1986) asserts that "culture is the central concept in anthropology." As such, society must apply practices adoptive in a cultural environment to solve conflict. Thus, the concept of peace is relative from one cultural environment to another. No wonder why, it is difficult to find world peace in a culturally diverse world. One of the major challenges of peace in the human society is that according to Fry (2007), human beings by nature are "warlike" with the quality of "sex differences in aggression, a catalog of barbarity, atrocity, and brutality." Therefore, how peace is restored among different groups of people remains relative.

The writer is of the view that the linguistic means to achieve peace is purely theoretical and relative in nature. What one may define as peace may not be the experience of peace in another place. For example, Chomsky (2003) mentioned that "the connection of how we should react to the crimes of others through humanitarian intervention remain a challenge." When others are guilty of crimes, we focus on the crimes and lament them, and we ignore or deny the same crime if committed by us. In other words, peace is defined from the perspective of the one who has the solution at the moment.

From the medical perspective, Kulkarni (1992:81) observes that an all-inclusive approach to health is the answer to peace because health and peace are symbiotic in nature. Kulkarni (1992:81) affirms that "a state of wholeness is a state of peace and the state of peace is possible when there is freedom not only from war and oppression but also from disease, poverty, and hunger." The challenge is that the superpowers strive for general peace is based on the devising syndrome of biotechnologies. The biotechnologies are devised to overcome the very biological and chemical weaponry the global superpowers produce. Consequently, viruses and other disease organisms are produced with the potential to wipe off and mutilate armies as well as a whole population.

In addition, the religious option for peace has been resolved at calling on all to form a unity known as the ecumenical movement for peace. Therefore, the difference in Christian doctrines appears to have been impeding the strive for global peace agenda.

It is noteworthy to mention that in all of the views mentioned about peace above, none supports the absolute derivative of peace. Rather, they all share and appreciate the concept of peace from a relative perspective. No wonder the Scripture points out that the more there is a cry of peace in the world, the more the state of anarchy (Mic 3:5; Exod 34:12).

The Concept of Peace from the Humanistic Perspective

A lot of definitions (Gultung, 1995:1, Abrams, 2001:3-10, Vesilind 2005:43, Scott Kin, 2008:83, UN 2020: n.d, UNESCO 2020: n.d) have been coined from the original Latin word *pax*, which is translated into English language as "peace." The writer has randomly captured and summarized a few of the many views on peace from the wealth of knowledge of profound scholars in the field of peace and conflict resolutions. To a large extent, the scholars are of the views that peace means "an agreement to end war," "to end dispute or conflict between two or more people," "the absence of war," "the use of force or control to bring stability into societies or nations," "the presence of justice/fairness, law and order," the acceptance and respect of human rights," "the freedom of individuals and nations," "a state of mind," "no interruption," "dignity, well-being for all," living together with our differences, etc.

There is also the idea of personal peace, which highlights the desire of personal stability and satisfaction in life. However, there is a fault with such a form of personal humanistic peace (Peter, 2010:476). Human beings without divine guidance cannot do anything to foster personal stability without taking into account the damaging consequences such actions may impose on the society or nation at large (Gultung 1995:1). The so-called personal peace is in effect a negative peace because it is detrimental to societal or government stability (Meererk, 1989:16). For example, a person may choose to steal from the government in order to be financially free and as well experience personal stability. This action, even though resulting into some form of personal peace and stability, it is relative in scope. It has the potential to hinder national or international development. The use of public items for the benefit of one person creates more harm than good in a society. It does not give peace to the defaulter in the real sense of the word.

It is further suggested that there is likewise the idea of external or positive human peace (Peter, 2010:476). This form of peace highlights the absence of organizational violence and conflicts. Unfortunately, it does not take into account the inner stability of the personnel as long as the organization is calm and stable externally to the outside world. In the quest for positive peace, there may be a craving for organizational turnover for the benefit of the proprietor (negative peace) more than the satisfaction of the majority who should rather benefit from the environment of positive peace.

The Challenge of the Human Made Peace

The leaders of the world, throughout centuries, have thrown aside the holistic-biblical prescriptive concept of peace. The replacement of the biblical peace idea with the humanistic concept has not proven anything good for human existence. In the writer's view, the peace concept that the world continues to suggest and offers to its inhabitants has not stopped violence, conflicts, hate speeches, wars, man-made disasters, internal-self conflict and abuses in the human society. Countless peace treaties by humankind have been developed, adopted, and applied, to no avail. The human society has continually failed to adhere to the divine guidance of what peace truly is. As mentioned earlier, the more the world and its inhabitants speak about their form of jaw dropping peace movements, the more the world and its inhabitant continue to face increased chaotic and challenging situations. This is resulting in more and more difficult and chaotic-conflicted predicaments around the globe.

Humankind continues to strategize and employ all forms of emergent jaw-dropping problem-solving stratagems from their standpoints in the name of peace. But this has yielded no real success. No wonder Christ informs the seekers of the biblical peace in this way: "Peace I leave with you; my peace I give to you. Not as the world gives do I give to you" (John 14:27, ESV). The human society shall continue to experience instabilities in all ramifications as long as the human way of finding peace remains the answer to the world's stability. The below Scriptural quotation provides an additional reason why the humanistic society is devoid of peace.

> … none is righteous, no, not one; no one understands; no one seeks for God. All have turned aside; together they have become worthless; no one does good, not even one. Their throat is an open grave; they use their tongues to deceive. The venom of asps is under their lips. Their mouth is full of curses and bitterness. Their feet are swift to shed blood; in their paths are ruin and misery, and the way of peace they have not known. There is no fear of God before their eyes (Rom. 3:9-18, ESV).

The human view of peace treaty is never beyond the face-value variation of some form of stability that the human society wishes to experience in the name of peace. In their understanding, they are doing something to remedy the pandemonium and instabilities the world faces continuously. The writer is of the view that thousands and millions of the United States dollars are spent regularly in the name of finding world peace. As a result, human beings are constantly on the lookout against any threats to it mundane connotation of peace. This view is in conformity with Weyel (2008: 8-15). He asserts that peace seekers are trying to maintain their form of peace and security by confronting those who jeopardize or breach their peace agenda through any acts of aggression against the violators. It is thus important to venture into a proper understanding of the concept of peace from the humanistic point of view.

The Quest for a Balance

There is an absolute and all-inclusive concept of peace which is prescriptive from the viewpoint of the Bible.

Notwithstanding, there is also a humanistic concept of peace which is in conflict with the biblical view of peace. It must be stated that the humanistic concept of peace is descriptive within a relative and incomplete scope of the word itself. Kollie (2018: 49-63) affirms that while the biblical concept of peace is original and divine, the humanistic view of peace disregards the influence of the Scripture in its definition of peace. Even though created by God, human beings have developed a mindset that they are the architect of their own achievements, without the guidance of the divine. As such, the humanistic view of peace rather than the divine, to a large extend, drives the concept of the peace movements in the human society across the globe.

According to Senehi et al (2010: 1-42), peace and conflict experts with the humanistic mentality believe that a person can truly find internal peace. Senehi et al (2010: 1-42), argue that to achieve such internal peace, it must begin within the self. In other words, one must search for truth from within, and must choose to be non-violent by self-standard. It further suggests that one must empower self to provide a sense of hope and self-commitment to non-violent actions. Senehi et al (2010:1-42) further opt that if a person succeeds in experiencing such internal peace, then he or she would be able to contribute to the external or positive peace movements. However, it is important to mention that the excessive quest for certain desires may result in suffering rather than finding peace. This view is supported by Singh (2008:43) because he mentions that "we do not have to be the slaves of unbounded craving." In other words, Singh (2008:43-44) is of the view that undue desire for a certain thing in the quest for peace or certain gadget that you only think of acquiring, might cause further sufferings. This is why the idea about self can be sometimes dangerous in finding personal peace.

In addition, the idea of "self" is relative to each person. What a person may consider as self-peace may not seem appropriate to another person. In essence, a peace agenda that is not holistic, objective, and Christ centered, is self-centered and narrow in application. Therefore, it cannot be free from bias in its implementation in the human setting.

Nonetheless, it is worth mentioning that peace and conflict experts with the humanistic mindset maintain that a person who has found self-peace is in the right position to contribute to external or positive peace movements. In this way, internal human peace is a prerequisite for external peace. In the human perspective, inner peace is difficult to achieve because of "the opponents of peace, who dispute its very value or dismiss it as soft or unrealizable" (Leckman, 2014:363). However, Senehi et al (2010:1-42) opt that those without internal peace do not have the transformative power to provide external or positive peace

The challenge here is that if peace is developed on self-aggrandizements, thinking peace globally will also be seen from the perspective of self-centeredness. In the writer's opinion, many leaders in the public and private sectors, without divine guidance think of enriching themselves rather than building positive legacy for the society or nation because their concept of peace is limited to self-will. Since the human concept of peace is relative in nature, the presence of force or control is sometimes used to bring people into the external environment of peace. Human beings have failed to acknowledge the limitation of the human reasoning; therefore, the quest for absolute peace can never be realized in the human society. As mentioned earlier, it must be stated that none of the humanistic idea over the centuries about peace has ever resulted into any lasting peace movement. Hartwig (2008:41) is right when he opts that a quest for peace solution is not possible for now. He further suggests that it may be possible in the future, when the world has changed. Is he referring to the eschatological peace? From the writer's view, there is currently an experience of individualistic peace that is not negative in nature because it has a divine source.

It should be mentioned that the humanistic peace in its variety should be the emergent jaw-dropping peace movement. Unfortunately, the human view of peace has boxed God's context of peace. Idiomatically, peace in the human society now appears to be like a chicken egg conveyed in a spoon by a young child to cover a kilometer distance. The fingers are crossed so that mistakes may not be made to drop the egg from the spoon.

Mission for World Peace

Early in 1891, world leaders organized a peace congress in Rome for the purpose of promoting the culture of peace in troubled and unstable parts of the world. Consequently, the International Peace Bureau (IPB) was established (Costa Bona, 2017:3). Tactlessly, the IPB could not maintain its goal of sustaining peace in the world. In no time, the Balkan war broken out (1911-1913). The unresolved conflict and irreconcilable differences between the great powers of Europe at the time further caused the World War I from 1914-1919 (The Balkan War. n.p). It is estimated that there were more than 40 million deaths and other casualties by the end of the senseless war (World War I, 2020: n.p). The desire for peace and the prevention of the repetition of the heinous suffering and destruction of lives and properties during the World War I informed the first peace conference in Paris, France on January 10, 1920 (League of Nations, 2020: n.p). Another peace organization was established. The League of Nations was organized as the first intergovernmental peace organization in the world as a result of the Paris peace conference. But in no distance future, the League of Nations failed to fulfill the expectation of fostering peace. It could not find meaningful solutions to the demands of preventing wars, sufferings, and destructions around the world. Accordingly, the League could not prevent the World War II (1939 to 1945) that followed. Regrettably, 60 million people died. Out of frustration, the League was formally dissolved on April 19, 1946. Another peace organization was established. The United Nations, on October 24, 1945, was founded a year after the end of World War II in September 2, 1945. The establishment of the UN did not also realize the desire UN goals. Prantl (2006: 8-9) is of the view that it began to play only a marginal role in the management of conflicts around the world. Thus, Paul and Nahory (2008: 29-38) state that one of the reasons why the UN does not still play a major role is that "The UN security mechanism has always been at the mercy of indecisive relationship among the self-proclaimed superpowers for world supremacy". A clear evidence is the geopolitical tension that broke up between the United States and the Soviet Union at the end of World War II. The result was the nuclear disaster that followed commonly known as the Cold War (Cold War, 2020: n.p). In the face of the UN, the cold war expended from the idea of containment, to a period of atomic supremacy, to a time of space race hegemony, to a period of the red scare, an anticommunist panic which took place in the US where more than 500 people in the name of communist subversion were led to lose their jobs because they were considered a part of a communist sabotage in the US. From the US, the cold war spread to other parts of the world through a growing concern of a perceived threat of the Soviet Union to take over the world. This resulted into lots of actual war conflicts around the world. In the presence of the UN Security Council, the world became "an antagonistic bipolar place for the affluent and underclass" (Cold War, 2020: n.p). To find solution to the escalated crisis, the United Nations adopted another approach for peace and conflict resolution by means of diplomacy instead of military action. As a result, the Strategic Arms Limitation Treaty (SALT I) was signed to prohibit the manufacture of nuclear missiles. Even though for this and other reasons, the Soviet's influences waned at some point in time, yet the United Nations could not still maintain peace. Paul and Nahory (2008: 29-38) also opt that "in a world torn by war and violence, there was a need for a far better Security Council to promote international peace and security and defend international law." For them, a solution could be possible in the future, when the world has changed. This assertion is supported by the view of Mbuende (2008:25) who mentions that the United Nations which began as a single unit to maintain peace and security among others around the world, has failed to solve conflict between and among the people of the world. The writer is further of the view that true change or real peace begins with the acceptance of the absolute-holistic idea of peace as prescribed by the Holy Bible. The failure of the IPB, the League of Nations, and the UN resulted into the creation of regional organizations to maintain peace in various regions of the World. A few of such regional organizations such as the North Atlantic Treaty Organization (NATO) for peace and defense in America and Europe failed to realize it goals. The Organization of African Unity (OAU), now known as African Union (AU) to restore peace in conflicted African countries failed to stand as a unit in the restoration of peace. Mbuende (2008:25) mentions that in the face of the AU there are still numerous untouched special needs of Africa in the areas of peace and security, and political, economic and social development. The failed NATO, AU, etc., further called for sub-regional mechanisms for the sake of restoring peace in their sub-regions. A few organizations such as the Economic Community of West African States (ECOWAS), the Southern African Development Community (SADC), etc., also failed in diverse ways to maintain the so-called humanistic concept of peace in their sub-regions. The list further extends down to individual countries' initiatives for peace. There has also been, still down to communities' vigilante for peace.

All efforts to institute international laws to prevent future unpredictable situations have always only promoted a fragile-temporal human idea of peace. The reality is that there is never going to be an absolute peace in the human society globally, because human beings have refused to subject themselves to the divine prescription of peace.

In summary of this sub-heading, Conti (2017: 15-30) reveals that the human concept of peace is relative in all effects. No move toward peace in the closing chapter of the 19th century and throughout the 20th century has truly worked well. It has been revealed that from 1870 to 1914, various empires wanted power and autonomy to the detriment of the stability of weaker empires. These moves did not provide world peace. Accordingly, Conti (2017:15-30) also opts that the American and the European powers sought to control colonial empires in Asia and Africa. This too did not provide world peace. Instead of the one world order for peaceful co-existence, imperialistic tendencies grew in the affluence nations such as the United States, Russia, Britain, and the likes. This did not similarly resolve to peace as well.

The feeding of patriotic sentiment furthermore developed within the suppressed underclass-colonized nations. This gave rise to a strong nationalist drive which gave birth to the struggle for freedom and independence in Africa especially in the twentieth century. But these moves have not provided peace. The independent nations witnessed the advent of disconcerting associations, organizations, and institutions in the name of keeping their peace. None of these moves has restored real peace in the world. The writer is of the view that all that is left is to patiently work toward the emergent jaw-dropping peace movements. This is because, all of the humanistic peace movements are just but fictions. The good news is that the biblical emergent jaw-dropping peace movements are absolute biblical facts that can be relied on.

Divinity and Peace Movement

It may interest you to know that the ideal emergent jaw-dropping peace movement is in reality, a biblical peace movement which is described in two phrases. The first phrase is an ongoing experience in our current world. As such, it is individualistic in nature. It is a present reality appreciated by many individuals around the world. The second has an eschatological implication. It will be experienced communally. In addition, it will be possessed only by those who are currently experiencing the first phrase of the ideal emergent jaw-dropping peace movement. In other words, the biblical reality of peace can only be experienced by those who have a meaningful relationship with God. The first phrase of this peace move has come. It will remain until the second phrase arrives at the Advent of Christ. It is therefore important to present the biblical ideal of absolute holistic peace in the next sub-heading.

The Absolute Ideal of Jaw-dropping Peace

The Old Testament (OT) provides a comprehensive and holistic definition of peace. It is found in an OT Semantic-Hebrew word known as *shalom* (Kollie and Kollie 2020:32-33). The word provides an all in all comprehensive meaning of peace, which should be considered as the ideal for peace and conflict experts. The word *Shalom* means, "peace," "well-being," "completeness," "soundness," "welfare," "be intact," etc. (Brown, Driver and Braggs, n.p). The biblical peace involves an elemental aspect of human life which refers totally to the soundness of the whole being, (2 Sam 17:3; Micah 5:4; Job 5:24) (Stendebach, 1987:17). Biblical peace extends beyond the prosperity of a person. It reaches out to the entire community at large. The biblical concepts of peace further mean righteousness which denotes the idea of straightness or conformity to a norm or right standard (Fountain, 1989:56). Such biblical peace affects every aspect of the current life, including personal character and responsibility, ethical behavior and practices, social concerns and conduct, righteous commitment and a holistic appreciation of God in all spheres of life endeavors.

This biblical peace means obedience which brings freedom from deadly diseases in the current life (Ex. 15:26; 23:20-26; Lev. 26:14-16; Deut. 5:32; 7:12-15; Prov. 3:7-8). It means the possession of strength to achieve in good business transactions, which is considered as a gift of God (Ps. 29:11; Ex. 15:2; 2 Sam. 22:3; Ps. 21:1; 28:7-8). Those who possess this peace appreciate its maintenance through healthy lifestyle and longevity activities (Fountain, 56). In other words, dying at a good old age is God's desire for those who appreciate and apply the principles of biblical peace in their daily interactions (Gen. 35:29; Judges 8:32; 1 Chron.

29:28). In essence, the OT provides a concept of peace that extends beyond the mundane to the celestial. It proposes that the second phase of the ideal jaw-dropping biblical peace resonates with the first. This means that in order to partake in the second wave of the ideal emergent-jaw dropping peace movements, each person must endeavor to develop a personal relationship with Christ through total and selfless dependence on the creator of universe (Kollie and Kollie 2020:32-33).

The New Testament (NT) also stipulates a comprehensive and holistic definition of an ideal jaw-dropping peace movement from a unique perspective. While there is only one key word in the OT which defines the first and second phrases of the ideal emergent jaw-dropping peace, there are several biblical Greek words which highlight the applications of absolute peace in general as well. Since this is not an exegesis paper, the writer has provided a theological reflection of a few of these words herein (Kollie and Kollie 2020:32-33).

The first word *Hugies* "whole" denotes the quality of the soundness of mental, rational, and intelligent wellbeing of a person (Matt. 12:13; Mark 3:5; Luke 5:31; 6:10 7:10; 15:27) (Luke, 308). Those who possess such *hugies* fruitfully cooperate as community dwellers by relating to one another in both physical and spiritual soundness of mind (Wilkinson, 1980:10).

The second word *Eirene* means tranquility in the absence of conflict. The term is opposed to conflict or internal disturbance. It envisions a peaceful and spiritual well-being that is experienced within a person who shares a salvific relationship with God. It covers all dimensions of the person's economic, political, family, and religious life (Miller, 1990:665). It connotes a wholeness or well-being through a restored relationship with God (Rom. 5:1; Eph 2:14-18; Col 1:20). This form of *eirene* covers a genuine relationship with one another (Mark 9:50; Rom. 12:18; 14:19; 1 Cor. 7:15; 2 Cor 13:11). It also brings internal relationship and satisfaction with oneself without a disadvantageous impact society or government as opposed to the humanistic kind of personal peace (John 14:27; 16:33; Rom. 8:5; 15:13), It expresses the idea of prosperity, quietness, and restful mind (Swartley, 2009:423).

The third *zoe* reflects a life which is a characteristic of an eschatological essence. It is a life which gives an assurance of a future life beyond death. It describes the hallmark of the coming age of peaceful life with Christ. Those who have meaningful relationship with Christ owns the *zoe* kind of life now which Christ also possessed during his first advent (John 5:24; II Cor. 5:17) (Swartley, 2009:423). It is a life that is in harmony with God's will while one awaits the everlasting bliss of peace (the phase two of the emergent jaw dropping peace). It is a free gift of Jesus to all who claims it (John 3:16; 10:10; 17:3). It helps the receivers to be at peace with God, fellow men, with oneself, and in readiness of the Advent of Christ (Wilkinson, 11).

The fourth is *teleios. It* conveys a sense of spiritual maturity. And only a sincere Christian in Christ can reach the attainable goal for which he or she is created to live and fulfill. It presents a sense of integrity, honor, and truthfulness in one's society (Wilkinson, 1990:24).

The last, *soteria* denotes the presence of God to "keep" or "protect" from serious peril. It provides deliverance from judicial condemnation now and then. It also offers cure from illness in order to stay in good health (Luke 1:77; 2:30; Acts 13:26, 47; Rom. 1:16; 10:10) (Foerster 1986:965). It further describes the idea of being responsible for the well-being of each other in the community (Detzler, 1986:338).

The concept of peace in both the OT and NT bring to light a commitment on the part of Christians to live in response to the guidelines or principles set by God. Notwithstanding, as believers, we cannot distance ourselves completely from the woes of sin. Christians are living in a sinful world. Therefore, the first aspect of the emergent jaw-dropping peace movement must begin with the understanding of the word peace as it is spelled out in the Bible. It begins with allowing Christ to be the captain of one's life at all times and in all decisions of life.

Only those who allow Christ to work in them will experience the second phase of the emergent jaw-dropping peace movement. This second aspect of peace shall not be experienced in a world of sin, but a world made new in its entirety (Rev. 21:1-4). You can begin to appreciate the eternal peace with God by living in the fullness of God's love. The reality about all these is that until humans realize that their source of existence originates with God, the world can never know the true concept of peace.

CHAPTER THREE

The Panorama of Peace and Global Religions

Oluseun Abel Akinpelu & Emmanuel O. Eregare

This chapter examines the major roles of some top global religions, their mission on peace and how they seemly fit into the master plan on the New World Order from the late twentieth century. The origin of the New World Order can be gleaned from the commonly accepted global religio-political concept. But by the early 1990s, the concept of the New World Order had rather resonated more on the political atmosphere especially during the reign of George Bush (Nye, 1992, 83-96; Freedman and Karsh, 1993, xxix; Slaughter, 1997, 183-197; Baker and DeFrank, 1995, xv; Mcgrew, 2000, 345-352). Skreslet (1997, 150-164) and Schroeder (2010, 25) opine further that the New World Order expresses a perception on a global change that has overtaken the purported ideals, as perceived by the global elite groups, to a world more orderly in its affair. Humanity surely needs a new order to salvage the insecurity, wars and rumors of wars, sufferings, climatic change and the disrespect to the rule of law that

Oluseun Abel Akinpelu (akinpeluo@babcock.edu.ng) is a Lecturer in the Department of Religious Studies, Babcock University and he is currently a PhD candidate. His area of interest is Biblical Studies, especially in the New Testament.
Emmanuel Orihentare Eregare is Senior Lecturer at the Department of History and International Studies, Babcock University, Nigeria, West Africa.

permeates the various societies (Freedman and Karsh, 1993, xxix). Nonetheless, the New World Order concept has played itself in various fronts since 1990s. The focus has been on the economic, social, political, technological and religious platforms. Recent discoveries also show that the world has experienced some notable incredible records of disaster, Patti (2010, 551) states that there have been irreparable acts of terrorism, earth-shattering disasters like pandemics that have been either natural or manmade, the resurgence of widespread armed international conflicts, global financial meltdowns, unbridled individual and corporate financial ethics violations, and the escalation of nuclear expansion by powerful nations. All these have posed a great upheaval on the landscape of the world with religious bodies. Consequently, these have generated the development of various approaches to create common grounds for a peaceful co-existence of man and global tranquility.

However, Arend (1993, 491) suggests that the emergence of the New World Order suggests the development of a global government that ensures a safe and peaceful international system. Slaughter (2014, 15) also classifies the New World Order as a global governance that is institutionalized to provide cooperation and contain the conflict in all nations. It is also to improve the global stewardship of the earth and reach minimum standards of human dignity.

The Elitist Global Religions

The number of the world religions is as vast as there are cultural and political diversities. According to Juan (2006, n.p.), research has shown that there are about five thousand religions across the world, and they are diverse in beliefs and practices. The world's top twenty (20) religions and its adherents include: Christianity, Islam, Nonreligious (Secular/Agnostic/Atheist), Hinduism, Buddhism, Chinese traditional religion, Primal-indigenous, African traditional religion, Sikhism, Juche, Spiritism,

Judaism, Bahai, Jainism, Shinto, Cao Dai, Zoroastrianism, Tenrikyo, Neo-Paganism, and Unitarian-Universalism. These religions range from billions to thousands of believers as in the order of priority. This section decides not to deal with the statistics as it varies over time but it just describes the level of their distinctive growth ratio which has always been constant. The global history of religions can first be traced to the three (3) Abrahamic religions which include Judaism, Christianity and Islamic religions. The first use of the term 'religion' was in the1590s to indicate the Protestants and Catholics while subsequent categorization of the world religions moved from four religions in eighteenth century to eight religions in 1870; a twentieth century survey identifies thirty-three principal world religions, which settles for a sort of 'G8 of major religions' in the world (Chidester, 2018, 45).

Efforts have been made at the global stage to foster an interfaith religious harmony in recent times in order to facilitate a new world order. According to Walsh (2012, 54), such actions by the United Nations include the convening of the Millennium World Peace Summit of Religious and Spiritual Leaders in 2000 at which the topmost religious groups were present. Subsequently, in August 2000, there was an Interreligious and International Federation for World Peace (an initiative of Rev. Sun Myung Moon). In 2004, the UN passed a motion for the "Promotion of Interreligious Dialogue". Another resolution was adopted in 2009 for the "Promotion of Interreligious and Intercultural Dialogue". In 2010, an annual "World Interfaith Harmony Week" to be celebrated each year during the first week of February was passed as a resolution. This chapter surveys the top ten global religions and their contribution towards the mission for world peace and order. The selected religions are Christianity, Islam, Hinduism, Buddhism, Judaism, African Traditional Religion, Sikhism, Bahais, Jainism and Chinese Folk Religion. This chapter also observes if there is any interconnectivity between the various global religions for global peace

Christianity

Christianity is the largest religion in the world which originates from the first-century Palestine (Johnson and Grim, 2013, n.p.) with about 2.3 billion adherents, making up nearly a third (31%) of Earth's 7.3 billion people (Hackett and Mcclendon, 2017, n.p.). The majority of Christians, according to a review (Cooperman, 2015, 5) are domiciled in sub-Sahara Africa (40%), South America, Latin America, the Caribbean and Europe. Tracing the history of Christian belief, H.J. Hillerbrand (2012, 2) opines that the history of Christianity is an history which began some two thousand years ago about Jesus of Nazareth who propounded a "striking religion" with a humble followership until He died "as a criminal", though rose from the dead, yet as hundreds of years passed till date, His mission to reach the world with a message of peace had been "stunningly successful."

Christianity is a religion following the model of the "Prince of Peace' (Isaiah 9:7). The term 'peace' is also based on a principle of the Old and New Testaments where humankind is expected to live peaceably with God and with fellow humans while emphasizing that the source and foundation of true peace and orderliness in the world is God, through the ministry of Jesus Christ (Gbotoe and Kgatla, 2017, n.p.). Even though Christ taught among people who were occupied by the military dictatorship of Rome, many of whom were sympathetic to a potential violent revolution, Jesus nevertheless calls for a life of non-violence. The biblical concept of peace suggests, not the absence of war and conflict, but "finding spiritual peace within oneself through a relationship with God" which transcends other concepts of global fulfilment of peaceful attainments (Brantmeier, et., 2010, 71). Such a spiritual experience brings peace and ultimately healing to the human life (Proverbs 13:30). Christianity centers on the principle of how to live at peace with oneself, with others and with the generality of the world (Philippians 4:4-9). No wonder, Jesus Christ described Himself as the Prince of Peace.

Islam

The Islamic global population is estimated about 1.8 billion, representing 23% of all people. There are two major branches of Islam – Sunni and Shia. Overwhelming majority (87-90%) of Muslims are Sunnis; about 10-13% are Shia Muslims (Hackett and Grim, 2012, 21). A larger population of the Sunnis is mainly found in Iran, Iraq, Bahrain, and Azerbaijan (Khalili, 2014, 41-47). This is the second largest religion in the world and it has a significant concern towards religious correctness - religious symbolism and rituals of worship (Denny, 1994, 1070). The Asian continent is home to most of the world's Muslims (71%), about 27% of Muslims live in Africa, 2% reside in Europe, 0.48% in America and 0.03 in Oceania (Kettani, 2010, 143-153; Nasr, 2003, 59-74).

The term peace (*salaam*) from the Islamic perception originates from the same root as the word Islam (*salim*) (Harper, 2007:11-22). This is positive in nature as it reveals that individuals receive peace as he or she enters into submission to the will of God (Wikipedia, 2021). It extends to making reconciliation with their non-Muslim and building peaceful societies even with their adversaries (Abu-Nimer, 2003). Islam believes in a Messianic figure in the end of times that will rid the world of injustice and evil. He will bring peace to the world. The public rather, through the binocular of Islam, views the term peace by the 9/11 incident in the United States in September 2001 triggers a negative worldview to the whole 'peaceful nature' of the Islamic religion" (Sachedina 2010, 333; Abu-Nimer 2003).

Hinduism

Hinduism is the third largest religious group in the world with about 1.2 billion adherents. It is a polytheistic religion with over 330 million gods and goddesses and one supreme and impersonal god known as *Brahmin*. It was originated in the present day Pakistan, with a faith system based on reincarnation and a caste system. It is confined within the Southern Asia region which includes countries like Afghanistan, Bangladesh, Bhutan, India, Iran, Maldives, Nepal, Pakistan, and Sri Lanka. India is home to the largest percentage of all Hindus (94%), followed by Nepal (2%) and Bhutan (1%). Hinduism, as a religion does not have a single founder; lacks a unified system of belief, a centralized authority and a bureaucratic structure. Most of their beliefs are simply a combination of traditions that are linked to a body of sacred texts called the *Vedas*. Common components include a belief in reincarnation (*samsara*) determined by the law of cause and effect (*karma*), and as well a belief in salvation which helps to transcend this cycle. "Hindus do not seek salvation, but desire to be released from their karmic debt to end the cycle of rebirth. This is called *moshka* and it is accomplished through works, devotion, and knowledge. It is a polytheistic religion which has a multiplicity of divine beings, which are centered on *Trimurthi* (a combination of *Brahma, Visnu, and Siva,* the deities deemed responsible for the creation, preservation and destruction of the universe) (Agarwal, 2015, n.p.; Soni, 2010, 310). Through the works of Gandhi, their concept of peace has been derived from the *Bhagavad Gita* text. Hinduism is a non-violent religion. It promotes a peaceful co-existence of man and raises higher righteousness. The Hindu religion believes in fighting against injustice and evil without physical force. This is believed to be one of the most powerful weapons ever devised by man for destruction (Anjum, 2017, 248-259).

Buddhism

Buddhism sprang up from Hinduism. Buddhism is non-theistic. It has no belief that a creator or god exists. It is a religion, though considered more of a philosophy and discipline, which follows the teachings of Siddhartha Gautama who was once a former Hindu prince. He has been known as "Buddha or the Awakened One" (Mark, 2020, n.p.). The global population of Buddhists is estimated as 535 million followers, which represents 8% of the world's total population. Cambodia has the highest percentage of its population as Buddhists with 96.9% of its population as Buddhists which is about 13.7 million out of 15 million. Buddhist countries include: Thailand, Myanmar, Bhutan, Sri Lanka, Laos and Mongolia. Mark (2020, n.p.) asserts that the four major beliefs in Buddhism are: (1.) life is suffering; (2.) the cause of suffering is craving; (3.) the end of suffering comes with an end to craving; and (4.) there is a path which leads one away from craving and suffering. Yen (2006, 91-112) submits that Buddhism is a religion of peace and non-violence. Therefore, Buddhism focuses its peaceful drive on the global peaceful concept of the Six Principles of Cordiality. These include a conscious and disciplined maintenance of bodily acts, verbal acts and mental acts of loving-kindness toward other group members, sharing of material gains with others, following the same codes of conducts, and holding the same view that would lead to the complete destruction of suffering. Some examples of the religion's effort to bring peace and relief include the establishment of The Buddhist Humanitarian Project, with a mission to provide relief to the Rohingya communities experiencing conflicts. Another approach devised by the Buddhism includes the International Network of Engaged Buddhists, which has worked extensively on humanitarian projects throughout Myanmar, Bangladesh, and India. Further, Buddhist Global Relief (BGR) is another non-profit organization founded in May 2008; it is an inter-denominational community of Buddhists and friends of Buddhism who address the plight of people afflicted by poverty, natural disasters and societal neglect. In 2015 alone, BGR distributed USD 336,600 across all its current projects, reaching about 15,000 people. The organization usually awards grants from USD 2,000 to USD 10,000 to fund projects. Typically, these might involve arranging emergency food aid or devising long-term strategies to increase food production, strengthen local capacity and promote long-term sustainability (Nitschke, 2016, 5).

Chinese Folk Religion

The Chinese folk religion has about 400 million adherents worldwide. It is a common religion for the Chinese culture, which includes a combination of Confucianism, Buddhism, and Taoism, and other local practices and beliefs. It includes the worship of forces of nature, ancestors, exorcism, and a belief in the rational order of nature. It also has to do with human beings and their spirits and gods in their ability to influence the universe and reality. Worship is devoted to many gods and immortals. The Chinese folk religion allows an easy incorporation of certain local beliefs and practices. It is syncretic in nature. Chinese folk religion is a faith whose theology, rituals, and officials are widely diffused into other secular and social institutions. It involves the traditional worship of local deities as that of the Buddhist and Taoist figures, astrology, the worship of animal totems, and ancestor worship. While Chinese folk religion is hard to define in the abstract, it does contain within itself numerous common elements. Chinese folk religion is not organized, nor is it equipped with theologies or theologians. Chinese folk religion has no fixed text. The emperor and the Chinese Government are open-minded about religion. By implication, they allow religions to co-exist. They are independent in nature yet they can syncretize. Religion is believed as a trend that must blend with the government. For example, love for one's religion should be equitable to the love for the country. China, over the years, has been in the movement of combing other religious groups that are ready to collaborate with their country. China has ever been having inter-religious dialogue with other religious groups even outside China as well. One Chinese folk religion aims at the collaboration with the religions of the world to defend ethnic equity, sufferings, defend the weak and ultimately achieve global peace (Liu Jinguang, 2013, 205-209; Zhigang, 2010:214-215).

African Traditional Religion

Lugira (2011, 36) states that the African Traditional Religion is polytheistic in nature. Recent studies show that it has about 100 million adherents worldwide in the continent of Africa and it was rooted in the pre-colonial era. The religion comprises of the total culture or traditions, norms, ethics and pattern of administration, religious beliefs and practices of Africans (Alokan, 2010, 4). It is not without other religious elements or gods. It covers the socio-political systems of Africans as well (Kanu, 2017, 32). African Traditional religion centers on the peaceful mission with the various ethnic groups through conflict resolution and making communal or inter-communal peace which deciphers to global peace. The medium for peaceful movement by the African Traditional Religions are through building broken relationships and making reconciliation among the members of a given community (Kanu, 2017, 33). This is to deemphasize competition and promote cooperation for a common good. This also implies that the peaceful concept of the African Traditional Religion fits into making the world a better place and promoting a peaceful co-existence of communities.

Sikhism

Sikhism is an Indian religion. It has about 26 million followers across the globe. Its geographical statistics is described as less than 2% of the Indian population. It has 80% of its followers living in the State of Punjab and about 0.3% of the world's population (Kaur, 2020, n.p.). Sikhism originates from Northern India in the 15th century. The teachings of *Guru Nanak* (the religion's founder), other enlightened leaders (gurus) and its holy text are basic to the religion. Sikhist's text is referred to as the *Guru Granth Sahib*. The word "Sikh" originates from a Sanskrit root which translates into "disciple" or "learning." Thus, Sikhs focuses on attaining salvation through the continual learning of God through personal meditation and rightful living. Sikhism believes in one God. It centers on the universal brotherhood of mankind. Peace movement in this religion seeks for reconciliation between warring factions in religious, social and political spheres and identifies the root causes. It then shows the way to a harmonious way of life; but if that fails, it is better to resolve such issues that may separate humans through violence and war which is fair and just (Balakrishnan, 2014, 45-48). Consequently, this provides the platform for unification for global peaceful movements and resulting to war if otherwise not consented to by the enemies.

Judaism

Judaism is a religion that makes about 14.7 million which is approximately about 0.18% of the world's population. It is the earliest of the three monotheistic, Abrahamic religions which include Christianity and Islam. Abrahamic religions, as the name implies, trace their origin to Abraham, who is a figure in the Hebrew Bible, New Testament and the Qur'an. Tradition teaches that the origins of Judaism are found in the covenant (divine agreement) between Abraham and God, dated to 2000 B.C.E (Tanenbaum, 2011, 5-6). The concept of peace, in the theology of the Jews, is *shalom*. It is derived from the verbal root *slm,* meaning "to complete" or rendered "completeness" or "wholeness", a state of personal perfection. The state that is devoid conflict; it is within this idea that the Jews see an emancipation from evil and the world crisis by looking forward to the time of the Messiah. It is believed that the Messiah will bring a perfect realistic peace to the world which is eschatological. Jung (1945, 388) reiterates that the Judaist religion believes that the only way to enjoy perfection or wholesome "peace" is by keeping to the tenets of the *torah,* the laws of God (Deuteronomy 23:8). In a rabbinic saying (Mishnah Avot 1:18), peace, truth and justice are the major principles upon which there could be a global peace. Does the world seek after peace, truth and justice? If the world pursues peace and justice without the truth the peace movement will be an illusion. Truth projects the completeness that God projects in the concept of peace movement.

For example, a classic scenario can be taken from the Jewish belief on peace rather than war as cited by the medieval Jewish

German Rhineland community in 1096. The Jews, in that period, gave up their lives willingly rather than resisting the marauding Christian armies just as the ancient Jews also offered to surrender to the tortures of the Roman conquerors of Palestine for the sake of the truth not only on peace and justice (Jung, 1945, 393).

However, there had been interfaith dialogues on peace by the Jews within the global community. They have had the *Standing Conference of Jews, Christians and Muslims in Europe* (JCM) established in 1975 (an annual dialogue conference for students of the 3 main faiths). The *Centre for the Study of Jewish-Christian Relations* was as well established in 1990, while the *Centre for the Study of Muslim-Jewish Relations* was founded in 2006. Between 2010 and 2014, three institutions (The Jewish Theological Seminary, Hartford Seminary and the Islamic Society of North America) worked together on academic workshops and community-based pilot projects, which were efforts at bridging the gaps on global religious conflicts. With the hope of bridging the gap between the political Israel and Palestine, Interfaith Encounter Association (IEA) comprising professionals and school groups were also established as an initiative of Judaism efforts at proving global peace (Magonet, 2015, n.p.). These efforts contribute to breaking down negative stereotypes; learning more about other faith groups (their rituals, ceremonies and basic tenets); and, most importantly, rehumanizing the "enemy".

Bahais Religion

The Baha'i faith is a world religion of about seven million adherents globally. It originated in the Middle East during the nineteenth century. It was founded by a Persian nobleman called *Baha'u'llah* (1817-1892) (Fozdar, 2015, 274-292). The faith advocates a 'one world' philosophy. It is a religion that bereft schisms. It does not have priesthood; rather, it has an elected circle of decision making representatives that operates at all levels. Baha' believes that God has made himself known through messengers as prophets Abraham, Krishna, Moses, Zoroaster, Buddha, Jesus Christ, Muhammad, The Bab, and Baha'u'llah. They have been sent to educate humanity on God and found the world religions. The writings of the last prophet, Baha'u'llah, are seen to be the modern day words of God containing not only past revelations but also new truths for the modern world (Were, 2005, n.p.). Bahá í teachings lay emphasis on the unity of all peoples, openly rejecting notions of racism and nationalism. At the heart of Bahá í teachings is the goal of a unified world order that ensures the prosperity of all nations, races, creeds, and classes (Smith, 2000, n.p.). It is a religion that believes also in the religio-political to relieve the world of the suffering from wars, the oppressive burden of military expenditures, embracing the cause of peace and instituting a universal framework for collective security and promoting the eradication of oppressive social ills which are the root causes of conflict and war in the world (Ferreira and Kalberg, 2017, 131-133).

Jainism

In addition to Hinduism and Buddhism, Jainism is one of the three most ancient Indian religious traditions that exist in South Asian religious belief and practice, with an estimated global population of about 4 million. Though Jainism shared similarities with Hinduism and Buddhism because of a common cultural and linguistic background, the Jain tradition must be regarded as an independent phenomenon rather than as a Hindu sect or a Buddhist heresy, as some earlier Western scholars believed. This seems to be the only religious group where devotees, monks and lay persons are required to be vegetarians. The idea of God who is a creator, protector and destroyer of evil does not exist in Jainism. It does not believe in a Supreme Being yet is not atheistic. It believes in a rigorous disciplined effort to bring everyone to a state of being able to conquer hatred, craving, anger, greediness, arrogance, upon which such can become a god of his own (Kamar, 2009, 3).

Every religion seeks to maintain peace. This study reveals that religious groups are mainly from different parts of Asia and sparingly from Africa. They are similar in the pursue of peace movements within and without their religious spheres commonly through a religio-political platform. They possess attempts to control the phenomena of war, sufferings, environmental order and peaceful co-existence of both their members and non-members. They are also susceptible to making peaceful associations with other religions. This latter is seemingly a fertile ground for the unity of the globe for global peace movements and maintaining order through the human wings of justice and peace to make the globe a better place to live. Truth becomes relative in their course for peaceful coalitions. Though truth is relative philosophically, this study centers on finding truth biblically which these religions devoid except for Judaism that has partial truth.

Global Peace Treaties

Alex Uguwkah

Global peace treaties are the common but legal instruments put in place by mankind to end wars and conflicts that pervade territories, nations and continents of the world. They are indeed instrumental and applicable worldwide which entrench it as global phenomena. Treaties are bridges between wars and peace. Treaties, in essence, provide a basis for an agreement between warring parties. Wars, battles and other domestic or international conflicts, whether armed or diplomatic, are often the outcome of disputes over natural resources or the struggle for power, influence and wealth. Examples of major conflicts of the world include, the Panic Wars, (264-146 BCE), a series of wars between the Roman Republic and the Carthaginian (Punic) Empire resulting in the destruction of Cathage; battle of Thermopylae (480 BCE); battle in Central Greece, Wars of Roses (1455-85) in the English history, 100 years' war was an intermittent war between England and France in the 14th-15th century over a series of disputes on the English and French claimants to the crown; Napoleonic wars

Dr Alexander Ugwukah (ugwukaha@babcock.edu.ng) is a Senior Lecturer in the Department of History and International Studies with special emphasis in Socio-economic History and International Relations. He has taught students for over ten years and published articles in both local and international journals.

which constitute a 23-year period of recurrent conflict in Europe; American revolution (1775-1783); World War I &II (1914-1918 and 1939-1945); Vietnam war (1954-1975); Korean conflict; Afghanistan war which started in (2001) triggered by the 911 attack by Al-Qaida and led by Osama bin Laden and so on. All these wars over the years have been negotiated or ended with different treaties. There are well over 5,000 peace treaties globally signed over the years to put an end to one war or the other. Usually, peace treaties are put in place by political or military leaders close to the end of hostilities in a dragging war situation. As a historical phenomenon, peace treaties emerge independently from one another in all major ancient civilizations of the world.

For the formation of the Modern International law of peacemaking, the dominant strand is the European type. Modern historiography has established a tradition of treaty making and peace making that starts with the Ancient Near East and passes via classical Greece to the Roman Empire. Through the survival of the Roman practices and the rediscovery of the Roman law in the 1th century, essential features of this tradition were woven into the peace treaty practice and doctrine of medieval and Modern Europe (Lesaffer, 2012:71).

In the context of colonization, European powers encountered other traditions and often had to adapt their own practices to local situations. However, in the 19th and early 20th centuries, the European and Western powers imposed their forms and ways of peace making upon non-Europeans. In general, three categories of substantial peace treaty clauses can be discussed. Firstly, there are the clauses that settle the disputes underlying the war and put an end to the state of war. Secondly, there are the clauses that deal with the legal consequences of war and put an end to the state of war. Thirdly, there are the clauses that regulate future peaceful relations between the belligerents, such as commerce and navigation (Lesaffer, Ibid). He further asserts that European peace treaties from the 16th to 19th centuries were particularly elaborate on the two latter issues thus, making them the foremost historical forces for the jus post bellum of the centuries. Before the 19th century, hardly any multilateral peace conferences were made. Even at the great multilateral peace conferences of the Early Modern age, peace was made through a set of bilateral peace treaties. Since the end of World War II (1945) and particularly since the end of the cold war (1989), peace treaty practice has undergone fundamental changes. Under the modern jus contra bellum, the lines between the state of war and state of peace have become blurred: 'Human rights, constitutional law and transitional justice.

As Akinboye and Ottoh (2011:251) have noted, "if the substance of international politics since the beginning of time is conflict and its adjustment among groups of people who acknowledge no common supreme authority, then the issue of Global Peace Treaties becomes a paramount instrumentality to achieve the adjustments and readjustments intended to regulate harmony among the nations of the world". However, the interest of this chapter is predicated upon Global Peace Treaties which is a prevailing solution to curb the prevailing conflicts among the relations of the nations of the world. The purpose of the chapter is therefore to analyze, discern and ascertain the functions of global peace treaties. Peace Treaties are legal agreements between the parties to an armed conflict or the armed conflict between them. One can broadly distinguish between two types of Peace Treaties. First, Peace Treaties in the strict sense, are agreements concluded between belligerent states in written form and governed by international laws that bring to an end the formal or material state of war between them. Secondly, agreements that are concluded between non-state parties where none of the warring parties are a government (Understanding Peace Treaties, 2004: n.p). It is a legal agreement between two or more hostile parties, usually countries or governments, which formally ends a state of war between the two parties. Peace treaties are different from other international documents that control conflicts because they are often the culmination of international peace discussions, and they seek permanent resolutions by establishing conditions for peace. A peace treaty is not the same as a surrender, where one party agrees to give up arms; or a cease fire, in which parties agree to suspend hostilities temporarily; or an armistice agreement, in which parties agree to stop hostilities, but do not agree to long term conditions for peace. Any, or all, of these documents, however, may precede the execution of a peace treaty between two parties. Conflicts might first end with the surrender of one party, or a compromised cease fire agreement. These might be followed by an armistice agreement, as in the case of the Korean War in 1953. In such circumstances, permanent conditions for conflict resolution may be finally enunciated in a formal peace treaty.

Peace treaties may also be distinguished from peace agreements. Peace treaties generally involve separate sovereign nation-states. In recent years, however, the international community has been compelled to reconsider how peace treaties might be used to resolve not only conflicts between nations, but conflicts within nations. Peace agreements, which serve similar legal functions as a peace treaty, are often negotiated between warring parties within one nation (Understanding Peace Treaties, 2004: n.p). Other specific circumstances from this base, international law evolved over the intervening centuries as the interaction evolved slowly over the intervening centuries as the need of international community become more sophisticated.

During the last century or so, concern with international law has grown rapidly. Globalization has significantly expanded the need for rules to govern functional areas such as trade, finance travel, religion and communications. Similarly, international treaties have been made on such subjects as genocide, nuclear testing, use of the oceans, climate change and human rights. Even the most practical of all activities, war and other aspects of national security have become subjects of international law. Climate change has become an unprecedented challenge for humankind due to its severe consequences for our environment. Especially in the last three decades, global warming has been increasingly, rapidly, and predominantly caused by the combustion of fossil fuels such as coal, oil and gas, as well as by continuing deforestation (Ruppel et al, 2013). Peace treaties are part and parcel of the International Law which has its beginning in the origin of states and their need to regulate their relations. In considering Global Peace Treaties, it is important to note that treaties grew gradually through the elements of the ancient Jewish, Greek and Roman customs and practices combined with newer Christian concepts to form the beginning of an international system law. The most famous of these was Holland's Hugo Grotius (1583-1645), the first scholar of International Law who wrote *De Jure Belli ac Pacis*- On the law of War and Peace. Grotius and others advanced ideas about the sources of international laws, its role in regulating the relations of states, and its application to war and peace (Rourke, 2009:278).

International treaties are therefore the primary source of international law. A primary advantage of treaties is that they codify or write down the law. Agreements between states are binding according to the doctrine of *pacta sunt servanda* (treaties are to be served/carried out). All treaties are binding on those countries that are party to them (have signed and ratified or otherwise given them legal constant). Moreover, it is possible to argue that some treaties are also applicable to non-signatories. An example of this is the Vienna convention on Diplomatic Relations of 1961 which codified many existing rules of diplomatic standing and practice (US Military History Companion/Peace, 2020: n.p). Conflicts have continued unabated in our contemporary world because of the domination of one group by another. The international environment is full of conflicts of various magnitudes and dimensions. There is a general view by scholars that conflict is a normal phenomenon in the interactions among humans, whether acting individually or collectively. The world society is a system of states competing with one another, all in a bid to seize what belongs to all and this intense competition among states results in conflicts. It must not be also ignored that the traditional view of self-interest has often been acknowledged as the reason why conflict is inevitable. Additionally, ideological conflicts have tended to create intense conflicts in the world. The cold war between the United States and Russia disagreed on certain resolutions on Marxism-Leninism against capitalism.

International hegemony, although difficult to explain is also an aspect of international conflict. The big powers' hyper active roles in the regions of influences help to exacerbate conflicts. At times, these conflicts may arise from territorial ambitions between two or more states. This is what is termed as conflict of interests. Holsti, (1967:141) has listed some factors that has led the world into conflicts which include; national prestige, the respect countries enjoy by virtue of their status abroad and worldwide, imperialism, acquisition, irredentism, diversionary strategy of leaders like religious and ideological extremism, mutual distrust and suspicious, sociological and political conflicts and Human Aggressiveness. Blainey (2011:251) on the other hand summarizes the collective impact of war. He asserts that "wars usually begin when two nations disagree on their relative strength and wars usually cease when the fighting nations agree on their relative strength. Agreement or disagreement emerges from the shuffling of the same set of factors. Therefore, for a treaty to end wars or conflicts often signed when two or more nations in the war have come to demonstrate their strength and who was right in the first place was signed between the Allied Associated Power and Germany. Another famous treaty was the Paris Peace treaties which signed on 10 February 1947. It was reached after the Paris Peace conference which lasted from 29 July to 15 October 1946. The treaties allowed the defeated Axis power to resume their responsibilities as sovereign states in international wars and to qualify for membership in the United Nation.

Figure 1: Tablet of one of the earliest recorded treaties in history, Treaty of Kadesh, at the Istanbul Archaeology Museum

Figure 2: The Treaty of Versailles, signed at the conclusion of World War I

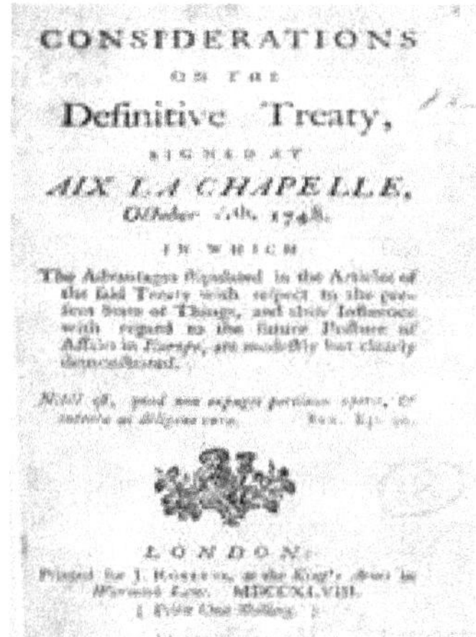

Figure 3: Considerations on the definitive treaty, signed at Aix la Chapelle, October 7/18th, 1748

Figure 4: Treaties of peace, good correspondence 1686

Another ancient Peace treaty is the five years' war (27BC to 22BC) between the Kushite Kandake (Queen), Amanirena and Augustus of Rome, a peace treaty which was signed in the year 21/20BC (Bell, 2008: n.p). The clash between the Kush and the Roman forces at Syene and Philae began as a border conflict. After an initial victory when the Kushites attacked the Roman Egypt, they driven out of Egypt by Gaius Petronius and the Romans established a new frontier at Hiere Sycaminos (Maharraqa). Mediators were sent from Kush to Emperor Augustus who was in Samos in the year 21/20BC when the peace treaty was concluded. The effect following the treaty was strikingly favourable to the Kushites in that the Southern part of the thirty-mile strip including Primis was evacuated by the Romans. Also, the Kushites were exempted from paying tribute to the emperor. On the other hand, the Romans continued to occupy the Dodekashoinos (twelve-mile lands) as a military border zone, so the frontier now lay near Maharraqua. It could therefore be said that an entente between them was beneficial to both. The Kushites were a regional power in their own right and resented paying tribute to Rome. The Romans also sought a quiet southern border for their absolutely essential grain supplies from Egypt without the constant war commitment and welcomed a friendly supply in a border region without raiding nomads. The Kushites perceived nomads like Blemmves to be a problem. The conditions were ripe for a deal. During the negotiations, Augustus granted the Kushite envoy all they asked for, and also cancelled the tribute earlier demanded by Rome Premmis (Qasrbrum) and areas North of Qasr Ibrin in the Southern portion of the Thirty-mile strip which were ceded to the Kushites as a buffer zone. Roman Emperor Augustus signed the treaty with the Kushites on Samos. The settlement brought peace and quietness on its Egyptian frontier. It also increased the prestige of the Roman Emperor Augustus, demonstrating his skill and ability to broker peace without constant warfare and do business with the distant Kushites, who a short time earlier had been fighting his troops. The respect accorded the emperor by the Kushite envoy as the treaty also created a favourable impress on Samos, including envoys from India and strengthened Emperor Augustus' upcoming negotiations with the Parthians. Another major feat of the peace treaty was that it ushered in a period of peace between two empires for about three centuries. Inscriptions treated by on an ancient temple at Hamadab, South of Pharde record the war and the favourite outcome from the Kushite perspective. Along with his signature on the official treaty, Roman Empire's Augustus marked the agreement by directing his administrators to collaborate with the regional priests in the erection of a temple at Denturi, and an inscription depicting the emperor himself celebrating local deities.

Middle Ages Peace Treaties

Wars and crisis did not abate with the transformation from the Ancient periods down to the Middle Ages, often referred to as the medieval period. From our list in this work, most of the peace treaties include the Treaty of Novgorod (1326), Treaty of Bretagne (1360), Peace of Lord (1454), Treaty of Madrid (1526), Peace of Catean-Cambresis (Lesaffer, ND). Other Peace treaties of the Medieval ages, particularly in England include, the Anglo-Saxon treaties, the treaties of the 100 years' war, treaties of the Duchy of Normandy, the treaty of Abercronvy, treaty of Action Anglo-Portuguese treaty of 1373, Treaty of Brigham, Boulogne Agreement, English Invasion of Scotland Treaty 1480, Treaty of London (1359) Treaty of New Castle 1244, Treaty of Paris (1303), Peace of Canterbury, Treaty of Amiens (1423), Treaty of Berwick (1357) Treaty of London 1474, Treaty of York 1464. All these treaties continued to restore peace in the troubled spots and territories of the European countries at the period before the gradual transformation to the modern period.

Historically, there was a time in man's evolution when religion was seen as an instrument for the regulation of societal behavior and a guide to the interaction of nations in the international arena. According to Akinboye and Ottoh, at that time of historical confection, there was a serious thought about political actors, who conceived the idea that sanctions, rules and regulations would only apply to nations outside their territory. The early application of rules and regulations vis-à-vis sanctions took root in the 15th, 16th and 17th centuries in Europe. The idea of regulation was constricted in the concept of legal rights and obligations with the development of sovereign states and whatever rules and regulations that existed to regulate or moderate behavior among states, grew out of the Chivalry by the ways knight were to behave (Akinboye and Ottoh, 2005:235). The church used this as well, while medieval Europe also incorporated natural laws and orders from Europe to guide the behavior of nations. For example, the church in 989 in the 10th century enacted the "Peace of God" which imposed restrictions on war, violence and squandering of any kind. A similar declaration, the Truce of God was established by Pope Bishop of Arles and the Abbot of Ching. The "Truce of God" first proclaimed 1027 prohibited fighting between Wednesday evening and Monday and also determined how people would fight, if at all. It also stated that nations should not engage in unjust wars and for a war to be just, it had to be established by an authority for legitimate reasons.

Another famous example would be the series of peace treaties known as the Peace of Westphalia which initiated the modern system of Nation-States. Subsequent wars were no longer over religion but resolved political issues of state. That encouraged Catholic and Protestant powers to ally, leading to a number of major realignments. The United Nations intervention in a war is an example of conflict that was ended by an armistice rather than a peace treaty with the Korean armistice agreement. The Korean War was a war between North Korea and South Korea. The war began on 25 June 1950 when North Korea invaded South Korea and ended unofficially on 27 July, 1953 in an armistice. This invasion was the first military action of the Cold War. By July, American troops had entered the war on South Korea's behalf. As far as American officials were concerned, it was a war against the forces of international communism itself. After some early back-and-forth across the 38th parallel, the fighting stalled and casualties mounted with nothing to show for them. Meanwhile, American officials worked anxiously to fashion some sort of armistice with the North Koreans. The alternative, they feared, would be a wider war with Russia and China–or even, as some warned, World War III. Finally, in July 1953, the Korean War came to an end. However, that war has never technically ended because final peace treaty or settlement has never been achieved.

A more recent example of a Peace treaty is the 1973 Paris Peace Accords that sought to end the Vietnam War. Treaties in the modern era continued to serve the purpose of bringing to an end the warring parties of the latter years from their territories and centres of government to end hostilities and wars. However, it must be pointed out that international law had begun to assume more complex standards which affected international relations and politics.

Modern Peace Treaties

In the strict sense, the history of modern international law really began with the Treaty of Westphalia (1648) where European power met and dissolved the empire of the church and broke into nation-states which, therefore brought about the concepts of sovereignty, territorial integrity, equality and non-interference. These principles formed the basis of modern international law and were reemphasized in the Treaty of Utrecht 1713. In the American and French revolutions of 1776 and 1789, respectively these ideas of neutrality in cases of boundary clashes between nations were settled using the principles laid down in the Roman law. Therefore, these are the factors that stimulated the growth of the international treaties. In 1760, there was an industrial revolution in Europe which brought trade in goods and services. It must be noted that in the same vein, towards the end of the 18th century, the French revolution erupted, precisely in 1789 because of the discontent which developed from the inequality in the French society. The inequities in the tax system which the first estate comprising all members of the Roman Catholic clergy and the nobles of the Second estate forced on the third estate, especially on the peasants eventually led to the French revolution. Soon, the revolution that followed brought the monarchy to an end, when Louis XV and his entire family, were sentenced to death on the guillotine (Burton, 1972:138). The rise of Napoleon Bonaparte in the years that followed and his determination to conquer and rule over Europe nearly succeeded but this obsession would eventually lead to his destruction (500) from 1806 to 1812 controlled most of the European continent after he defeated Austria and Russia. He attempted the defeat of Britain but failed because of the British Naval Forces. His empire crumbled finally in 1814, when enemies struck from all directions and the Allied forces defeated him and banished him to the island of Elba, which lay off the coast of Italy. He soon escaped and returned to France as Emperor once again for 100 days before the countries of Europe united again and defeated him in a battle at the Belgium village of Waterloo in 1815. This time, he was banished to the South Atlantic Island of Helena where he died in 1821.

While his impact on the continental to Europe is arguable, some felt he established religious freedom, the abolition of serfdom and noble privileges and the institution of the Napoleonic code of Law. Out of his 15 years of rule, 14 years were spent in Wars, which really characterized him as a Warrior as he caused Europe many years of bloodshed. After his defeat, the people of Europe were sick of war and longed for peace. The essence of this narration is that Europe was at war for years which only came to an end with the congress of Vienna. The main goals of the congress of Vienna were to settle conflicts among the Great powers of Europe consisting of Britain, Prussia, Austria, Russia and France and to strike a political balance among these powerful states. To reach their goals, the congress of Vienna first created small buffer states along the borders of France, which was still considered as the main threat of the Peace of Europe. Then Austria, Russia, Prussia and Britain in what came to be called the concert of Europe agreed to meet periodically to guard the Vienna settlement and keep the peace of Europe. This was the first international effort to keep and solve shared problems in such a diplomatic manner. It must be asserted that the concert of Europe kept the European peace for the next 50 years without any major war.

The Crimean War

The Crimean War which began in 1853 was the next big armed clash in Europe after 1815. The professed reason for the war between France and Russia was the administration of Holy places in Palestine which was under the jurisdiction of the weak Ottoman Empire. The conflict pitted French, British, Italian and Turkish troops against Russia. The Crimean War was a statement, when Austria which had remained neutral threatened to enter the War on the side of the British, French, Italians and Turkish in 1855, Russia sued for peace. In 1856, the warring countries gathered at Paris for a Peace conference. This conference resulted into another important treaty herein known as the treaty of Paris (1856). This treaty in its manifestations insulted and hurt Russia in several ways. The most important was the ban on all Russian battleships on the Black sea. This development left the Russian Southern border undefended leaving Russia weaker. Another important result of the Peace conference in Paris was a secret pact France made with Italy to help out Austria from two Northern Italian states, paving the way for Italian unification (1858-1870).

Treaty of Moscow / Treaty of Brotherhood

Another important peace treaty is that which was an agreement between the Grand National Assembly of Turkey (TBMM), under the leadership of Mustafa Kemal Atantwk and

Russia under the leadership of Vladimir Lenin signed on 16 March, 1921. Turkey's borders, as well as those of Georgia, Armenia and Azerbary defined by the treaty are still in existence. After the shutdown of the Russian Sukhoi Su-24 over the Syria-Turkey border in November 2015 and the rise of Russian-Turkish relations, members of the communist Party of Russia proposed annulling the Treaty of Moscow. Initially, the Russian foreign ministry considered that action to second a political message is the government of Turkey President, Peace Tayyip Erdogan. However, Moscow ultimately decided against the idea in its effort to deescalate tensions with Ankara.

The Treaty of Versailles (1919) is possibly the most notorious of peace treaties and is blamed by many historians for the rise of National Socialism in Germany and the eventual outbreak of the Second World War in 1939. The costly reparation that Germany was forced to pay the victors, the fact that Germany had to accept sole responsibility for starting the war and the harsh restrictions on German rearmament were all listed in the Treaty of Versailles and caused massive resentment in Germany. The peace treaty signed in the Hall of Mirrors on June 28, 1919 signified the end of the First World War. The outstanding personalities that drew the Treaty of Versailles included President Woodrow Wilson of the United States of America, Georges Clemenceau, the Prime Minister of France and Lloyd George, the Prime Minister of Britain. Germany was not represented at the Versailles Treaty. The overriding principle governing the territorial settlement at the Versailles Treaty was self-determination.

Germany considered the terms of the Versailles Treaty too severe and vindictive against her, with special reference to the payment of reparations, the loss of Alsace and Lorraine, the loss of her overseas territories, the loss of the Eastern part of Germany to Poland (where over $2^1/_2$ million Germans resided), the reduction of her naval power, the numerical inferiority of her armed forces etc.

Worse still, apart from territorial losses, Germany was made to deliver large quantities of coal to France, Belgium and Italy. Therefore, to Germany, the terms of the Versailles Treaty were too harsh and severe. The German delegates that received the terms had this to say

> "We are well aware of the weight of hate that is here directed against us". Even Lloyd George, the British representative commented thus on the terms of the Treaty of Versailles "The terms are written with the blood of fallen heroes…" (Fadeiye, 2016:139-143

Thus, the problems created by the Versailles treaty led to the Second World War in 1939 which ended in 1945. After that, there were other conflicts which attracted peace treaties. Given the volume of global peace treaties in the world which as earlier noted, is more than 5,000, the best that can be is to list out some of the most important of these treaties organized chronologically in order to give us an idea of the length and breadth of Peace Treaties in the world since the ancient periods. The list of treaties is organized chronologically by the years they were signed. 628- Pact of Al-Hudaybiyal; 754- Donation of Pippin; 756- Donation of Pippin; 843- Treaty of Verdun; 1201- Treaty of Venice; 1326- Treaty of Novgorod; 1360- Treaty of Bretigny; 1370- Priests Chantes; 1454- Peace of Lord; 1489- Treaty of Medina Campo; 1494- Treaty of Tordesillas; 1526- Treaty of Madrid; 1548- Ausburg Laterun; 1559- Peace of Cateau-Cambresis; 1596- Union of Pirest-Litovsk; 1617- Treaty of Stolboro; 1648- Peace of Westphatia; 1654- Pireyaslaw Agreement; 1657- Treaty of Wehlau; 1659- Peace of the Pyrennes; 1660- Treaty of Copenhagen; 1661- Treaty of Carchs; 1667- Treaty of Breds; 1670- Treaty of Dover; 1678- Treaty of Nijmegen; 1679- Treaties of Nijmegen; 1689- Treaty Merfchiknsk; 1699- Treaty of Carlowitz; 1706- Trfeaty of Altranstadt; 1707- Act of Union; 1709- First Bawier Treaty; 1713- Second Bawier Treaty; 1714- Treaties of Rastatt and Baden; 1715- Third Berier Treaty; 1718- Treaty of Passarowitz; 1733- Pacte de Famille; 1737- Walking Purchase; 1739- Treaty of Belgrading; 1743- Pact de Famille, Treaty of Abo; 1718-

Treaty of Ax-la-chapelle; 1755- Gianti Agreement; 1757- Treaty of Alinagew; 1761- Pacte de Famill; 1763- Peace of Hubertusbing, Treaty of Pans; 1768- Treaty of Masulipatam; 1772- First Partition of Poland; 1773- First Treaty of Bangras; 1774- Treaty of Kucuk Kaynarca; 1775- Second Treaty of Banaras; 1776- Treaty of Purandha-between Peshiwa of the Marutha and the British East India company in Calcutta; 1778- Franco-American Alliance; 1779- Convention of Wadgaon; 1783- Peace of Paris, Treaty of Geogrevsk- ended the United States War for independence. Represent England was Richard Oswald, Chiefnegotiator under the Earl of Shelburne, the Secretary of State; 1784- Second Treaty of First Stanwik; 1790- Treaty of Varals; 1792- Treaty of Jessy

1793- Second Partition of Poland; 1794- Jay Treaty; 1795- Pinckney's Treaty; 1797- Treaty of Compo Formio; 1802- Treaty of Amiens, Treaty of Bussein; 1803- Lonesiana Purchase; Treaty of Deogaon; Treaty of Surji-Arjungaon; 1805- Treaty of Pressburg; 1807- Treaties of Tilsit; 1809- Treaty of Armarts and Treaty of Canack and Treaty of Schonbrunn; 1810- Strangford Treaty; 1812- Treaty of Bucharest; 1814- Treaty of Chaumont, GTreaty of Ghent and Treaty of Kiel and Treaty of Paris; 1815- Treaty of Paris Napoleon Bimenpate; 1817- Rush-Bagot-Agreement; 1819- Transcontinental Treaty; 1833- Treaty of Hunkar Iskelesi; 1840- Treaty of Wantangi; 1842- Webster –Ashburton Treaty; 1846- Bidlak Treaty; 1848- Treaty of Guadalupe Hidalgo; 1850- Clayton-Bulwer Treaty; 1851- Treaty of Kuldja; 1853- Gadsden Purchase; 1854- Treaty of Kanagawa; 1855- Bowring Treaty; 1856- Treaty of Paris- to end the Crumean War; 1858- Harris Treaty; 1862- Treaty of Saigon; 1867- Alaska Purchase; 1868- Nagodba; 1874- Chinese Engagement; 1874- Pangkor Engagement; 1875- Reciprocity Treaty; 1878- Treaty of San-Stefano; 1881- Treaty of Bardi; 1882- Triple Alliance; 1918- Treaties of Brest Litovsk; 1919- Treaty of Versailles; 1921- Four Power Pact; 1921- Treaty of Moscow; 1949- Geneva Convention; 1963- Nuclear Test Ban Treaty; 1966- Tashkent Agreement; 1967- Outer Space Treaty; 1972- Anti

Ballistic Missile Treaty; 1992- Kyoto Protocol; 1993- Chemical/Weapon Convention.

An attempt has been made to consider Global Peace Treaties from the ancient period to modern times. It is hardly practicable to write on every peace treaty since the beginning of times. The least that this chapter has done is to present the ideology of Global Peace Treaties since the beginning of times. The earliest recorded Peace Treaty, although it is rarely mentioned or remembered was between the Hittite Empire and the Hayaza-Azzi confederation around 1350 BC. The treaty was completed between the Hittite and the Egyptian empires after 1274 BC. After which several others followed as depicted in the above list of Peace Treaties. Equally, an attempt has been made to consider the theoretical dimensions which influenced the inauguration and signing of these peace treaties. It must be noted that the role of peace treaties cannot but be a paramount instrumentality to achieve the adjustments and readjustments intended to regulate harmony among the nations of the world. Without peace treaties, it is obvious that the world would be at a stake of unending conflicts. That is why efforts have always been made by world leaders to institute these global peace treaties, knowing fully well that every party that signs such a treaty would be bound by the dictates of such global peace treaties. It is in this realm that this work has considered the position and functions of global peace treaties. Though peace treaties are human efforts, some were made, some parties were satisfied, some parties were not satisfied, no equity in the justice made, peace made over the ages seem not to be permanent. However, peace is still being sought for. This will be a human continual effort until the coming of the Prince of Peace, Jesus Christ.

CHAPTER FIVE

New Testament Overviews on the New World Order

John Apiah

The attempt of humanities to find, maintain and enjoy peace is an ongoing quest throughout recorded history. History is repleted with efforts by individuals, societies, and inter-continental communities and various nations to enjoy lasting peace on earth. Political and economic ideologies have been formulated and religious institutions such as the World Council of Churches, Religions for Peace, Catholic Peacebuilding Network, and the Council for a Parliament of the World's Religions have arisen all under the guise of achieving peace on earth. However, peace seems to elude its pursuant. Political upheavals, economic downturns, health crisis-epidemics, and pandemics all seem to thwart humanity's attempt to achieve world peace. What is the Judeo-Christian tradition on global peace? This chapter tries to present a theological study on the Judeo-Christian perspective on international peace, with a focus on the New Testament (NT).

The concept of peace in the NT is a "A theological reading of the New Testament implies putting the Bible on a pedestal;

John Appiah (john.appiah@vvu-edu.gh) is a Senior Lecturer at the Department of Theological Studies, Valley View University, Oyibi, Accra, Ghana, West Africa. He is currently the Head of Department of Theological Studies at Valley View University.

setting it apart from and assigning to it a special place among other literature not imbued with sacred authority" (van Zyl, 2008: 135). The theological analysis employed in this chapter assumes the authority, infallibility, historical reliability, inner harmony, and inspiration of the Bible (van Zyl, 2008: 135; Fowl, n.d: xiii). This study assumes the authority of the Scripture as the word of God (see Kelley 1).

The idea of peace and the New World Order are revealed in this chapter through the biblical and historio- apocalyptic worldview (Paulien 26-27). The apocalyptic studies provide a glimpse of hope to humanity (see Y. Collins, 2011: 447). "The apocalyptic also portrays God's overarching control of history. Apocalypses see the world as evil and oppressive, under the apparent control of Satan and his human accomplices. But the current world order will shortly be destroyed by God and be replaced with a new and perfect order, corresponding to Eden. The final events of history involve a severe conflict between the old order and the people of God, but the outcome is never in question. Through a mighty act of judgment, God will condemn the wicked, reward the righteous, and re-create the universe" (Paulien, n.d: 21-26; Evans & Porter , n.d: 43; J. Collins 14, Strand 19; Rodriguez 9-14; A. Collins, 1986, 7; A. Collins, 2011: 447-457).

The chapter is aimed at the NT. However, the Old Testament would provide the basis for presenting the NT concept of peace. For this chapter, the following terms are defined: New World Order- Biblical metanarrative–as "the storyline of the Bible" (Combis, n.d: 118). The biblical concept of peace lies within the broad biblical metanarrative on the great struggle between Christ and Satan. The Bible posits that God can establish universal peace on earth (Rivers 1, 4).

Old Testament's Concept of Peace

In the beginning, God created a perfect world (Gen 1:31). There was a perfect harmony between God and human beings, nature and the ecosystem. There was a perfect trust, openness, sharing, harmony, and fellowship (Gombis, n.d:118). Adam and Eve enjoyed perfect peace on earth before the entrance of sin during their earliest stay in the garden of Eden.

However, the perfect peace God projected for humanity at creation did not last. Sin cut it short because Satan deceived man from God's lofty character to disobey God which is sin against God (Gen 3). Sin thereby caused separation between humanity and God. The separation also occurred between humankind and his neighbour. Humanity and nature also separated (Gombis 118; Jemison 132). With this separation, Adam and Eve hid from God (Gen 3:8). Also, Adam and Eve became ashamed of their nakedness and started playing the blaming game in self-defense (Gen 3:7; Gombis, n.d: 118). Nature also would not yield its full capacity (Gen 17-19; Gombis 118). Consequently, sin brought mistrust, shrewdness, selfishness, disharmony, and further separation between God and man and man with his fellow man (Gombis 118).

Arthur Freeman identifies three dimensions of sin: (1) Sin describes the problem that one has with oneself (one struggles with oneself and is not able to do what one intends). (2) Sin also enters into the nature of one's relationship with others, relating to a failure in the relationship and harm of others. There are communal aspects of sin as well as interpersonal. (3) Sin describes failures or rebellion in one's relationship with God. In the Judeo-Christian tradition, not only is the relationship with God affected by one's relationship with oneself and others, but all life and actions are in God's presence. To disobey God is the primary sin and the source of all others" (Freeman 23). Sin takes the peace God intended for humanity at creation.

Adam and Eve fell from their original state of sinlessness to sinfulness. They fell from their special union with God into a separation from God (Jemison 131). (Jemison 132).
God, therefore, has put enmity between humanity and the serpent (Jemison 134) (Gen 3:15). Jesus, the seed of the woman, would have

to die to save humanity (Gen 3:15). Humanity rebelled against God (Isa 1:2, 3). In rebellion, humans separated themselves from God (Isa 59:1, 2-3). God would do away with the world, He would create a new world (Isa 65:17). God yearns for the rebellious humanity (Hos 11:7, 8; Jemison 134).

The Fall of humanity has also affected nature or the ecosystem or climate change. Profound changes have taken place in the world since man first disobeyed God or sinned against God. The field was cursed; thorns and thistles would grow in the field (Gen 3:17, 18). The earth experienced flooding (Gen 7:12), and desertification (Deut 32:10; Jemison 134). Satan began to claim the rulership of this world (Gen 3; John 12:31; 14:30; 16:11). "The whole creation groans and labours with birth pangs until now" (Rom 8:22; Jemison 132).

The Fall of man had a more significant effect on humans. The consequences of the Fall on humanity (Adam) include fear of God's presence (Gen 3:10); blaming the wife for his sin (Gen 3:12); the *field* was cursed because of Adam (Gen 3:17); The burden of work was increased for Adam (Gen 3:18); the experience of death (Gen 3:19; 5:5); He lost the glory of God that covered him (Gen 3:21); He lost his perfect Eden home (Gen 3:22-24); and Adam experienced the death of Abel, his son (Gen 4:8). Moreover, humanity (Eve) would experience enmity with the "serpent" (Gen 3:15). Eve would suffer the pain of childbirth (Gen 3:16), and her husband would "rule" over her. Again, her desire would be for her husband (Gen 3:16; Jemison 132-133).

The descendants of Adam and Eve have also been experiencing separation from God (Isa 59:1, 2), enmity with the "serpent" (Gen 3:15), Murder (Cain), death (Abel; Gen 4:8), an abundance of wickedness, sin (Gen 6:5), God will punish humanity that remains in sin (Gen 9:5, 6), and eventually, God will destroy humanity (Gen 6:6), humankind faces impending death and destruction (Mal 4:1), humanity has become subject to death (Rom 5:12-14), and a sense of condemnation; humans have become sinners (Rom 5:18, 19). Humans have become slaves to sin (Rom 6:20); humans have become enemies of God (Rom 5:10; Col 1:21), humans die because of Adam's sin (1 Cor 15:22). Humans, since the coming of sin have become deceived by Satan (2 Cor 11:3). Humans have been walking in the futility of their minds (Eph 4:17-19). Each child is born into a sinful human family rather than a sinless one. Each child has inherited the weaknesses and perverted tendencies resulting from sin. Each child has been subjected to death. Each child possesses inherited tendencies toward sin (Jer 17:9; Rom 3:9, 10; 1 Cor 15:22; Eph 2:2, 3). Each child carries the responsibility for the sins he/she commits (Eccl 12:14; Ezek. 18; Rom 3:23; Jemison 132-133).

As a result, humanity has no peace on earth. Throughout the Bible, God has promised to restore peace to humankind. He did it through Jesus Christ. In the New world order, real peace is possible by accepting Jesus Christ as one's Saviour and Lord. After exploring the background to peace on earth, the next section proceeds with the New Testament's concept of peace.

New Testament's Concept of Peace

The Greek, εἰρήνη, may be translated to peace, harmony, or tranquility. In the NT, εἰρήνη can refer to 'a state of traquility, exception from the rage and havoc of war' (see Luke 14:32; Acts 9:31; 12:20; 24:2, Thayer 1599). εἰρήνη can also connote peace/harmony/concord between individuals in the NT (see Matt 10:34; Luke 12:5; Acts 7:26; Rom 3:17; 14:17, 19; 1 Cor 7:15; 1 Cor 14:33; Gal 5:22; Eph 2:15, 17; 4:3; 2 Tim 2:22; Heb 12:14; Jas 3:18; 1 Pet 3:11, Thayer 1599). εἰρήνη can allude to the Hebrew *shalom*, meaning 'security', 'prosperity', felicity' (see Matt 10:13; Luke 2:29; 7:50; 8:48; 10:6; 11:21; Act 16:36; 1 Cor 16:11; 1 Thess 5:3; Heb 7:2; Jas 2:16; Thayer 1599). εἰρήνη can refer to the Messiah's peace/salvation (see Luke 1:79; 2:14; 19:38; Theyer 1599). εἰρήνη can refer to 'the tranquil state of a person being assured of salvation' (see John 14:27; 16:33; Rom 8:6; 2 Pet 3:14; Rom 5:1; 15:13; Eph

6:15; Phil 4:7; Col 3:15; Thayer 1599).

The Hebrew equivalent, shalom, infers a sense of welfare and health. In a general sense, shalom denotes one's relationship with God. The NT ε ρ νη may allude to one's relationship with God (see Mark 5:34; Rom 1:7; 1 Cor 1:3; 16:11; 1 Thess 1:1; Jas 2:16). In a specific sense, ε ρ νη connotes messianic salvation (See Luke 2:14; John 16:33; Rom 5:1; Eph 6:15; Phil 4:7; Gingrich 57).

In the NT, God is the author, source, and promoter of peace (Greek, ε ρ νη), Rom 15:13, 33; 16:20; 1 Cor 14:33; Phil 4:7, 9; 1 Thess 5:23; 2 Thess 3:16; Heb 13:20. People who are reconciled to God, through Jesus Christ, experience inner peace, Rom 8:6; 2 Pet 3:14. These people are to seek and maintain peace with their neighbours, Rom 14:19; 1 Cor 7:15; Gal 5:22; Eph 2:14, 15, 17; 4:3; 2 Tim 2:22; Heb 12:14; Jas 3:18. When a city or society accepts Jesus Christ, it enjoys peace, Luke 19:42. In the NT, humanity would enjoy peace (Greek, ε ρ νη) when they associate themselves with Jesus Christ. Jesus brought peace on earth when He became man, Luke 2:14. Jesus gives peace to those who accept Him, John 14:27; Col 3:15. He guides others to a way of peace, Luke 1:79. Those who accept Jesus have peace with God, Rom 5:1. Jesus came to inaugurate the kingdom of God/heaven on earth. People who associate themselves with the kingdom of God experience internal peace through the indwelling of the Holy Spirit. Repentant sinners are recreated to reflect the character of Jesus Christ on earth. With the recreation, the broken relationship has been restored. Jesus' followers experience peace with God, neighbour, and nature on earth. They will experience eternal peace when the kingdom of God is consummated (Rev 21:1-7).

The Concept of Peace in the Canonical Gospels

The message of the Gospel is the announcement of the coming of the kingdom of God. The kingdom of God on earth is the arrival of that new reality in which the brokenness of creation will be restored (Matt 3:1-2; 4:17; 10:5). God, through Jesus, is restoring the broken nature, climatic or ecosystem. Jesus would remake society according to its original design. He would restore peace on earth.

Humanity would enjoy this peace by (1) listening to Jesus and repenting of their sins, (2) repenting of their sinful social practices, and (3) reorienting their lives according to how Jesus is redeeming and restoring humanity (Gombis 120). With these, humanity would enjoy peace on earth again. Thus, God has set Himself to reclaim what has been lost—the three relationships, (1) humankind to God, (2) humanity to humanity, and (3) humanity to nature (Gombis 120-121). Jesus is to redeem what has been broken or degenerated. Through sin, humans lost peace on earth. Through Jesus, God is set himself to restore peace on earth. When a person accepts Jesus Christ, he/she has peace with God (Greek, ε ρ νη). This inner peace manifests itself in one's attempt to establish peace with his neighbours. The story of Jesus' encounter with Zacchaeus attests to this fact. When Zacchaeus experienced salvation (peace with God), he attempted to restore peace with his neighbours by his willingness to restore what he had extorted from them fourfold (Luke 19:1-10).

In John 14:27 and 16:33, Jesus promises His followers peace on earth. John 13-17 contains Jesus' farewell discourses delivered at the Last Supper. Jesus' farewell speech in John (13:31-17:26) emphasizes Jesus' unity with the Father and the work of the Paraclete, or "Spirit of Truth" (14:16-17). Jesus pleaded with the Father to keep His followers united (17:9-11, 20-22), (16:1-15). In John's view, Jesus imparts the promised Paraclete (advocate, or spirit) at His resurrection, merely by breathing on the disciples and saying, "Receive the Holy Spirit" (20:21-23). The risen Lord's action recalls the creation scene in Genesis 2 when Yahweh breathes into Adam's nostrils "the breath of life," making an animate being (Harris, n.d: 471). By this act of recreation, John seems to indicate that Jesus Christ and the Father reside in Jesus' followers through the Paraclete -the Holy Spirit-(17:23). And that it is through the indwelling Paraclete, working in the followers of Jesus that the unity among the followers is assured. The unity between humanity and neighbor seems to imply that the separation that occurred between them after sin is being repaired. This unity results from the repaired unity between humanity, who accepts the salvation offered through Jesus Christ, and God. If this postulation is true, then the concept of peace between humanity and God and humanity and his neighbor is found in Jesus' farewell message in John 13-17.

Jesus' farewell message in John 13-17, is sandwiched between Jesus under the shadow of death, John 11-12, Jesus' death and resurrection, and their implications, John 18-21. Whereas, John 11-12 points to Jesus as the Messiah who is to die; John 18-21 recounts His death and its implications. The literary context of Jesus' farewell message is that Jesus' death has made the unity between humanity, which accepts God's offer of salvation through Jesus Christ and neighbor possible. Thus, when a person associates himself/herself with Jesus Christ, he/she is recreated. As a recreated person, he enjoys peace on earth. And that it is through the indwelling Paraclete-working in the followers of Jesus that they enjoy peace in Him on earth (Luke 2:14; 19:42; John 14:27; 16:33).

The peace Jesus offers His disciples, however, is not what the world offers (Matt 10:34; John 14:27). The world would hate them (John 16:1-4, 33). Jesus' followers would not be disturbed by the apparent hatred because He has promised them eternal peace on His return (John 14:1-3; Peters 1). With this assurance, they will experience peace on earth. They are God's children (Matt 5:9). Their presences invoke peace to a place (Matt 10:12; Luke 10:5, 6). The present life of the Christian on earth, however, is warfare (Matt 10:34, John 16:33; See Punt 7; Peters 1). Thus, the Gospels portray peace as a result of the indwelling of the Holy Spirit in a Christian. Peace on earth to the Christian, however, is an irony. Whereas, the Christian enjoys inner peace with God, he/she has to endure persecution by the world in peace.

Moreover, the city or society that accepts Jesus Christ experiences peace (Greek, ε ρ νη). The woes of Chorazin, Bethsaida, and Capernaum seem to point to their rejection of Jesus and refusal to repent (Matt 11:20:24). Jerusalem had rejected Jesus, and subsequently lost the intended peace it would have enjoyed (Luke 19:42).

The Concept of Peace in the Pauline Epistles

The concept of peace in what has traditionally been accredited to Paul as the author is that peace is from God (Rom 1:7; Gal 5:22; Eph 2:14; Phil 4:7; Col 3:15). Christians, through Jesus Christ, have peace with God and neighbour (Rom 5:1; Eph 2:14-18; Col 1:20; 3:15; 1 Thess 5:13). Their friendship with God helps them endure troubles on earth (Rom 5:3-5). They are to seek peace and do their best to live at peace with people (Rom 12:18; 1 Cor 7:15; 2 Cor 13:11; 2 Tim 2:22). They are to bear the fruit of peace as an evidence of being controlled by the Holy Spirit (Gal 5:22-23). They lead peaceful lives (1 Tim 2:2). The followers of Jesus would enjoy inner peace with God.

The followers of Jesus promote and maintain peace with their neighbours (Rom 14:17, 19). In Rom 14:14-23, Paul explains that maintaining peace with one's neighbor should motivate a Christian in what he/she eats. In the view of Paul, one should not eat or drink what would be a source of offense to the weak in faith. Thus, peace with a neighbor ought to be the guiding principle in one's relationship.

In 1 Cor 7:15, Paul asserts that God calls Christians to peace (Greek, εἰρήνη). In 1 Cor 7:15, Paul addresses the issue of a Christian with an unbelieving spouse. The Christian should be faithful to the unbelieving spouse if the latter wants to maintain the marriage relationship. However, if the unbelieving spouse wants to leave the marriage, the Christian counterpart should not be held responsible for the spouse's decision. The guiding principle is that God has called Christians to peace, (7:15).

Galatians 5:22 presents peace (Greek, εἰρήνη) as a fruit of the Spirit. Peace (Greek, εἰρήνη) is listed among the fruits of the Spirit (with love, joy, longsuffering, kindness, goodness, faithfulness, gentleness and self-control). The fruits of the Spirt are contrasted with the works of the flesh: adultery, fornication, uncleanness, liciviousness, idolatry, sorcery, hatred, contentions, jealousies, outbursts of wrath, selfish ambitions, dissensions, heresies, envy, murders, drunkenness, revelries, and the likes (5:19-21). People who demonstrate the works of the flesh will not inherit the kingdom of God, v. 21). Those who reveal the fruit of the Spirt walk in the Spirt, and belong to Christ, vs. 24-25. The concept of peace is further evident in v. 26 where the Galatian Christians are admonished live at peace with one another in vs. 16-26.

In Eph 2:14-18, Jesus Christ, through His death on the cross, has broken down the enmity between the Jews and Gentiles. He has established peace between the two. The Greek ε ρ νη translated peace, is used three times in the pericope, vs. 14, 15, and 17. Thus, Christians, Jews and Gentiles are now one in Jesus Christ before God. In Eph 4:1-6, Christians are to walk in unity. Jesus Christ is the source/author of Christians' peace (Greek ε ρ νη), v.14. Christians are, therefore, to unite in peace. The purpose being called Christians is to live at peace with their neighbours. Unity is a hallmark of the Christian community.

Thus, Paul understood peace as a gift from God to Christians. They ought to live at peace with God and neighbour. Having explored Paul's concept of peace on earth, the study proceeds to investigate the concept of peace in the General Epistles. Jesus' death has made the unity between humanity, which accepts God's offer of salvation through Jesus Christ and neighbor possible.

The Concept of Peace in the General Epistles

This section investigates the concept of peace in what has traditionally been termed General or Catholic Epistles. The purpose is to examine the concept of peace on earth in these Epistles. A Christian is to demonstrate the wisdom of God by leading a peaceful life (Jas 3:17). A Christian is to show peace as a fruit of righteousness. He/She should make peace with people (Jas 3:18). The Christian's knowledge of God, the Father, and Jesus Christ brings peace to him/her (2 Pet 1:2). 1 Peter 3:8-12 exhibits the concept of peace. Since Christians are called to blessing, they should maintain peace with themselves. To ensure peaceful co-existence, love, compassion, tenderheartedness, and courtesy should guide their relationships as Christians. Verses 10-12 allude to Ps 34:12-16, which admonishes a lover of life to, among others, pursue peace (Heb. Shalom; Greek ε ρ νη). Having explored the concept of peace in the General or Catholic Epistles, the study proceeds to investigate the concept of peace in the book of Revelation.

The Concept of Peace in the Book of Revelation

This section investigates the concept of peace in the Book of Revelation. The Book of Revelation portrays a cosmic battle between Christ and Satan (see Rev 12:7-12; 13:1-18). The struggle which began in heaven (12:7, 8) ends up in Satan coming to the earth (Rev 12:9-10). The result of the battle leaves no peace for the inhabitants on earth (Rev 12:10-12). Satan and his confederation of evil powers and accomplices will be destroyed (Rev 19:17-21; 20:1-15). God will establish His Kingdom that He has promised, where evil shall be no more (Rev 21:9-27). When the new Heaven and the New Earth is established, there will be peace on earth (Rev 7:1-17; Rev 14:1-5; 22:1-5).

Revelation 21:3-4 portrays the creation of a new heaven and a new earth. The immediate literary context of Rev 21:3-4 points the new heaven and earth. First, John saw a new heaven and a new earth, the New Jerusalem-the dwelling of God- descending from heaven, vs. 1-2. Then, John heard a voice from heaven confirming what John saw -God tabernacles with His people, vs. 3-4; cf. Exod 25:8,9, 40. The reconciliation is consummated. Humanity and God is reunited. Moreover, the One who sat on the throne said, "Behold, I make all things new." John is commanded to write because these words are true and faithful (John saw and heard), vs. 5-8. Thus, the immediate literary context of Rev 21:3-4 is that "all things are made new."

The broader literary context of Rev 21:3-4 points to (1) The fall of Babylon, in which Satan and his confederation of evil angels and evil human accomplices are defeated, judged and destroyed after the 1000 years. Death and Hades are destroyed (Rev 18-20). God puts an end to evil and decay. This present world will be no more (2) The new heaven and the new earth will appear. God tabernacles with humans. The New Jerusalem will come after what comes (Rev 21)? The New heaven and the new earth will then be inaugurated and three (3) things that sustain the new system of things will be -the river of life, the tree of life (its leaves are for the healing of the nations), and the throne of God and of the Lamb are in it, they shall reign forever and ever (Rev 22:1-5). The following may be implied to form the broader literary context of the nature of the new world order, Rev 21:3-4: (a) This present world dominated by Satan and evil will pass away. (b) God will re-create the earth after His original plan. (c) God's reign will be established on earth. (d) God would unite with humanity into eternity. (e) Humans, who are saved, would be united. (f) Humanity would unite with nature. (g) Peace will be established on earth. Thus, the book of Revelation climaxes the concept of peace in the New Testament. The separation that occurred in Gen 3 because of sin would be reversed. Humanity would once again unite with God, neighbor, and nature, climatic change will be restored to its original and better form.

In sum, the Bible portrays a cosmic struggle between Christ and Satan. The battle, which started in heaven, resulted in Satan being banished down to the earth. When Adam and Eve sinned, Satan took control of the earth. With Satan's reign, peace eluded the inhabitants of the earth. God has intervened to restore peace on earth. Jesus Christ is God's chosen agent to restore peace on earth. People who accept Jesus as their Saviour and Lord enjoy inner peace now on earth though they may face persecution from evil powers and their human agents. Those dominated by evil, will pass away. God will establish righteousness. Peace will return to the earth. After determining the biblical concept of peace on earth, the study proceeds to the analysis of the study. Evidence from the Bible and present human experience seem to affirm the biblical concept of peace. The Bible claims that sin has affected the peace God intended for humanity on earth. The separation from self, neighbour, nature, and God has made it impossible for humanity to enjoy peace on earth. The New Testament's concept of human peace is linked with one's acceptance of Jesus Christ as personal Saviour and Lord. When an individual accepts Jesus into his/her life, he/she enjoys inner peace with God. The ultimate restoration of peace on earth will occur at the Second Coming of Jesus Christ. At that time, Satan and his evil forces and human accomplices will be destroyed. The world will be re-created. The redeemed would enjoy perfect peace.

CHAPTER SIX

Covid-19 and Global Peace -Keeping Mission

Marcelo E. C. Dias

For to us a child is born, to us a son is given,
and the government will be on his shoulders.
And he will be called Wonderful Counselor,
Mighty God, Everlasting Father,
Prince of Peace (Isaiah 9:6, NIV)

This pandemic, of unprecedented dimensions, led to a reconfiguration characterized by social isolation and quarantine of virtually everyone. Almost all was affected, not only at work, but also in education, recreation, and religion. To avoid agglomerations, religious temples generally suspended services and celebrations, especially guided the faithful of the risk group to stay at home and had to "reinvent" (Jeffery, 2010: n.p). The coronavirus pandemic has significantly challenged religiosity and its practices, such as: worship, community, teaching, proclamation, and

Marcelo E. C. Dias (Marcelo.dias@unasp.edu.br) graduated in 2016 with a PhD in Religion (World Missions) from Andrews University. Currently, he is a professor of Applied Theology for undergraduate and graduate programs at the Brazil Adventist University (UNASP). Recently, he has been involved in research on discipleship and the spreading of new Adventist church models in Brazil, a discipleship program for youth from the ages 10-40 window, and a movement that has, in the last five years, sent more than 600 people to mission projects in 16 countries. He is married to Ana Dias, who teaches in the School of Education at UNASP, and they have an 11-year-old daughter, Alissa Lauren.

mission. Although no one knows exactly how society will reorganize, leaders are already beginning to plan the next steps, and the Church must reflect on these movements.

Almost as a magnifying glass, this pandemic helped to identify conflicting challenges in different realms of life. For example, interpersonal relationships were challenged by social distancing and proximity while in quarantine. However, this apparent opportunity drew attention to these challenges. Statistics indicates a possible record number of divorces in China (Prasso, 2020: n.p), a significant increase in the United States (Rosner, 2020: n.p), Saudi Arabia (Barakat, 2020. N.p), and South Africa (Pace 2020) especially due to confinement. Another worrying fact is that, during this period, women that are victims of violence increased by 44.9% in the State of São Paulo, Brazil (Bond 2020), while those numbers doubled in China and in the United Kingdom (Bellizzi et al. 2020).

The relationship with the vulnerable groups at risk in society has also been highlighted, especially the homeless, people with comorbidities, and the elderly. During the pandemic, many solidarity initiatives have demonstrated the best of humanity. Sacrifice and love for others marked many moments. However, all predictions indicate that the post-pandemic period will be characterized by even greater social challenges. The pandemic could double the world's malnutrition and lead 265 million people to starvation, according to a UN alert (Chade, 2020: n.p). The UN has already pointed to the first famines of the coronavirus era in Yemen, South Sudan, Northeast Nigeria and the Democratic Republic of Congo (Gladstone, 2020: n.p). In Brazil, for example, the number of the unemployed people already exceeds 13 million and could reach 40 million. In some states, almost 20% of the people are in these conditions (Viera and Scaramuzzo 2020).

In the international context, the relationship between science and religion is another hotly debated issue. Although, discussions about the relationship between science and religion are not new, during the pandemic, in some contexts more than others, there were positions that confronted scientific medical instructions on how to behave during this period. While the prevailing official orientation was based on social isolation, some groups insisted on challenging this position (Shapiro 2020). Religion has come to the fore in the many times that this positioning has been justified with religious arguments. Some of these included the idea of disregarding science and relying on God's power or ignoring instructions and joining a chain of fasting and prayer. This attitude was strengthened by the clashes and hesitations of some evangelical churches in adhering to measures of social isolation (Yee, 2020: n.d).

This is a challenging scenario for finding global peace and health in the new world order, even from a religious point of view. How can missiology elucidate Christian mission for times like these? What is the mission of Christians in the post-coronavirus pandemic context?

The Prime Minister of Peace

Medemer became the fashion word in Ethiopia in 2019. Literally, the word in Amharic means "addition," but it can also be translated as "unite." The mischief is the result, at least partially, of the performance of the young Prime Minister Abiy Ahmed as a peacemaker of the country and the northeast region of Africa. In essence, this philosophy proposes that different and even contrary ideas can dialogue and generate inclusion and cooperation (important values of Ethiopian culture). This emphasis on working in harmony, despite poverty and ethnic challenges, especially in relation to the neighboring country of Eritrea, earned Abiy Ahmed last year's Nobel Peace Prize. Internal conflicts in recent days have cast doubt on the effectiveness of *medemer,* which will continue to be tested in the region (Ahmed, 2019: n.p).

Ahmed is not the only world leader that has undertaken a mission to foster peace; Mahatma Gandhi, Martin Luther King Jr., Nelson Mandela, for example, are recognized for the impact of their leadership on the development of human rights in different countries.

The Prince of Peace and Christian Mission

Christian mission is centered in the understanding about Christ. The biblical narrative "moves from the universality of the Father's creation to the particularity of the Son's incarnation, death, and resurrection, and then again to the universality of the Spirit sending God's people into the entire world to proclaim the message of salvation and the coming kingdom" (Ott et al., n.d: 61).

Among the Old Testament messianic prophecies, those of Isaiah are especially relevant in considering this "other ruler." According to Isaiah 9:6, the ruler in the prophecy is a prince and the defining word is *shalom*. *Shalom,* which includes the idea of peace, has a much broader meaning related to well-being—the harmony of life in an integral way, in all its dimensions. That was the promise to Judah (Goldingay, n.d: 43). Their ruler would be the Prince of Peace, *Sar Shalom* (in Hebrew).

The idea of a kingdom of peace was not strange to the people of Israel. Melchizedek was the "King of Salem," (i.e. "of Peace"); the name Solomon, an important ruler of the people, means "the peaceful one;" and Isaiah himself had prophesized the Messiah's reign of peace (2:4; 9:5). It was a message of hope that worked as a reminder of God's previous promises and how they would be fulfilled despite all the terrible circumstances the nation faced under King Ahaz, which included idolatry and the desecration of the Lord's temple (Smith, 2007:242).

The Kingdom of Peace

The kingdom of peace prophesied would be based on the identity of its ruler and on his actions; Christ is peace and He establishes the peace. The prophecy in Isaiah chapter seven- "the virgin will be with child and will give birth to a son, and will call him Immanuel" (7:14)-was primarily fulfilled in Isaiah chapter eight. The preceding chapter has the promise of a delivering king, the Bible mentions the birth of a boy, whose name is Maer-Salal-Has-Baz (meaning "swift are the spoils, speedy is the plunder"). This was the second son of Isaiah and he was a sign to the people about the conquest of Syria and Israel. However, Immanuel is mentioned once again in verse 8.

> Mention of the name Immanuel is a reminder that Israel might have had God with them (see on ch. 7:14). They completely forfeited God's presence, and Judah nearly so. Many of the leaders and people of Judah had forsaken the Lord, and as a result His presence could not be with them. But others, a small remnant, were faithful, and they would be saved. It was primarily for their benefit that this message was given (Nichol, 1977:141).

This is part of the context of chapter 9; "an abrupt shift takes place between the gloom of 8:22 and the light of 9:1. A promise is given of the return of lands that had been humiliated by the capture of the Assyrians" (Carter and McLeod, 1972:396). That prophecy refers specifically to Jesus, the one who would fulfill the words of Isaiah 700 years later, as an angel revealed to Mary (Lk. 1:32-33).

When Christ was born, angels praised Him and referred to that aspect of His mission by saying "Glory to God in the highest heaven, and on earth peace to those on whom his favor rests" (Lk. 2:14). The coming of Jesus represented a new government and a new ruler, kingdom and king, that would reign forever ("He who was seated on the throne," Rv. 21:5). Later, Paul, in his writings, would introduce the "God of Peace" (Pp. 4:9, 1 Th. 5:23).

Coherent with His being, Christ established peace (Cl. 1:19-20). Jesus' ministry was the divine initiative of reconciliation, even though the context of Jesus' ministry was not very peaceful. It included poverty, migration, mocking, discrimination, criticism by religious leaders, betrayal by a close disciple, unfair trials, and death on a cross. Ultimately, His mission has been related to the cosmic reconciliation. Paradoxically, the reconciling purpose of the cross is to restore the harmony of the original creation (2 Co. 5:11-21).

> Our Lord Jesus Christ came to this world as the unwearied servant of man's necessity. He "took our infirmities, and bare our sicknesses," that He might minister to every need of humanity Matthew 8:17. The burden of disease and wretchedness and sin He came to remove. It was His mission to bring to men complete restoration; He came to give them health and peace and perfection of character (White, 2002:59).

While teaching about salvation in Christ to the Romans (5:1-11), Paul uses two metaphors; a relational metaphor connected with the idea of reconciliation and a legal metaphor connected with the idea of justification. The result is peace with God: "Therefore, since we have been justified through faith, we have peace with God through our Lord Jesus Christ" (v. 1).

Christ established peace by preaching about peace, forming a community of peace, and sending His followers on a peacemaking mission. Among all the preaching of Jesus, the Sermon on the Mount (Mt. 5-7) is the *locus classicus* of Christian peacemaking. Following the teachings and the values of the Sermon on the Mount, mean to develop Jesus' peacemaking ways. Among those teachings, one finds anger and reconciliation (5:21-26), not resisting an evil person (5:38-42), loving one's enemies (5:43-48), forgiving (6:12, 14, 15), and not judging others (7:1-5) (Stassen, 1991:37).

Christ preached peace for a world without peace. His use of terms such as opponent (5:42), gentiles (5:47; 6;7; 6;42), enemies (5:43-44), and unrighteous (5:45) conveys the idea that His message of peace is for everyone and not only His disciples (Love 2020:5). The world of Jesus was characterized by much evil expressions, such as legalism, agnosticism, polytheism, racism, chauvinism, and immorality. Therefore, reconciliation with God is inseparable from reconciliation with people. God's plan includes the integration for all creation in Christ (Lausanne, 2020: n.p).

> The gospel is a message of peace. Christianity is a system which, received and obeyed, would spread peace, harmony, and happiness throughout the earth. The religion of Christ will unite in close brotherhood all who accepts its teachings. It was the mission of Jesus to reconcile men to God, and thus to one another (White, 1911:46-47).

Christ also established a peaceful community of followers (Ep. 2:11-22). Christ's peace is embodied by the church, which becomes an instrument of peace (Ep. 4:3; 6:15), by overcoming the divisions between Jews and Gentiles and, therefore, transforming into a prototype of God's kingdom. As White points out, "the spirit of peace is evidence of their connection with heaven. The sweet savor of Christ surrounds them. The fragrance of the life and the loveliness of the character, reveal to the world the fact that they are children of God" (White 1908). Peace among God's people should be as much a fact as a command. As Bosch warns, "if we reject the road of reconciliation, we are crucifying Christ anew (Livingston, 2013:339).

Christ points out that His peace does not mean absence of difficulties, but the possibility of remaining calm and confident in the certainty that God is in control. He does not "give to you as the world gives" (Jo. 14:27). Because Christ is peace, "in me you may have peace. In this world you will have trouble" (Jo. 16:33). This concept seems like Martin Luther King Jr.'s remark about "a negative peace which is the absence of tension" versus "a positive peace which is the presence of justice" (King 1963).

Paul reminds Christ's followers that they should "as far as it depends on you, live at peace with everyone" (Rm. 12:18), after all, "as members of one body you were called to peace" (Cl. 3:15). There is no expectation that people who do not know Christ will have peace and reconciliation. But if followers of Christ do not experience reconciliation, there is no church. It is the denial of the identity of the church

Finally, Christ sends His followers on a peacemaking

mission. Christ's followers are people of peace who take the gospel of peace. In the gospel commission of John (20:21), the expression "Peace be among you" (*Shalom Aleichem,* in Hebrew) is repeated three times. The disciples were afraid, hiding even after the testimonies about the resurrection of Jesus. They were afraid of what the people would think and do about them. Jesus' first words to His disciples were not a command, but a blessing. The blessing of peace is an essential element of the fulfillment of the Great Commission. Christ's followers enjoy peace as they share the gospel.

In the first missionary encounter between Peter and Cornelius, there is a clear presentation of the gospel. "You know the message God sent to the people of Israel, announcing the good news of peace through Jesus Christ, who is Lord of all" (Ac 10:36). "If he is truly Lord of *all,* then the gospel *and* Christ's peace are for all peoples, not just the people of Israel" (Polhill, 1992:261).

> Christ's followers are sent to the world with the message of
> peace. Whoever, by the quiet, unconscious influence of a
> holy life, shall reveal the love of Christ; whoever, by word or
> deed, shall lead another to renounce sin, and yield his heart
> to God, is a peacemaker (White 1908).

Therefore, the church is a sign and an agent of peace. As Bosch points out, "the church is a reconciled community and a reconciling community" (Livingston, 1992:255).

> We need to understand peace witness as a continuum,
> beginning from peace with God, moving into peace with
> ourselves, our families, our churches, those of other faiths,
> work colleagues, at national and international level, and,
> most challengingly, with our enemies. Each Christian will be
> at a different point on the continuum, and must be
> encouraged to move on through it (Widjaja, 2007:280).

The Hope for Peace

The United Nations (UN) currently coordinates 13 Peacekeeping operations around the world. These missions help countries to walk the difficult path from conflict to peace. Despite all this mobilization for peace, global spending on weapons is approximately $1.8 trillion. The annual cost of wars is estimated $1 trillion. In contrast, all UN peace operations reach a maximum of $50 billion which is even a small fraction of what is spent on wars (UN Peacekeeping, 2021: n.p).

The world includes a history and a legacy of racism, black slavery; holocaust against the Jews; apartheid; ethnic killings; decimation of indigenous populations, interreligious violence; Palestinian suffering, caste oppressions, tribal genocides. Before the pandemic, it was estimated that there were currently 40 million people in slavery (more than 200 years ago) (Hodal, 2109: n.p). Migration had reached historical levels for several reasons that had led to human trafficking, female and child subjugation on all continents. In addition to the 600 million people with some kind of disability (the largest minority in the world) (WHO), there were continued crises of poverty, health conditions such as HIV infection and ecological challenges. Christians who, by their actions or inactions, contribute to these tragedies, seriously disregard their testimony of the gospel of peace.

Based on the biblical understanding and seeking to make a difference in the current scenario, one of the missionary tendencies is the mission of peace. In such a violent and hostile world, Christians are positioning themselves in difficult areas where ministries of mercy, compassion and pacification are needed. Those are places where unreached people live in contexts of violence, whether Muslim, Hindu, Buddhist, or secularist context. They are adopted as places that need to be ruled by the Prince of Peace (Sunquist, 2016: n.p).

Don Richardson's *Peace Child* has become a paradigmatic history for missiology. The couple of young missionaries in 1960s dedicated themselves to living on Irian Jaya, part of Indonesia, with the cannibal Sawi tribe. After learning their language and culture, they were still having difficulty communicating the gospel story. Amid conflicts with neighboring tribes, however, they learned about the peace-child custom, which is a ritual to establish a covenant of peace.

> When I saw you exchanging children, at first, I was horrified," he began. "I kept saying to myself, 'Couldn't they make peace without this painful giving of a son?' But you kept telling me, 'There is no other way.'" He leaned forward and, in accordance with Sawi custom, placed his right-hand palm down on the floor. "You were right," he said. Every eye in the manhouse was fixed on him as he continued. "When I stopped to think about it, I realized you and your ancestors are not the only ones who found that peace required a peace child" (Evans and Parker, 2001:111).

The Mission of Peace Today

The first advent was the inauguration of God's kingdom and the Second Advent will be its consummation—the ultimate realization of all things, including perfect peace. Between the Pentecost and the Parousia, Christians must live and promote the kingdom of peace. The mandate is to be missionaries, peacemakers, and evangelists (gospel of peace). However, there must be congruence between the message (the gospel of peace), the mandate (to pacify and evangelize), and the performance (the fulfillment of mission). *Christians preach peace, work for peace, and imitate the Prince of peace.*

The reflection on the pandemic showed that it is not enough to give time and put people together. Greater awareness of the collective requires guidance on what to do and how to deal with relationships. The church has the potential to guide in the education of children, conjugal relationships and, above all, in the communion with God. Despite the good initiatives that exist, more need to be done to develop spirituality in the home.

Christians, especially, have solidarity as part of their identity. There is an expectation that by rediscovering the joy and meaning of a life of service, many will continue to live this way. These moments of mission involvement can be transformative! People have discovered that they do not have to choose between speaking about Jesus and showing His love; between serving and saving. They do not have to balance good deeds with the proclamation of the gospel because the two dimensions are indivisible sides of the same coin. Mobilizations for vulnerable people due to increased social inequality through forms of relief, protection, and financial aid, will be important in the post-pandemic context.

In the debate on science, politics, and religion, perhaps, the most worrisome are not the opinions expressed, but above all the extremism and imbalance adopted in some discourses. The Adventist Church has sought to harmonize faith with science by understanding that God has used all resources for the blessing of His children.

In countries where Christians have increasingly occupied the public sphere, this panorama places even more responsibility on Christian witness are expected. Are their testimonies contributing to a good reputation for the faith they profess? Or have they often reinforced the stereotype that Christians are homophobic, irrational, exclusivist, incoherent, and sexist, among other traits?

A recent survey by the Pew Research Center revealed that the majority of U.S. adults (86%) believe that there is some kind of lesson for humankind to learn from the pandemic, and about a third (35%) believe this lesson was sent by God (Pew Research 2020). The post-pandemic world offers opportunities for new spiritual leaders to wake up and engage this context. In times of crisis, God has offered opportunities for the world to reflect on its condition, recognize divine sovereignty, decide to follow His paths, and mobilize to live His will. Jesus, on the occasion of His ascension, explained that the establishment of His kingdom, especially the time of it, could not be fully understood by His disciples, but that they had a mission "both in Jerusalem, as in all Judea and Samaria, and even at the ends of the earth" (Ac 1:8).

In addition to the eschatological understanding of the present times, it is important to reflect on these elements from the perspective of the mission. The apocalyptic sensitivity will only be truly adjusted if, in times of crisis, people become active witnesses of God's love. As Newbigin emphasizes, a healthy escathology fosters missionary engagement (Newbigin, 2008:135) "If there ever was a time when serious reflection becomes everyone who fears God, it is now, when personal piety is essential. The inquiry should be made, "What am I, and what is my work and mission in this time?" (White, 1992:73) An optimistic look at this moment concludes that this is a great opportunity for reflection, revival, and mobilization.

The church should be a place where people study, practice and proclaim peace, but the gospel of peace must be proclaimed peacefully. That does not mean proclaiming it with less excitement and courage. Adventists should reflect the shalom-making ministry of Jesus, which can be found in its own tradition of teachings and practices of wholistic ministry (Krause 2014:59). The identity of a Christian is to be a peacemaker; and the distinction of the remnant is its biblical identity.,

Christian evangelism must not attack other children of God, impose political or religious positions, or create division in the church (for example, young people versus elderly). Christians must promote peace in the family, in the church community, in the neighborhood, in the larger community, and around the world.

Earthly kingdoms advance through greed, war, and oppression. The kingdom of God advances through justice and peace, the peace that will reign eternally in the new heaven and in the new earth. The promise of Isaiah 9:7 must be claimed today:

Of the greatness of his government and *peace there will be no end*. He will reign on David's throne and over his kingdom, establishing and upholding it with *justice and righteousness* from that time on and *forever*. The zeal of the Lord Almighty will accomplish this (Is 9:7).

CHAPTER SEVEN

Global Pandemics and Global Health

Olayemi O. Adeoye

Pandemics are infectious disease epidemics with a profoundly extensive distribution, involving multiple countries and possibly the whole world. They are not a new phenomenon and can be tracked back to the Dionysian Era, Before Christ (BC). Beliefs and perceptions about their origin, etiology and outcome were shaped by the overarching worldviews about diseases in the era in which they occurred. Records of the early pandemics were poor, and most were lost over time. However, with modern epidemiological tools and archeological skills, valuable details are unraveled. Although technological development and medical advancement have helped to mitigate the grave effects of pandemics on humans, their occurrence has proven inevitable. This chapter explores a historic genealogy of global pandemics and their etiology, perceptions, impact, global response and a recommendation on their management and prevention.

The world-renowned astrophysicist, Carl Sagan, once said that "to understand the present, you have to know the past." This

Olayemi O. Adeoye, MBBS, PHD, MPH (oadeoye@llu.edu) is an Assistant Professor at the Departments of Pharmaceutical and Administrative Sciences and Basic Sciences & Center for Perinatal Biology under the school of Pharmacy and Medicine respectively in Loma Linda University, California, United States of America.

could be true for infectious disease outbreaks caused by the same etiologic microorganism, each time. These large-scale epidemics, known as pandemics, transcend international boundaries and involve multiple countries, possibly the entire world. In the case of the current COVID-19 pandemic, which took the world by surprise, plunging it into a global health and economic crisis, so far, the virus is yet to align entirely with Sagans' hypothesis. This is partly because the virus is novel. Humans have endured pandemics for a long time and have every time outlasted the scourge but not without paying a massive price of losing lives and livelihood. The first major pandemic recorded outside of biblical accounts occurred during the Peloponnesian war between two Greek cities, Sparta and Athens, between 430 BC and 404 BC (). Before this pandemic, known as the Plague of Athens, a flu-like pandemic occurred in the Babylonian empire in 1200 BC, but it was not adequately recorded (z, 1921:n.p) ; ,2001:572-579).

In contrast, Thucydides, a Greek historian and military general, recorded the significant pieces of the Plague of Athens, and epidemiologists have since referenced his work (, 2009:456-467). Since the Plague of Athens, at least 20 considerable pandemics have occurred. These outbreaks had diverse origins, etiology, course, and outcomes. Whereas, viruses caused most pandemics in history, some were bacterial or parasitic. Although viruses are the main culprits in true global pandemics, many patients died from bacterial co-infections and complications. Pandemics occur due to various risk factors, including environmental changes, geographic spark and spread risks, global cooperation failure, and inadequate preparedness. Pandemics impact human health via increased morbidity and mortality as well as economic and social turmoil.
There has always been a love-hate relationship between the human race and the microbial world. Microbes serve multiple beneficial roles in human life, including vitamin synthesis in the gut (, 2011:771-785), the maintenance of cavity and epithelial immunity via normal microbiota (, 2012:4-14), the industrial manufacture of drugs, and genetic engineering (, 2009:5-16) to name a few. Despite

this, microorganisms continue to be the primary culprit for the largest number of human morbidities and mortalities via epidemics and pandemics. Pandemics are not a new theme. They have impacted both the human race and the animal kingdom for centuries (, 2016:n.p). Human exposure to these microbial pathogens can be tracked back to the early primitive times when humans hunted for their food and drank water from sources shared by their lower animal counterparts. Whereas, some pathogens affect only humans, the most infectious agents that have caused pandemics in history are carried by animals (, 2010:1636-1640). These pathogens that cross-species from animals to humans cause diseases that are referred to as zoonotic diseases. The human quest for the sustenance of life exposed them to these animal reservoirs of infectious agents such as bacteria, viruses, and parasites. Additionally, hunting aided the spread of the infection or disease. During the Neolithic age, when agriculture was established to sustain the increasing demand for food for the rapidly expanding human population, societal interactions became a significant route of transmission of disease (,2018: 323-340). Pandemics in history spread to varying extents, with some affecting only a couple of countries and others, multiple countries, possibly the entire world as with the current COVID-19 pandemic. This chapter focuses on the "true" global pandemics that had a worldwide distribution and global mortality of over half a million (*Table 1*). A few other pandemics with mortalities less than 1000 per episode are presented in figure 2 for reference.

Table 1

Pandemic	Period	Common Name/Strain	Type of Organism
Influenza	1847 to 1848		Virus
	1889 to 1890		
	1918 to 1920	Spanish Flu/ H1N1	
	1957 to 1958	Asian Flu/ H2N2	
	1968 to 1970	Hong Kong Flu/ H3N2	
	2009	Swine Flu /H1N1	
3rd Plague	1855 to 1960	Bubonic Plague	Bacterial
Encephalitis Lethargica	1915 to 1926	EL	Idiopathic, Viral or Bacterial
Psittacosis	1929 to 1930	Psittacosis	Bacterial
7th Cholera	1961 to 1975	Cholera - El Tor Strain	Bacterial
HIV/AIDS	1981 to present	HIV/AIDS	Virus
Severe Acute Respiratory Syndrome	2002 to 2004	SARS	Virus
Mumps	2000s	Mumps	Virus
Middle East Respiratory Syndrome Coronavirus	2012 to present	MERS-CoV	Virus
Western African Ebola Virus	2013 - 2016	Ebola	Virus
Zika Virus	2015 to 2016	Zika	Virus
Corona Virus Disease 2019	2019 to Present	COVID-19	Virus

Table 1: Shows a list of selected true global pandemics and their corresponding occurrence periods, common names and the type of pathogen that caused them.

Historical Overview of True Global Pandemics

Pandemic Influenza

Some historical but not optimally scientific records of the signs and symptoms of respiratory disease outbreaks in the BC era suggest that influenza may have occurred in humans earlier than 1580, which was the consensus year of the first global flu pandemic (Kuszewski and Brydak, 2000:188-195). Since then, at least four major true global flu pandemics have occurred (Table 1). The Spanish, Asian, and Hong Kong flu pandemics occurred in the 19th century and originated from China, whereas the Swine flu pandemic occurred in 2009 and originated from Mexico. Each of these flu pandemics accounted for over 0.5 million deaths worldwide. The

Spanish flu pandemic is the worst of all pandemics in the human race's history, with a mortality of up to 50 million (Figure 1) (Saunders-Hastings and Krewski, 2016:n.p).

Figure 1

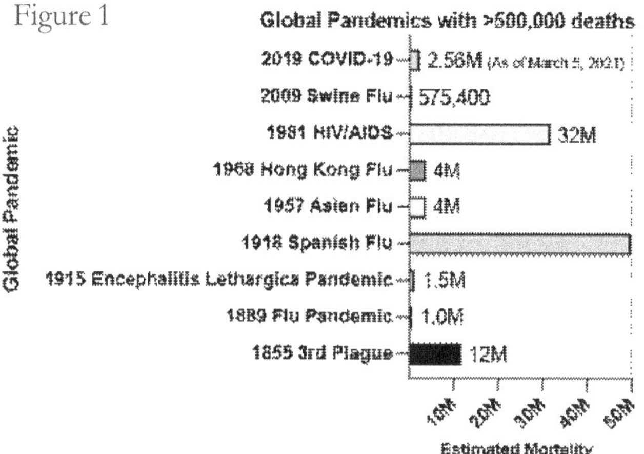

This bar chart shows selected true global pandemics that resulted in the death of greater than half a million people. The 1918 Spanish flu had the highest mortality of approximately 50 million and the current COVID-19 pandemic has claimed the lives of 2,560,995 as of March 5, 2021 (WHO).

Figure 2

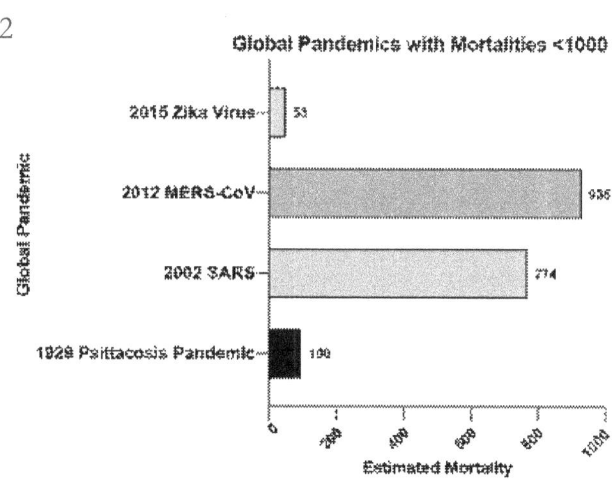

This bar chart shows the global pandemics that resulted in mortalities of less than 1000 persons. Some of these pandemics recurred in other years; values shown here are year specific.

To infect a human being, the influenza virus must gain entrance into the host body cells, attach to the respiratory epithelia, hijack the transcriptional and translational machinery to form its constituent proteins, which are subsequently assembled into a mature virion; before finally exiting the initial host cell to infect adjacent or neighboring cells. These processes are made possible by two glycoproteins known as: hemagglutinin (H) and neuraminidase (N), present on the virus' surface. Except for the Spanish and Swine flu that had the same etiologic viral strain, the other flu pandemics were caused by different viral strains formed either by a molecular alteration (antigenic drift) of the genetic codes for the surface glycoproteins or the formation of a hybrid virus from the re-assortment of the two co-infecting influenza viruses (antigenic shift) (Kim et al.,2018:174-183).

The 3rd Plague - Bubonic Plague

People often get confused about the Plague. This is because the word "Pandemic" is frequently used interchangeably with the word "Plague," which means – strike or blow, in its Greek origin. Plague is a zoonotic disease caused by a bacterium known as Yersinia pestis, which is harbored in rodents. Rodent fleas are the vectors that transmit this bacterium from infected rodents to humans. Before the 3rd Plague, there were the 1st and 2nd pandemics, which did not exhibit a profoundly widespread transmission. However, with the 3rd outbreak, it originated in China and initially spread to Hong Kong, where it was identified by and named after Alexandre Yersin; then Europe before spreading to the rest of the world (Bramanti et al.,2019:2018-2429). Estimates of global deaths from the 3rd Plague were 12 million (*Figure 1*), with many more others experiencing varying levels of febrile illnesses from being infected. The high lethality of the Plague earned it the opportunity of being used as a biological weapon. Once waring groups figured out that it could be used as a weapon of mass casualties and death by aerosolizing the causative bacterial agent, its use became widespread in winning wars (Riedel, 2005: 116-124- "Plague: From Natural Disease to Bioterrorism")..

Encephalitis Lethargica

Encephalitis Lethargica is a neuropsychiatric disease whose exact etiology remains largely unknown. It was commonly referred to as "sleeping sickness," even though it is different from the African Trypanosomiasis, a tropical disease caused by S. brucei and transmitted by its vector – tsetse fly. The world experienced a pandemic of Encephalitis lethargica (EL) between 1916 and 1930, which closely overlapped with the Spanish flu pandemic (Foley, 2009:143-150). Because symptoms exhibited initially by patients mimicked those of the pandemic flu, H1N1 was hypothesized as EL's probable cause. Several other research has suggested other likely viral causative microbes, e.g., poliovirus and bacteria such as Clostridium botulinum and Streptococci (Dourmashkin, 1997:515-520). The most widely accepted etiologic agent is H1N1, even though the research showing causal relationships is sparse (Henry et al.,2010:566-571). Victims of the EL pandemic experienced initial flu-like symptoms such as lethargy with later and chronic neurological symptoms such as hypersomnolence and ophthalmoplegia (the loss of control of the muscles that control eye movement) as well as psychiatric symptoms such as parkinsonism and schizophrenia-like symptoms (Henry et al.,2010:566-571). During the EL pandemic, victims' symptoms were robustly characterized by a neurologist named Constantin von Economo in Vienna in 1917. His documentation about the widespread nature of the disease was accurate and the disease was popularly referred to as the Von Economo disease. EL was proposed to have originated from Romania in 1915, reaching Vienna in 1916 and other parts of

Europe in the late 1900s because of soldiers' mass movement during World War I. Historic literature reveals that EL probably started much earlier than 1917 when it was officially diagnosed.

Earlier seen diseases such as English sweats, Rafania, mal Mazzucco, Nona, and Krieblkrankheit may well have been EL, considering the similar nature of symptoms and signs exhibited by patients (Hoffman and Vilensky, 2017:2246-2251). Since the end of the EL pandemic in the 1930s, no large-scale outbreaks have been seen, although sporadic cases are seldom seen. Killing up to 1.5 million people worldwide (*Figure 1*), the 1916 EL pandemic remains one of the top 10 pandemic killers in human history.

HIV/AIDS

The phylogeny of the Acquired Immune Deficiency Syndrome (AIDS) and its causative organism, Human Immunodeficiency Virus (HIV), can be traced back to the African Chimpanzee. Although many unknowns concerning infectious diseases exist in the interphase between humans and animals, it is well established that the HIV type II as well as type I, which is the culprit microbe for the AIDS pandemic, are a result of cross-species re-assortment of the Simian Immunodeficiency Viruses (SIVs) naturally harbored by primate mammals of African descent (Sharp and Hahn). Although SIVcpz (SIV from chimpanzees) does not cause an immune deficiency in non-human primates, humans infected with HIV over time, without adequate treatment, suffer from severe immune disorders. The molecular signature of human infection with HIV is a severe attenuation of the CD_4^+ (T-Helper cells) cells and a consequent aberrant immune response, which ushers in several opportunistic infections s (Williams and Burdo, 2009:400-412). As with other pandemics, the formal identification and diagnosis of HIV and its chronic sequel, AIDS, started with the observation of unusual symptoms, signs, and death in patients infected. The initial official diagnosis was made in 1981 when infected gay men (men who have sex with men – MSM) in the US presented with previously unseen symptoms such as hairy leukoplakia (white patches in the mouth), thrush, pneumonias and certain unique malignancies which manifested as dark purple skin and face patches (Greene, 2007: 94-102). Apart from homosexual men (a term rarely used now), other groups of individuals in which early cases were found were Hemophiliacs, people of Haitian descent, and individuals using Heroine, which was why AIDS was initially called the 4H disease early in its history (Marc et al., 2010:2089-2097). Post-1981, researchers received several monetary grants that funded the research that would eventually trace the virus' genesis back to the 1920s along trade routes in the Democratic Republic of Congo (DRC). Further study involving a posthumous analysis of blood samples retrieved from a man who had died in Kinshasa, DRC, in 1959 revealed the first verified case of HIV infection n (Faria et al.,2014:56-61).

International trade, industrialization, and globalization contributed to the rapid spread of the HIV pandemic (Gayle and Hill, 2001: 327-335). Sexual relations with infected individuals in the infection hot zones accounted for the early cases seen in the West. There are multiple means of the transmission of the virus with a geographical trend, which may suggest one or more of these: heterosexual prostitution, gay sexual relations, intravenous substance abuse, parenteral administration of blood and blood products, and mother-to-child transmission. Sub-Saharan Africa and Southeast Asia continue to be the hardest hit regions by this HIV/AIDS pandemic (Cock and Weiss, 2000: A3-9). Whereas developed countries have enjoyed more access to antiretroviral medication and AIDS management expertise, there continues to be a palpable disparity in the availability of these drugs to patients in developing countries. Unless a cure is discovered, it is anticipated that this pandemic will continue well into the future.

Covid-19

The world was not ready when this current pandemic hit. Pandemics are not an everyday occurrence, so we who are alive and living through this current COVID-19 pandemic are making history. COVID-19 is a severe respiratory disease caused by a novel strain of the coronavirus known as the severe acute respiratory syndrome (SARS), coronavirus 2 (SARS-CoV-2) (Kamel Boulos and Geraghty, 2020: 8). The scientific community continues to have scholarly debates on the most appropriate name for this new virus, which was initially named 2019-nCoV (Zhu et al., 2020: 727-733) by the World Health Organization (WHO). The novel virus, recently renamed by the International Committee on Taxonomy of Viruses (ICTV) on February 11, 2020, reflects the nomenclature of a previously known virus (SARS), which caused an outbreak in 2003. Both viruses are genetically similar, although they are entirely different. SARS-CoV-2 originated from a seafood market in Wuhan, Hubei Province, China, in December of 2019 (Coronaviridae Study Group of the International Committee on Taxonomy of, 2020: 536-544). Epidemiological contact tracing of patients who had presented to the hospital with a previously unseen and an atypical form of pneumonia led to the market site. The novel virus was subsequently isolated from the human respiratory epithelial cells of the patients who were all adults and admitted into an adult hospital. Despite the Chinese officials' public health measures to contain the COVID-19 outbreak and limiting it to Wuhan, the virus spread to other parts of China within a brief period and subsequently to other countries. Much speculation and not so covert criticisms have been targeted at the Chinese government for not sharing the much-needed information about the novel virus early enough with other countries and warning other nations about what was likely to become a pandemic. Because of this late notification, many countries worldwide were caught unawares with no concrete emergency preparedness measures on the ground when their citizens started dying from the disease. As of October 5, 2020, 35.5

million people have been infected by the virus, of which 1,043,447 deaths have been recorded globally. Scientists have unequivocally stated that cases and deaths will continue to rise until a vaccine and/or treatments are discovered and made available in adequate quantities globally.

Perceptions and Beliefs about Pandemics

Diseases have always been viewed through the lens of the prevalent worldview of the era in which they occurred. Before the Renaissance, early in the human history, never-before-seen events, including diseases, were explained via cause and effect themes. A prominent explanatory theme for diseases was the inhalation of foul air, and where these explanations were impossible, disease causations were attributed to some malicious supernatural powers or the divine (Riva et al., 2014: 1753-1757; Tountas, 2009: 185-192). Correspondingly, remedies were sought from divinity experts such as traditional healers, witch doctors, and occultists believed to have the powers to drive those maladies away (Tountas, 2009: 185-192). Throughout history, peoples' beliefs and perceptions about a pandemic or a threat of its occurrence have always been influenced by their understanding of the pandemic.

The historical records of the Plague of Athens between 430 – 426 BCE serve as one of the oldest pandemic records' resources that were pivotal to understanding pandemics in the early human history. Thucydides, an army general and historian with no formal medical knowledge or training, was the one who eloquently recorded the Athenian Plague (Littman, 2009:243-255; Thucydides, 1980:230-232). He wrote about the symptoms and signs experienced by those infected by the bug that caused the pandemic and the role of human behavior in its spread (Riva et al.). The late Greek era ushered in the foundation on which the modern field of medicine was built. Many of the supernatural explanations for diseases were challenged and largely debunked, even though some of those elements still exist in different quarters of the world.

Several historic writings recorded the refute of the supernatural worldview by the Greeks (Tsiompanou and Marketos, 2013: 288-292). The public health concepts of preventive avoidance and immunity were birthed and made famous through a careful observance of the pandemic's spread. Over time, people who lived in the Greek era figured out that society's seclusion, later termed "quarantine" of infected and sick individuals, and the avoidance of contact with them prevented the spread of the disease. Similarly, some individuals were observed not to exhibit any symptoms or signs despite their exposure to sick individuals; this was later termed immunity. It is essential to acknowledge that Hippocrates, popularly ascribed the title "Father of Medicine," was pivotal in the Greek era in challenging some of the previously held beliefs and concepts about the causation and transmission of diseases (Martin and Martin-Granel, 2006: 976-980).

Many Greek era developments and science were built upon in the Roman era, which spanned 0 to 500 CE. During this period, the Antonine Plague, the Plague of Cyprian, the Plague of Justinian, and the first Plague Pandemic occurred (Spyrou et al., 2019: 323-340).

Claudius Galenus, also known as Galen, was a major player during this period. The field of public health experienced tremendous shaping and development by the Romans. Many present-day public health codes and structures were conceptualized, designed, and built during this period. Public restrooms, sewage disposal, market cleaning days, and public hand washing basins were some of the structures constructed (Badash et al.,2017:e1018). Galen lived through the Plague of Antonine and documented the symptoms and signs of infected patients (Littman and Littman, 1973: 243-255). Perceptions and beliefs about the pandemic were shaped by medical knowledge, which was on the rise during this period. Keen attention was focused on the disease's pathogenesis and progression, which was "smallpox-like" with characteristic skin lesions, fever, diarrhea, and throat inflammation (Haas, 2006: 1093-

1098). The Cyprian Plague closely followed the Antonine Plague and the pathogenesis of both diseases suggested to the Romans that they were new and emerging. Over time, their hopes were slightly raised from the observation of some infected people who recovered and were subsequently protected from getting reinfected; this was later termed immunity.

During the late medieval period, when the "Black Death" killed more than one half of the European population and up to 150 million globally (DeWitte, 2014: e96513), people's perceptions and beliefs resulted in less than desirable reactions. People resorted to the suspicion of the stranger, scapegoating, targeted societal ostracization, and illegal quarantine (Nelkin and Gilman,1988: 361-378).

At the beginning of the modern epoch to this present time, because of the robust technological advancement in science and mass communication/media and the discovery of the first vaccine by Edward Jenner in 1796 (Riedel, 2005: 21-25 "Edward Jenner and the History of Smallpox and Vaccination"), beliefs and perceptions about infectious diseases pandemics were altered dramatically. Perceptions of people are profoundly influenced by the information pedaled by news media outlets, which often align with partisan views or stance. Whereas scientists say one thing, politicians who have a formidable influence on the news media outlet say another in order to support their political aspirations (Limaye et al., 2020: e277-e278). It is a no-brainer to wear masks during infectious disease pandemics, which are spread via aerosols; however, wearing face masks was politicized to the point that some global leaders were not modeling it to their citizens (Limaye et al., 2020: e277-e278). The other extreme involves some news outlets that pedal doomsday to make their political opponents look terrible considering the upcoming elections. The worse the imagery of the pandemic, the better for the opposing party, but the worse it is for the ruling party (Hoffman, 2020: 273-374).

Risks and Causes

For centuries, the scientific community has struggled to articulate the exact causes of pandemics exhaustively. However, no specific etiology has been identified each time pandemics occur, multiple factors have been shown to increase the odds of their occurrence (Madhav et al., 2017: n.p). Additionally, a mature body of literature shows that pandemics have occurred more frequently in the last century than any other time in history (Ross et al., 2015: 89-94). Thus, the question that remains is "what changed in the last 100 years?" We know so far that the following factors/activities have changed dramatically over the last century: land exploration, urbanization, population explosion, poverty, increased trade and globalization, industrialization, and outer space activities, all culminating in a gross disruption of the natural ecosystem (Madhav et al., 2017:n.p).

The environment, which was neatly defined by Einstein as "everything, not us," could be equally a blessing and a curse to the humanity, especially when humans adopt the role of dominating it as opposed to being stewards of it (Bourdeau, 2004: 9-15). Indeed, as cliché as it may sound, reckless human behavior that adversely affects the environment and worsen global warming contribute in part to the increased prevalence of pandemics (Shope, 1991: 171-174). With the growing global industrialization, the need for and the rate at which land-use changes have occurred has increased. Given that land use is very closely related to the incidence and prevalence of emerging infectious diseases, correspondingly, land use changes significantly alter the rate of occurrence of these infectious diseases, which have hit pandemic levels over the last century. Additionally, most of the pathogens responsible for the pandemics that humans have endured have their origins in animals that human beings share the environment with (McFarlane et al.,2013: 2699-2719). The crossing of species by disease pathogens is impacted by changes in land use (Boni, 2008: C8-14). These changes alter the pathogen lifecycle, breeding, density, distribution, virulence factors, vectors, and structural adaptability changes. When the environment changes, some pathogens undergo mutative changes in the genes that code for some of their surface markers (antigenic drift) and/or adopt a hybrid form by exchanging genetic material with other microorganisms present in the host at the same time (Taubenberger and Kash, 2010: 440-451). Apart from the impact of human activities, including the building of cities, exploring of the outer space and fostering of international trade, on emerging infectious diseases, failure in ensuring efficiency in pandemic early detection and surveillance, emergency preparedness, information sharing, reporting, and a coordinated global response also increase the risk for pandemics.

Despite the numerous efforts of the international public health agencies such as the WHO and the UN in building capacity in impoverished countries while fostering a coordinated and effective global response to pandemics involving more affluent countries, much remains to be achieved. Countries always seem to resort to an individual and siloed response to pandemics that creates global gaps and promotes the transmission of these infectious diseases. This siloed approach to pandemics, complicated by the limited and unevenly distributed resources, creates a patchy and ineffective response. Another significant risk for pandemics is the massive gap in knowledge about their cause, research capabilities, and overarching national and global policies on protocols to follow when they happen. Together, these risk factors continue to increase the odds of pandemics happening and their consequent effects including increased morbidity, mortality, socioeconomic and political uncertainties.

Impact of Global Pandemics on Global Health

The World Health Organization defines health as "a state of complete physical, mental and social wellbeing and not merely the absence of disease or infirmity." Correspondingly, this section explores the impact of global pandemics on human physical, mental, and social health.

Physical Health

Some of the public health advocated steps in limiting the spread of infectious diseases during extended outbreaks such as pandemics include sheltering in place, wearing face masks, and degerming, including but not limited to regular washing of hands. Additionally, venues and events that host public gatherings are advised to be avoided. These steps usually result in the closure or lock down of public facilities like schools, parks, gymnasia, salons, and recreational facilities (Xiang et al., 2020: n.p). Although, physical distancing slows or curbs the spread of an infection, it adversely affects individuals with medical conditions impacted by a lack of physical activity. When advised to stay at home, for people with obesity, they are more likely to be sedentary than they usually would; for patients with other cardiovascular illnesses like hypertension, peripheral vascular diseases, and cardiomyopathies, their odds of developing complications increase (Ghanemi et al., 2019:110042). During pandemics, people stockpile and consume more canned foods that contain salt-based preservatives like nitrates. High salt diets worsen medical conditions, such as hypertension and kidney diseases. Fresh foods such as leafy vegetables and fruits become scarce during pandemics because farmers who are typically low-income earners and are more predisposed to getting infected may stop working due to ill-health.

Additionally, the refill process and delivery of medications needed by patients may be affected. Financial difficulties from layoffs and furloughs during pandemics also affect citizens' purchasing ability, resulting in inferior health choices being made. Adults who retain their jobs but may need to work remotely from home split their time between getting their job done and helping their children with school. This reduces the amount of time they have for self-care, including exercise and other physical activity (Ainsworth and Li, 2020: 291-292).

Pandemics significantly impact the physical health of children and young adults. When schools are closed, and children have to attend classes remotely, they tend to sit for long periods in front of the computer, which could cause headaches, eye disorders, and fatigue. Because physical activity during the regular school recess is eliminated with remote learning, children and young adults tend to gain weight more with a higher chance of becoming overweight or obese (Xiang et al., 2020: n.p).

Older people are almost always severely impacted by infectious disease outbreaks. This is because many of them have pre-existing health conditions that get worse during pandemics. As people age, their body systems also wane in structure and function, especially their immune/lymphatic systems. Thus, seniors are more likely to be infected by the pathogens responsible for pandemics and they suffer from complications resulting from the initial infection (Ainsworth and Li, 2020: 291-292).

Frontline workers such as emergency response personnel, doctors, other healthcare staff, postal service workers, and grocery store workers are especially at risk of getting infected by a pandemic bug. The situation is worsened because some of these essential workers are low-income earners and immigrants with other risks and vulnerabilities.

The spread of infectious pathogens during pandemics is seen more in crowded populations such as refugee camps, concentrated homeless sites, shelters, military bases, and camps. For developing countries that typically experience a significant poverty level and often live in crowded households, disease transmission is accelerated (Ainsworth and Li, 2020: 291-292).

Mental Health

During pandemics, infected individuals experience significant fear of dying from the infection, while non-infected people experience tremendous anxiety and fear of getting infected. Patients with diagnosed psychological, psychiatric, or behavioral conditions such as anxiety disorders, major depressive illnesses, post-traumatic stress disorders, schizophrenia, and bipolar disorders experience worsened symptoms. A robust body of literature shows that domestic violence, child abuse, and neglect significantly increase during pandemics even though reported cases decrease. Because schools and hospitals are closed during pandemics, many salient signs of abuse usually detected by teachers and caregivers are missed. Social distancing and sheltering-in-place result in people experiencing loneliness and isolation, which may further worsen their mental health. During stay-at-home orders, children and young adults that would normally play with their peers either in school or in their neighborhood experience boredom, loneliness, depression, crying spells, loss of concentration, and heightened irritability during sheltering-in-place orders (Javed et al., 2020: 292).

Social Health

The wellbeing of an individual is not only reflected in their physical health but also in the social interactions they develop with family, friends, and other people in their society. Social distancing, lockdowns, and sheltering in place of healthy, uninfected individuals and the quarantine of infected citizens adversely affect people's social and mental health. This effect was worse in the past than now; thanks to the technological developments that birthed social media and smartphones through which people communicate and stay connected (Wiederhold, 2020: 197-198). Nonetheless, humans are social beings that continuously feel the need to socialize with people they identify with. It is also not unusual for people to be suspicious of people outside of their immediate circle as potential infection sources. Countries shut their borders and quarantine visitors to their country. Pandemics are generally viewed as diseases of the visiting stranger. People tend to view themselves as the vulnerable ones that could be infected by other people (Tognotti, 2013: 254-259). This suspicion is worse for individuals who are from the countries where the pandemics originated. When this is not properly managed, pandemic associated nervousness could morph into hostility, xenophobia, or even hate (Mamun and Griffiths, 2020: 102073); however, some authors have suggested that people tend to pull together more than pedal hate during pandemics (Cohn, 2012: 535-555).

Economy

The threat of an impending pandemic or an actual pandemic always takes a toll on the global market. During pandemics, infected workers are asked to self-quarantine, and healthy workers may be advised to work remotely from home to maintain their social distance. Whereas, these sheltering-in-place steps help to curb the easy and rapid spread of the causative agents, over time, national productivity and revenue drop precipitously (Szucs, 2006: 6776-6778). Stocks, bonds, and shares always plummet, and the global financial crisis or meltdown almost always happens during pandemics. Infected individuals are quarantined, treated, or managed by experts.

Companies and corporations are usually compelled to reduce their expenditure during pandemics; hence, many people tend to get furloughed or laid off outright (Meltzer et al., 1999: 659-671). Small business sole proprietorships are always the hardest hit population during pandemics. Big corporations experience financial hardship but are usually the first to be considered for government aid. Together, these economic effects adversely affect the national revenue and the gross domestic product (GDP). For countries that are already impoverished, pandemics' economic consequences occur much faster than for affluent countries.

Due to the shutting down of countries' borders, international trade, imports and exports are affected, resulting in the scarcity or inflated costs of imported commodities. Additionally, fear-mongering results in citizens' excessively stockpiling groceries and other consumables. Retail stores may resort to the rationing of consumables and commodities. Responsible governments prioritize testing availability, treatment, if any, research, and the development of vaccines. All these activities cost much money, which many developing countries lack.

Since history suggests that pandemics will always occur, all nations must discover and adopt means by which their impacts could be minimized in terms of human physical, mental and social health as well as the global economy. The following are the suggested topical considerations to minimize pandemic impacts:

Surveillance System and Emergency Preparedness

All countries should prioritize their existing national surveillance system or create one if they do not currently have one. Surveillance systems help to identify cases and they are an effective means of reporting them to the health and human services departments or other corresponding entities. National emergency preparedness plans should include funding, trained personnel, communication systems, military support, and expertise availability.

Public Health Education

People worldwide still have different beliefs and perceptions about pandemics, many of which are scientifically flawed. These non-scientific beliefs and perceptions affect how these individuals view and respond to pandemics. For example, people who do not believe in wearing masks or maintaining social distance may put others at risk. Also, people who dispel conspiracy theories about vaccines create a significant challenge in getting people to do the responsible thing in protecting themselves and others. Public health experts should be granted funds to help with the education of the public when pandemics hit.

The Elimination of Siloed National Response and the Enhancement of Global Response

Global resources are not equally and homogeneously distributed. Some countries are endowed with more resources and wherewithal to respond aggressively and promptly to pandemics. Because a threat of an epidemic in one country is a threat of a pandemic to the rest of the world, every nation should show an interest in building their capacity to detect and respond effectively to pandemics. Affluent countries should support the impoverished countries in building their capacity in readiness for a potential pandemic.

Prioritization of Mental Health Support

Although pandemics severely impact people's mental health, national risk assessment, and responses do not always reflect mental health support's prioritization. Because of the nature of pandemics and the need to curb the transmission of the pathogen almost always involves sheltering-in-place and home quarantine, the need for mental health support further increases. Country authorities need to be aware of this fact and prioritize the voting of funds.

Enhanced Global Cooperation and Communication

One of the major criticisms of the Chinese government about the handling of the current COVID-19 pandemic is the late notification of the rest of the world about the initial cases and early genome sequencing research done on the virus. Consequently, other countries were not optimally prepared for the avalanche of infections and deaths that would follow. This is a classic example of how a lack of early, influential, and continuous communication as well as a lack of global cooperation during global pandemics could worsen their natural and often inevitable effects on global populations.

Comprehensive Economic Package for Small Businesses

Pandemics crash global markets because of the significant decline in the earnings of government or public-owned businesses, big corporations, and small businesses. Whereas, public companies and big corporations typically benefit from bail-out or stimulus packages to save them from collapsing, small businesses literarily die. Since pandemics are neither predictable nor easily prevented, the focus of all countries of the world should include planning for early mitigation and minimization of the economic impact. One way this could be attained is for legislators to vote on a comprehensive plan to earmark an appreciable amount of funds to bail out small businesses when pandemics occur. A small business should not have to shut down or die because of a pandemic they did not directly cause.

Special Health Insurance Coverage for Frontline and Essential Workers

People still have to eat, send and receive mails during pandemics, including medications and other life-saving gadgets. Thus, essential workers risk their lives and their families to ensure that these crucial aspects of life are still operational. Additionally, healthcare workers whom the world has suddenly realized to be heroes and heroines, put themselves in harm's way by going into hospitals to take care of the infected, sick and dying patients. In many instances, these healthcare providers deal with the mental trauma of seeing their patients in so much pain, discomfort, isolation and the agony of dying without their loved ones around them. Essential workers, as well as healthcare frontline workers, must be prioritized in the global response to any pandemic. International governments must prioritize the establishment of specific health insurance or coverage for these workers. Should these essential workers ever get infected in the line of performing their duties, there should be a rich amount of resources to take care of them.

Also, because of the challenging environment they work in and the associated mental trauma, there should be resources to help meet their mental health needs.

CHAPTER EIGHT

A Biblical Response to the New World Order

Robert Osei-Bonsu & Samson D. Dakio

Crises are coextensive with human life. So long as there shall be life on this planet, crises shall occur. They may erupt from different levels, including the socio-political, ecosystem, economic and religious planes. Humans have survived difficult and perilous moments in her history. Some of these challenging experiences nearly brought the human race on the verge of extinction. Such dramatic events include the two World Wars, natural calamities, climatic changes, and epidemics such as the novel Covid 19 pandemic. Humans have, since time immemorial, distinguished themselves by their ability to address their issues.

This is a reality perceptible in the number of federated initiatives materialized in local and international organizations such as NATO, the United Nations, and its subsidiary institutions such as the World Health Organization (WHO). These organizations have the mandate to harness their efforts and resources to relieve or eradicate the suffering of humankind. In all its wisdom, the

Robert Osei-Bonsu, PhD, MEd (osei-bonsur@aua.ac.ke) serves as the Program Leader of the PhD Biblical-Theological Studies program at the Theological Seminary of the Adventist University of Africa, Nairobi, Kenya.
Samson Dawé Dakio (sdawe@vvu.edu.gh) is with the School of Theology and Missions at the Valley View University, Accra, Ghana.

challenge is that the world does not know God, as indicated in 1 Cor. 1:21.

Meanwhile, any attempt to solve problems apart from God is bound to fail; this is where Christians must come in. The religion of Christ stands for peace. Those who profess to know Christ must likewise be ambassadors of peace wherever they go. This leads to the following questions: What has been the contribution of Christianity in peace-making and global crises management in history? Can Christians be the answer to the pending global challenges of the globe? What does the Scripture say about the current sequel of events leading to the end of the world? These questions shall constitute the stature of this chapter. The chapter employs an exegetical approach to ascertain the biblical stance on past, present, and future global crises.

I. Christianity's Basic Concerns about Peace and its Role in the Search for Global Peace

Christianity is a religion of peace per the nature of its founder, Jesus Christ. Throughout His earthly ministry, He lived as a peacemaker and taught His disciples and the masses to emulate Him. Jesus taught, among others, that "Blessed are the peacemakers: for they shall be called the children of God" (Matt 5:9, KJV). He also taught His disciples in Matt 5:39 that "But I say to you, that ye resist not evil: but whosoever shall smite thee on thy right cheek, turn to him the other also" (KJV). Christ's messages of peace changed the then known world. History bears witness that due to Jesus' statements, many Christians refrained from using force and weapons to defend themselves and are mostly conscientious objectors. Under the first Roman emperor, Augustus, Christianity experienced exponential growth due to the peaceful conditions he [Augustus] created (Morgan 1996:196). Christians were free to worship their God in security.

However, under Emperor Nero, the Christian community experienced awful persecution that inhibited the young religion (197). Emperor worship through symbolic objects was the order of the day. Any person who refuses to pay homage to the emperor was deemed an enemy of the state. During this challenging period, many Christians, including Bishops Ignatius and Polycarp, were killed because of their devotion to the cause of Christ (1996:197). Christianity was referred to as an illegal religion (*religio Ilicita*) because it was seen as a threat to the public order. Besides, Christians would not worship or offer incense to the emperor in conformity to the day's standard. History testifies that Nero (AD 54-68) was the first to perpetrate systematic persecution of Christians in AD 64. He had some believers torn into pieces by wild animals, and others set alight as torches in the dark (Winks et al. 1992:108). Being a Christian alone in the first century was a sufficient reason to be victimized.

Under Emperor Trajan Pliny the Younger (AD 110-111), who was the governor of Pontus and Bithynia then, executed Christians based on the mere allegation that they were Christians. Any accused individual who had acknowledged three consecutive times to be a Christian was executed. The persecution reached its apex under Diocletian, who had decided to wipe away Christianity from the Roman Empire in AD 303 (Winks et al. 1992:109,197). However, God was still in control of things. After the division of the Empire into East and West, God raised a certain emperor called Constantine. Overseeing the Western part of the Roman Empire, he became a friend of Christ's religion. Through him, Christianity became a *religio licita,* meaning that it was recognized and accepted by the empire. Fortunately, this religious freedom culminated in the Edict of Milan in AD 313, when the liberty of worship and other privileges were pronounced for all religions (1992:197). By the year AD 380, Christianity had grown to gain the status of the official religion of the Roman Empire under Emperor Theodosius. Up to this point, the Church had never resorted to violence in any form to proselytize anyone. However, Christianity was spreading rapidly like a wildfire despite the ruthless persecution that Christians went through at some points (Winks et al. 1992:122).

However, the interference of the State in the affairs of the

Church had paved the way for an incestuous union between the two parties. The sell-out of Christianity can be attributed to its quest for peace. It ensures that the sequel of events was characterized by religio-political movements in Eastern and Western Europe.

I.   A Paradigm Shift in the History of the Christian Church: From Peace to Terror

From the sixth century, after the pagan Rome's demise around AD 476, Christianity experienced the darkest period of its history until the end of the medieval period (Winks et al. 1992:128; Ferrell 2003:81). This period, usually known as the Middle Ages or Dark Ages, was a period of political and religious unrest. The period was called Dark Ages, not because the sun and the moon had ceased to play their functions, but precisely because of the vicious activities perpetrated at that time. A series of events occurred during that period that made humanity retrograde in terms of human civilization.

It is no secret to students of the Bible and history that the year AD 538 was a milestone in the Christian Church's history. From AD 538, the Roman Catholic Church, through the papal system, began to rule with an iron hand after the destruction of the last Arian tribe, the Ostrogoths (Ferrell 2003:81). This oppressive rule of the Church lasted till 1798 when the papacy fell victim to a deadly wound. Pope Pius VI was captured by Napoleon's general, Alexander Berthier, and imprisoned in Valence, where he passed on a year later (Ferrell 2003:72, 75). During the 1260 years that span from AD 538 to 1798, the Church perpetrated many atrocities on people in God's name. When we talk about the persecution of Christians, we can think of the suffering of the Waldenses, the St. Bartholomew Day Massacre (August 23, 1572), the Spanish Inquisition, the Crusade against the Albigenses, and the 30 years' war (1618-1648), a lengthy religious conflict in which it is estimated that both military and civilian casualties, protestants and catholic, exceeded 8,000,000 (Mervyn, 1985). This lugubrious period of the Church is well depicted in Daniel 7. In these centuries, the Little

Horn persecuted the saints of the Most High God, blasphemed against His holy name, and eclipsed Christ's earthly ministry through the sale of indulgences and the confession of sins to priests. The Church tried to shift attention from the mediatorial role of Christ to the authority of the Church on earth.

Among the sordid activities of the Church during the Middle Ages emerged the practice of the crusades under the auspices of the Jesuits. They would do anything to defend the papacy. The crusades were wars sometimes called 'holy wars' between Christians and Muslims. Verily, they were "military expeditions undertaken by the Western European Christians between 1095 and 1270, usually at the behest of the papacy, to recover Jerusalem and other Palestinian places of pilgrimage from the Muslim control" (*Change your Life Biblically* 1997-2001:134). By extension, the term crusade could also apply to 13th-century wars waged against pagan people, Christian heretics, and the papacy. In other words, crusaders viewed themselves as soldiers of Christ and were the military arm of the papal policy (1997-2001:134). The very first Crusade in the history of Christianity was expedited in 1095 by Pope Urban II. This is an excerpt of the proclamation of the said Crusade:

> Let those who are accustomed to wage secret wars wastefully even against Believers, go forth against the Infidels in a battle worthy to be undertaken now and to be finished in victory. Now, let those, who until recently existed as plunderers, be soldiers in Christ; now, let those, who formerly contended against brothers and relations, rightly fight barbarians; now, let those who recently were hired for a few pieces of silver win their eternal reward (Winks et al., 1992:239).

It was a call for Christians to kill in the name of the Lord from the "vicar of Christ"; a need to maim and kill for the "course of Christ." A critical assessment of the above quotation does not look like a pope's discourse but rather like that of a gang leader. The message of Urban II was received with much excitement by the audience with cries of "God wills it." The Crusaders had been trained with an ideology akin to that of terrorists in modern times. They [crusaders] were made to believe that they were thus serving God by taking away innocent lives. Again, "if a man were killed doing this work of God, he would automatically be absolved of his sins and assured of salvation (*a plenary indulgence*)" (Winks et al., 1992:238). This is akin to what some jihadists are doing today in different countries in the name of religion and God. There are similarities between what the Christian Church under the leadership of the bishop of Rome did during the crusades and the sins being perpetrated by some jihadist elements.

When believers are indoctrinated to such a level, then there is a cause for alarm because such individuals would be ready for anything, be it good or bad. Without going further, the citation of Urban II gives an idea about the extent to which the Church had apostatized during the Middle Ages. Nevertheless, this period had known some peace movements, but the Crusades eclipsed them.

The Church that used to be a partisan of non-violence had gradually become an advocate of violence and terror. Indeed, the Church had digressed from its *raison d'être*, which is, to preach the Gospel and be a haven for all. Making the eulogy of violence and terrorism is not part of the mandate that Christ had given His Church. It must, therefore, be acknowledged that Christianity has not always been a religion of peace, especially in the medieval period.

The Reformation period was not peaceful either. It was characterized by a high tension between the Roman Catholic Church and the Protestant Churches that came out of her. None of the reformers had it easy; be it Martin Luther, John Calvin, or Zwingli, it was at the peril of their lives that they did minister. In short, the Reformation was a tumultuous period in the Church's history. The aftermath of this period was characterized by "nationalism and increased militarism: it was a tragic contradiction that World War One was fought almost entirely between nominal Christian nations—a monumental failure of Christianity to prevent the war ("Christianity and Peace," 2020:2).

Moreover, the Thirty Years' War was another fatal conflict in the History of Christianity. This war was fought among Catholics and Protestants in Central Europe between 1618 and 1648 and it claimed over eight million souls, making it one of the deadliest conflicts in human history. This war is reminiscent of the fourth Crusade launched from 1202 -1204 by Pope Innocent III, who directed the mighty Crusade against fellow Christians instead of maintaining the pressure against the Muslims who had controlled the city of Jerusalem (Küng, 2005:259). Küng explains that this attack was perpetrated against the Byzantine city of Constantinople to affirm Rome's supremacy. This act was contrary to the primary purpose of the Crusades that were meant for Muslims. It becomes imperative to concede that Christianity has never fully reflected its founder's peaceful image apart from the first five centuries of its history.

Nevertheless, this dark page in Christianity's history cannot obliterate the many other glorious pages that characterized it thereafter. In fact, after several centuries of spiritual lethargy, the Church had reclaimed its rightful position, which is championing peace in the world.

Recent Global Crises: The Christian Church in Search for Global Solutions

In recent years, the crises that have arisen include humanitarian crises and climate change matters. In the face of these global challenges, the Church has been greatly involved in seeking solutions. Several ecumenical movements attempt to contribute their quota to resolving the challenges of the moment. What is the role of God's Church in bringing relief to our suffering world? The Church should not remain passive when the globe is in dire straits. However, it is becoming more and more preoccupying when the demarcation between the Church and state is gradually fading away.

The danger inherent to that fact is that history is likely to repeat itself. Religious liberty tends to suffer a loss when the Church tries to assume the state's role and vice versa. In the same vein, experience has proven that fundamental rights such as religious liberty are often infringed upon in initiating the new world orders. On this subject, the *Seventh-day Adventist Minister's Handbook* has this to say:

> Given the Seventh-day Adventist understanding of the great controversy and the climactic events of human history involving the union of Church and state that will eliminate the free exercise of religion and result in persecution of the faithful remnant, the department seeks to monitor and interpret current trends that may reflect the prophetic scenario ("Ministerial Association," 2009:69).

As the years go by, the observation is that the Catholic Church and some ecumenical movements are at the forefront of international affairs. They have taken upon themselves the responsibility to play the first roles in bettering the world's dire situation.

The World Council of Churches (WCC) highlights its new challenges, thus:

> The ecumenical process, which led to the formation of the WCC was not only a response to the gospel imperative of Christian unity. It was also an affirmation of the call to mission and common witness and an expression of a collective commitment to the search for justice, peace, and reconciliation in a chaotic, warring world divided along with race, class, and competition national and religious loyalties. ("History and Structure," 2020: par. 6; emphasis original).

The WCC was created in Amsterdam in 1948; the conciliar body includes more than 300 churches—Protestant, Anglican, Eastern Orthodox, and Oriental Orthodox (Hick, 2020: par. 1). For the past decades, this movement has played a tremendous role in alleviating the suffering of many in the times of crisis. Over five decades ago, Pope John XXIII sent an Encyclical to warn about the terrible outcomes of war and offered hope and solutions when the world was on the verge of experiencing a nuclear war (Ceballos 2016:286).

Pope Francis has championed the issue of climate change and global warming. A decade ago, in 2009, Pope Benedict XVI had stated that, "The way humanity treats the environment influences the way it treats itself, and vice versa (Brecha, 2020: par. 6)." In his Encyclical, Pope Francis addresses: "an extensive range of environmental problems, such as global warming, loss of biodiversity, hazardous chemicals and waste, marine pollution, destruction of forests, monoculture plantations, lack of clean drinking water, and social problems such as inequity, greed, and poverty (Ceballos, 2016:286). Ceballos believes that the publication and outreach of *Laudato Si'* by Pope Francis played a role in many critical global discussions and very likely had some influence on the outcome of the historic Paris Climate Agreement of December 2015 (COP21) (Ceballos, 2016:286). Laudato Si': On Care for Our Common Home is an urgent appeal from Pope Francis, addressed to every person living on this planet for an inclusive dialogue about how we are shaping our world (**"General Secretariat United States Conferences," 2020: par.1**). In section 13 of the Encyclical, Pope Francis expressed his hope thus: "The urgent challenge to protect our common home includes a concern to bring the whole human family together to seek sustainable and integral development, for we know that things can change" (Ceballos, 2016:287).

The recent interfaith dialogue aimed at uniting, as much as possible, all the religions or denominations of the planet behind a common cause, the welfare of mother earth. However, how can it be possible? All religions, denominations, and world leaders are to put aside their differences because, as the US President John F.

Kennedy posited, what unites us is more significant than what divides us (Kennedy, 2020: par. 7). If this initiative is praiseworthy, at the first glance, it must be pointed out that there is an untold and hidden agenda. Any union between individuals or groups that is not grounded on absolute obedience to God becomes suspicious. This kind of unity is akin to that of the antediluvian people who, contrary to God's word, decided to construct the tower of Babel to remain together and make a name for themselves (Gen 11:1-4). It ensures that this kind of quasi-incestuous union likely presages other global crises.

In fact, in the name of restoring the earth and its ecosystems, some nations have already begun to restrict fundamental freedoms that point to the institutionalization of Sunday worship. This quotation is apropos:

> Not long ago, Sunday used to be a day of rest, a day of spiritual renewal, a day for families to come together, but we have changed Sunday from rest to shopping, flying, and driving. However, in the context of excessive carbon dioxide emissions into the atmosphere, which brings catastrophic upheavals, we can restore Sunday to a day for Gaia, a day for the Earth (Kumar, 2020: par. 3).

Some world leaders have already started advocating for no or less work on Sunday to mitigate the dire effects of increasing global warming. Kumar explains that the complete ceasing of activities on Sunday is believed to have therapeutic values on human beings and the planet earth (Kumar, 2020: par. 5). Pope Francis has made an official appeal to world leaders or politicians to consider taking drastic measures against this global phenomenon (Pullella, 2020: par. 1). The Pope further enjoined the United Nations' Summit thus:

> There, governments will have the responsibility of showing the political will to take drastic measures to

achieve as quickly as possible zero net greenhouse gas emissions and to limit the average increase in global temperature to 1.5 degrees Celsius concerning pre-industrial levels, following the Paris Agreement goals (Kumar, 2020: par. 3).

On the 17-18th September 2014, the World Alliance of Religions' Peace (WARP) Summit was held in Seoul, Republic of Korea. This summit brought together over 2000 *people, including prominent religious leaders, to sign a peace agreement. The agreement stated that,*

Religious leaders must unite their religions as one under the Creator to bring all wars to an end and leave world peace as a legacy to future generations. Representatives of the UN should make the utmost efforts to enact an international law for the cessation of all wars and contribute to world peace ("Peace Agreement Ceremony," 2020: par. 4).

The current trend of events indicates that the future for religious liberty appears bleak because there is a plurality of opinion on what qualifies as liberty or freedom. The perception of nations when it comes to freedom differs. Differently put, contrary to general belief, the worst is yet to happen in the human history.

II. Exegetical Analysis of Matthew 24:3, 6-8

The above background study has shown that this world has always been in crisis. Despite all the teachings of Jesus on peace, the world is still in dire straits. Christ taught, among others, that His followers are to obey and maintain a cordial relationship with their governing authorities (Matt 22:21; cf. 1 Pet 2:13, 14); they are to love one another and remain united (John 13:34-35; 15:12, 17; 17:11, 21-23); they are never to retaliate. With these teachings, the world is expected to experience peace. Unfortunately, this has not always been the case because of the fallen human nature. It ensures that the

Scriptures depict an apocalyptic picture of this world's future, some sporadic biblical passages hammer on that fact.

A Lexical-semantic Analysis

Matthew 24 is a significant chapter in the New Testament (NT) owing to its eschatological focus. Many Christians consider this passage to be one of the most convincing biblical pieces of evidence about Christ's second coming. The chapter has some link with chapter 23. Matthew 23:38 reads: "Behold, your house is being left to you, desolate"! This verse comes at the climax of Jesus' invective against the religious leaders of His day.

The disciples' questions to their master were triggered by the statement made in v. 38 and 24:2 about the plight of Jerusalem's temple. Verse 3 states: "Tell us, when will these things be, and what *will be* the sign of your coming, and the end of the age?" Some scholars argue that the last two syndetic clauses must function as a single question because a single Greek article governs them (Mounce, 1990:222). It follows that the disciples' concern was to know two things: (1) When will these things (i.e., the desolation of the temple) take place? (2) When will the world come to an end? The disciples thought these events would occur simultaneously or in rapid succession (Nichol, 1977:5:496).

In response to these queries, Jesus does not give them a specific timeline. Instead, He points them to some signs that are prerequisites for the temple's desolation and His subsequent coming. However, those signs are not in themselves the proofs that the end has come. They are only precursory ones. These signs include: (1) People other than Jesus will claim to be the Messiah; (2) Wars and rumors of war will abound; (3) International hostility and enmity will also be universal; (4) Famines and earthquakes typify the natural disasters that will often make people wonder if the end is near, but nothing may be deduced from them; (5) The next concern is "pestilences," "plagues" or "disease" the Bible makes it clear that it will permeate the last days. The world will be afflicted with diseases far worse than the Coronavirus. There will be a time of trouble with death on a scale never seen (Bloomberg, 1992: 353).

The purpose of this brief analysis of Matt 24:3, 6-8 is to ascertain the significance of this passage in the on-going debate on the global crisis and the search for a New World Order. Matthew 24:6-8 states: "You will hear of wars and rumors of wars but see to it that you are not alarmed. Such things must happen, but the end is still to come. [7]Nation will rise against nation, and kingdom against kingdom. There will be famines and earthquakes in various places. [8] All these are the *beginning (archē)* of *birth pains (ōdin)* (NIV)." This passage does not present many exegetical challenges. Nevertheless, a close look at vv.3, 6, and 8 is crucial to this study. A concise lexical analysis of the terms *archē* "beginning" and *ōdin* "birth pang," *telos* "end," and *synteleia* "end" will provide insight into the subject matter.

ōdin

ōdin is a close word to *odynē*, meaning "a pang or throe, grief or sorrow, pain, or travail" (Strong, 2007:1652, 1685). In secular Greek, the words *ōdin*es "birth pangs," and *ōdinō* "to suffer birth pangs," likely denoted the cries of women at the commencement of their labor (Bertram, 1974:667). The noun *ōdin* is used in passages such as Mark 13:8 and Acts 2:24. Mark 13:8 states that wars, earthquakes, and famines will mark birth pangs (*ōdinōn*). 'Acts 2:24 says, "And God raised Him again, putting an end to death's agony." It may be observed that the meaning of "birth pangs" *ōdin* may be the same in these three passages. The meaning is best construed metaphorically than literally. In other words, *ōdin* may be construed as any great pain that Christ's disciples may experience before His Second Coming. Mounce concurres with the foregoing when he states that the Greek *ōdin* in Matt. 24:8 is used for the terrors and torments that precede the Messianic Age (Bertram, 1974:223). Again, "Matt. 24:8 relates the expression' beginning of sorrows' to all the eschatological happenings that he [Jesus] depicts" (depicts" (Bertram, 1974:672). The woes are believed to point to the imminence of the redemption and the parturition of the new people of God in the eschatological future (Bertram 1974:672). When *ōdin* is used in the singular, it denotes the travail or pain of childbirth, as in 1 Thess 5:3 (Zodhiates 1992:1497-1498). When used in the plural (i.e., *ōdinōn*), it warns of the sorrows that would follow wars, famines, and other catastrophes (Matt. 24:8; Mark 13:8; LXX: Job 21:17; Nah. 2:10 [Zodhiates 1992:1497-1498]).

The verb *tiktō* appears about 215 times in the LXX and usually translates the Hebrew verb *yālad*. In the NT, *tiktō* occurs chiefly in the Matthaean and Lukan birth narratives of Jesus and John the Baptist; *tiktō* portrays more the physical reality of giving birth (Luke 2:6f, 11). In other words, *tiktō* is a more drastic word and is used in passages that depict the reality of labor (John 16:21; Rev. 12:3). It expresses the idea of travail, danger, and stark realities of childbirth (Bauer, 1986:1,186). In John 16:21, the words *tiktō* and *lypē* are used respectively to translate "travail" and "sorrow." This verse describes what a woman goes through before she gives birth to a newborn baby. The word *lypē* has the following semantic range: "the pain of the body or mind, grief, sorrow," while *tiktō* stands for "to beget, bring forth." It ensures that both *ōdin* and *lypē* may be used interchangeably. However, *lypē* is a more specific term for literal pain resulting from childbirth. Josephus employs the word *ōdin*es only on an OT basis to mean labor or pregnancy, which usually entails pain (Bertram 1974:671). Exodus 1:19, for example, points out that the midwives realized that Hebrew women deliver (*tiktousin*) faster than their Egyptian counterparts. Bertram explains that *ōdin*es and *ōdinō* "are used for Hebrew words that denote pregnancy as such with no special thought of the painful experiences involved" (Bertram 1974:669). This implies that the OT does not exclusively use the words *ōdin*es and *ōdinō* to denote pain resulting from the process of giving birth. For example, the critical passage, Gen. 3:16, which stands as the foundation of childbirth pains, uses *lypē* rather than *ōdin*es to translate the Hebrew words *'e'eb* and *'i'ābōn*. A close look at the various usages of the verb *ōdinō* leads to the concession that *ōdinō* is best translated as "to cause to a tremble or quake," which has no reference to bearing or being born, as in Job 39:1 (Bertram, 1974:669).

Based on this brief analysis, it is fair to argue that the term *ōdin* "birth pang" is best construed as a broad term that may refer to pain due to childbearing or suffering caused by the unfolding of the end time signs. However, the use of the plural *ōdinōn* "birth pangs" in Matt. 24:8 clearly indicates that only the pains or sorrows caused by end-time cataclysmic events are in view. We now turn to the word *archē*, "beginning."

archē

This word *archē* occurs 55 times in the NT to mean beginning or commencement (Weiss, 1990: 161); Bietenhard 165). Weiss argues that *archē* always signifies the 'primacy' of time, place, or rank. In Greek philosophy, *archē* acquires a special meaning to denote a point at which something new begins in time (Müller, 1986:1,164). In the OT, *archē* is used to translate over 30 Hebrew words, including *rō'š* "head, top" and *rē'š t* "beginning" (Coenen, 1986:1: 164-165). The NT uses the term *archē* in a manner akin to that of secular Greek to denote the first point in time and to indicate an area of authority. In the NT, *archē* may connote the commencement of something within time. For example, in Mark 1:1, *archē* stands for the beginning of the Gospel. In Mark 13:8, *archē* points to the beginning of the sufferings leading to the close of the age. In John 1:1, *archē* refers to an absolute beginning, that is, before time, as it is counted today. *archē* may also refer to a passive beginning, such as the beginning of a line, road etc. The term *archē* sometimes connotes "power, authorities, rulers," as is the case in Luke 12:11; 20:20; Titus 3:1. In these passages, *archē* is used collocational with *exousia* "authority" to refer to the civil or religious authorities of the Jews.

Matthew 24:8 states that the cataclysmic events described in vv. 5-7 will be but the beginning of birth pangs. The context suggests that a temporal usage of the word *archē* is in view. It designates the point of a new beginning in a temporal sequence (Delling, 1985:81). In other words, *archē* in v. 8 denotes the starting point of the troubles leading to the destruction of the Jerusalem temple and, ultimately, the Second Coming of Jesus. It follows that Matt. 24:8 and Mark 13: 8, which narrate the same event, use the term *archē* about the cosmic woes that will culminate into the Second Coming of Christ.

History bears witness that this world has already experienced wars, famines, earthquakes before the destruction of the Jerusalem temple. The practice of war was not foreign to the Israelites. These wars between Israel and heathen nations occurred in the context of 'holy war.' That is, in the context of the conquest of the land of Canaan. Such war was perceived as Yahweh's battle on behalf of His people. Hence, Yahweh was seen as 'the Divine Warrior.' Prophets were even consulted before engaging in war (1 Kgs. 20-22). With the advent of Christ, the practice of 'holy war,' however, came to an end. Yet, Jesus warned His disciples about the resurgence of wars as one of the end-time signs. "The wars and rumors of wars in the apostolic times foreshadowed the end of the Jewish nation, so the international turmoil and strife of our day presage the end of the world" (Nichol 5:497).

In addition to wars, the world was supposed to experience a series of famines and earthquakes heralding the commencement of troubles preceding the end of time.
The *Seventh-day Adventist Bible commentary* points out that there were altogether four significant famines during Claudius' reign spanning from A.D. 41 to 54 (5:497). Again, "there were a series of major earthquakes between A.D. 31 and A.D. 70. The worst of these was in Crete (46 or 47), Rome (51), Phrygia (60), and Campania (63)" (Nichol 5:497).

The above calamities were expected to happen before the destruction of Jerusalem, and they did. Nevertheless, the temple's demolition in AD 70 was not supposed to mark the end of sorrows.

That period would only mark the commencement of the apocalyptic woes.

telos/synteleia

In the LXX, *telos* has some Semiotic equivalents such as *sōph* and *qē* translated as "end." *sōph* and *qē* "are used for *telos* only in precise or generic indications of time" (Delling, 1985:51). *telos* has a rich semantic range, including "goal, result, reward, conclusion, close" (Delling, 1985:52). Delling argues that the word in the sense of "conclusion" links *telos* with the eschatological events that are yet to occur at any rate in the Synoptics and 1 Cor. 15 (Delling, 1985:55). He explains that the context suggests that the *parousia* is in view, especially in Matt 24:14 and Mark 13:7.

synteleia is used extra biblically to connote several things, including "a common accomplishment," "common performance or cooperation," "conclusion, ending" (Delling, 1985:8:65). In the LXX, *synteleia* is translated as "execution" about the crossing of the Jordan in the book of Josh. 4:8. It is also used in Job 26:10 to mean "end or boundary." In Nah. 1:8, *synteleia* is used for "destruction" to translate the Hebrew word *kālāh,* which means "completion, complete destruction, annihilation, or consumption."

Some scholars point out a difference between using the two terms *telos* and *synteleia* rendered "end." Jeannine K. Brown argues that the use of *telos* in Matt. 24 refers to the destruction of the temple, while *synteleia* refers to the end of the age (2015:275; Delling, 1985:66). Gerhard Delling (1985:66) explicitly states that the use of *synteleia* in Matt. 24:3 materially points to eschatological events that have not yet occurred. The term *synteleia* occurs six times in the NT, of which five are found in the book of Matthew (13:39, 40, 49; 24:3; 28:20). All these occurrences point exclusively to the end of the world (J. K. Brown, 2015:275; Balz, 1993:309). This does not negate the fact that *telos* can also connote eschatological events, as Delling points out. This seems to be the case in Matt. 24:14; Mark 13:7; and 1 Cor. 15:24, where the use of *telos* points to the end of the world. In

Matt. 24:14, for example, the preaching of the Gospel of the Kingdom to all the nations is said to be the *sine qua non-condition* for the coming of the end of time. Therefore, it is to state that the difference between *telos* and *synteleia* is best ascertained contextually. Nevertheless, it is clear from the Scripture that the use of *synteleia* is scanty, and each occurrence points to the eschatological Day of the Lord. Although some scholars picture the fall of Jerusalem and the Second Coming of Jesus as a single event in history, the caution is that the precursory signs and the events are not conflated (Stefanovic, 2007:108-109; J.K. Brown, 2015:275). The birth pangs that had begun some time before the temple's destruction are to last until the consummation of the age (*synteleia*).

Based on the above analysis, it may be argued that the various catastrophic signs that heralded the destruction of the temple of Jerusalem will reach their *terminus ad quem* at the second advent of Christ. This implies that this planet is not going to get any better. Generally speaking, the Scriptures depict an apocalyptic picture of the future of this world. Jesus did not promise anywhere that this globe will be a peaceful place for His followers. On the other hand, He promised that He will be with them through all their trials (John 17:15; 16:33; cf. Isa 43:1-2). Therefore, it may be concluded that the use of the word *synteleia* in Matt. 24:8 is not fortuitous. It was a deliberate attempt on the part of Matthew to draw the awareness of his audience to the fact that the cataclysmic events that will precede the destruction of Jerusalem will not end, but they will rather begin the apocalyptic woes. As believers living in the twenty-first century, the fulfillment of this biblical prophecy is undeniable. Since the destruction of Jerusalem in AD 70 to date, the world has experienced fiercer global crises.

Therefore, it may be concluded that Christians are not to expect a world free from troubles. They are to pray for the strength to cope with whatever comes their way. Christians will hardly derive joy and happiness from external circumstances, but only in their close relationship with Christ shall they find inner peace. All human attempts to achieve a new world order devoid of suffering seem to be a lost battle. Christians are expected to play their role as the salt and light of the world (Matt. 5:13-14).

Nevertheless, they must always bear in mind that they are only pilgrims on this globe. Their citizenship is not of this earth but in heaven (Phil 3:20). The new world that humanity and precisely the redeemed will be ushered into is establishing the kingdom of God on earth at the *Parousia*.

The study has embarked on an exegetical survey in order to ascertain the biblical response to the on-going global crises affecting humanity. The background study has laid the foundation for the analysis. It has shown that global problems do trace their origin back to the fall of humanity. As a religion of peace, Christianity has played a significant role in promoting peace in the world. However, it must be recognized that at some point in history, the religion of Christ has been found guilty of several atrocities, including the Inquisition and the Crusades.

The exegetical study has revealed that crises will mar life on this globe until Christ's second advent. The analysis has established the eschatological import of Matthew 24:3, 6-8. In the entire chapter, Christ dealt with two distinct but related events, namely the destruction of Jerusalem's temple and the end of the world. These two events are associated with each other in the sense that: (1) similar global events that preceded the destruction of the temple will also herald the end of the world; (2) the actual destruction of the temple foreshadows that of the world.

The use of the term *synteleia* in Matt. 24:8 is paramount to understanding the sequel of events that are currently undermining the tranquillity of the globe. The catastrophic happenings during the apostolic and post-apostolic times were meant to herald the impending destruction of Jerusalem's magnificent temple. Those events did not mean that the *Parousia* was at hand. Instead, they meant that trouble had just begun. The birth pangs are expected to be a part and parcel of life till the second appearance of Christ.

Simply put, Matthew 24:3, 6-8 has revealed that humanity has experienced wars, famines, and natural calamities before the destruction of Jerusalem's temple. It is expected that more of these portentous tragedies will continue to sadden humanity till the appearance of Jesus Christ. Therefore, it is an illusion to hope that the current condition of this world will improve in the future. Such speculative enterprise runs counter a clear-cut 'thus says the Lord'.

It follows that any human agenda including papal and ecumenical endeavours for a world free from wars and suffering is doomed to failure. Today, the religious bodies' active involvement or movements in resolving the world's most challenging problems may have some adverse effects on personal and religious freedoms.

Based on the above, Christians must be abreast of the times in which we live. They must be conscious of the fact that they cannot turn this world into a paradise. Such a perception of things would be utopic. However, they can be a catalyst for a better world by positively influencing their respective milieus.

Therefore, the study concludes that this world has nothing good to offer, especially to believers in Christ. On this globe, it is unrealistic to hope for a life devoid of troubles. However, with Christ, it is possible to experience true peace and happiness, even amid global turmoil. The birth pangs are meant to usher in a new era of eternal bliss. Only those who endure till the end of the sorrows shall be saved.

The study makes the following recommendations: Christians must live the faith they profess, then the world will get better. It is high time religion ceased to be used as a means to fuel conflicts around the globe. For that matter, Christians, especially religious leaders, must subscribe to a non-violence ideology as preached by the master teacher, Jesus Christ. Also, Christians must tread cautiously in their endeavours to help resolve the pendent challenges of the globe. They must always strive to be a part of the solution and not the problem. Christians and ecumenical entities must make sure to guarantee religious liberty and all individual freedom of conscience. Finally, in the quest to find a new order for a peaceful world, Christians must be proactive enough in making the difference between the sacred and the mundane.

CHAPTER NINE

Biblical Prophecy on the New World Order

Nsengumuremyi Ananie

There have been various interpretations on the Covid-19 pandemic. Majority believe that the novel corona virus has paved way for the institutionalization of the New World Order. Such a view, in the general sense, has been upheld by the majority of the Christian groups even among the Seventh-day Adventists. Thus, this chapter employs the exploratory research design. The inquiry centers on the biblical prophecy as it indicates that there are no tangible evidences that Covid-19 is leading to the biblical New World Order.

The secular new world order, in the political realm, is referred to as "a new period of history evidencing dramatic change in the world political thought and balance of power. In a sense, the New World Order is primarily associated with the ideological notion of the global governance of new collective efforts to identify and understand, the worldwide problems that go beyond the capacity of individual nation-states to solve" (Wikipedia, October 2020). In a general sense, the political new world order sounds as having good

Nsengumuremyi Ananie (ananienseng@yahoo.fr) was born in 1966 in Rwanda. He has a Masters of Theology in Church History and a Masters of Business Administration in Management. Since 2000, he teaches at the Adventist University of Central Africa in the Faculty of Theology.

intention on human well-being. Having all nations identify, understand, and address the worldwide problems together as a team is not in itself a problem for some Christians challenge. The thought-provoking aspect of the definition is in the solving of a "worldwide problem" in the world political thought.

Nonetheless, the New World Order is also a concern for conspiracy theories whereby "the common theme in conspiracy theories about a New World Order is that a secretive power elite with a globalist agenda conspires to eventually rule the world through an authoritarian world government—which will replace sovereign nation-states—and an all-encompassing propaganda whose ideology hails the establishment of the New World Order as the culmination of history's progress". It is in the same line that "many influential historical and contemporary figures have therefore been alleged to be part of a cabal that operates through many front organizations to orchestrate significant political and financial events, ranging from causing systemic crises to pushing through controversial policies, at both national and international levels, as steps in an on-going plot to achieve world domination (Wikipedia October 2020). It is in that vein that, when covid-19 started its ravaging journeys that Christians and non-Christians have been accepting the allegation that the Covid-19 is a means in the hands of worldly secret powers to achieve the New World Order. Consequently, there is a need to understand Covid-19 in the line with the biblical new world order. Here, the biblical new world order (Revelation 17:12-14) is expected to be more accurate than the political new world order and especially the one referred to by conspiracy theories.

The Bible and the New World Order

Taking a lift from the definitions of the New World Order, there have been the phenomena of changes in the history of the human race. Changes are not new in the biblical mind. Actually, the new world order, if we take them as changes in governance, is a theme that has been marking every step of the human race towards the end of its earthly history. The book of Genesis opens up the pace setters' changes in government as the time our first parents were chased out of the Garden of Eden (Genesis 3:22-24); also, during the biblical flood, things changed in a radical way (Genesis 9:1-3). The implication of these aforementioned changes is the conflict between good and evil. What these epochs share in common is the crime, sufferings, climatic change and the rejection of the law of God. This has led to the total disturbance of the human nature. Hence, humanity is led to the new ways of living and leading in its dealings. Paul writing to Timothy, reminded him that the end time period will be marked by people who are lovers of themselves, lovers of money, abusive, lovers of pleasure rather than lovers of God, etc. (2 Timothy 3:1-5). People with such anti-values are always ready to do anything to achieve their plans.

Today, crime is fast becoming a major menace that is changing the way in which many people live. These changes encompass all ramifications of human life; that is political, social, religious/spiritual, welfare, and physical world (Matt 24:7). "As the end draws near and the conflict between the satanic and divine forces intensifies, these calamities will also intensify in severity and frequency and it will find an unprecedented fulfillment in our time" (Ministerial Association 2005).

The Bible, though not using the term the new world order, refers to the changes that will be orchestrated by the human powers (best out of the earth) toward the culmination of the history of the human race. The book of Revelation especially, refers to the worldwide policies that will put an end to religious liberty, carrying with them serious restriction measures in the economic domain: "He also forced everyone, small and great, rich and poor, free and slave, to receive the mark …so that no one could buy or sell unless he had the mark, which is the name of the beast or the number of his name" (Revelation 13:16-17). According to the same prophecy, the powers of the world will agree to surrender theirs powers to the Beast so that it may accomplish its agenda. "For God has put it into their hearts to accomplish His purpose by agreeing to give the beast their power to rule, until God's words are fulfilled" (Revelation 17:17). Before the coming of Jesus Christ, Paul also refers to the rise of the man of sin, the man of lawlessness who will oppose God and exalt himself over God, proclaiming himself God (2 Thessalonians 2:1-4). Here, it is clear that the cornerstone of the new world order is worship. His secret power, as Paul said, started working during his time and will continue to do so till the man of sin will be revealed (2 Thessalonians 2:7). Is the secret elite (conspiracy) the one referred to by Paul here? The agents of the coming New World Oder as conceived by the conspiracy theory seems to be also referred to in the writings of White (1978: 5-6) that calls Christians to beware of secret societies and confederacies:

> "As we near the close of time, there will be greater and still greater external parade of heathen power; heathen deities will manifest their signal power, and will exhibit themselves before the cities of the world, and this delineation has already begun to be fulfilled... All needs wisdom carefully to search out the mystery of iniquity that figures so largely in the winding up of this earth's history. God's presentation of the detestable works of the inhabitants of the ruling powers of the world who bind themselves into secret societies and confederacies, not honoring the law of God, should enable the people who have the light of truth to keep clear of all these evils".

Reading, the above citation, four issues in line with the New World Order can be noticed: First by saying: "as we near the close of time, there will be greater and still greater external parade of heathen power"; she is underlining that the future will be different, that means that things will not continue to be as they were or are; changes will occur. Secondly, this change will not be a natural change rather; it will be coming from the deceitful plans of "the ruling powers of the world" which will not allow people to grasp their internalities from their externalities. Thirdly, this change will not be coming in isolation context rather the ruling powers of the world will "bind themselves into secret societies and confederacies". Lastly, the purpose is to rebel against the Creator of the universe by rejecting His law.

As these societies are secret and seem to be friendly to the Christian faith, some Christians are eager to unite with them. To warn such Christians, White (1946) wrote: "While there may be in these societies much that appears to be good, there is, mingled with this, very much that makes the good of no effect, and renders these associations detrimental to the interests of the soul". The secret societies, do not reveal the real reason for their association, their outward is totally different from their inward. It seems that they associate with one another for horrible plans while enveloping their real nature with humanitarian activities. As Bradley says: "the most visible and vocal protectors of morality are the very people who are working behind the scenes to destroy it" (Parker 2015).

White accounts her experience the time she received the vision relating to secret societies in the following words: "I have been permitted to look in upon these secret societies, their feasts, their order, their works, and my prayer has been: Hide them from my sight forever. Let me not understand more" (White 1978). This experience is not different from Bradley's as he advances more in research about secret societies. He also said that, "the more I have researched, the more alarming my discoveries have been… I have woken up to the possibility that we are not free, that we do not control our destinies, and that we are the puppets, not the masters" (Parker 2015).

It is not possible that two or more persons at once have an idea to come together for a common interest without a promoter. There is always a promoter behind every human association. The new world order in the biblical context is being promoted by Satan, the ancient serpent, the dragon. His intention is just to make a war against those who obey God's commandments and hold on to the testimony of Jesus (Revelation 12:17). White underlines that Satan, making war against the godly through secrecy, under cover, in the following words: "A power from beneath is working to bring about the last great scenes in the drama; Satan coming as Christ, and working with all deceivableness of unrighteousness in those who are binding themselves together in secret societies" (White 1992). What does it mean? All those that unite in evil societies make themselves, knowing it or not, the allies of Satan.

White and the Bible do not doubt that the main character in this last great scene is Satan. He is the one influencing the enemies of God to bind themselves together in secret societies. These secret societies are not named in White's (1980) writings, but one of them, the Free Masons, is referred to: "There are those who question whether it is right for Christians to belong to the Free Masons and other secret societies". The Free Masons is the only one that is explicitly listed in White's writings, though, others are there, but they are not explicitly named, nonetheless they were known by her.

The coming of the man of sin ranges among the steps of the conflict between Satan and God (II Thessalonians 2:9-10). The Counterfeit miracles, signs, wonders, and every sort of evil will be used to deceive people. Can covid-19 be one of these evils that Satan and his allies are using to lead to the new world order? According to many evangelical Christians in the US "COVID-19 and other irritations of our times are rather a 'foreshadowing' of what will come upon us in the end of times. The pandemic thus appears as a wakeup call" (Alder & Schaublin 2020). The disease, therefore, became a socio-political force all over the world. Among the measures adopted by many governments in the world to prevent the spread of COVID-19 was to ban public gatherings and close the places of worship (Bwire 2020).

White, even though in a different context, refers to what is to come in the future, she does not provide the exact picture of what is to be the world to come. This is not due to her will but to the lack of accurate information. "We are not now able to describe with accuracy the scenes to be enacted in our world in the future" (White 1980). She noticed that "the mark of the beast is exactly what it has been proclaimed to be. Not all in regard to this matter is yet understood nor will it be understood until the unrolling of the scroll" (White 1946). The prophet Isaiah, though he is not pointing the intended, noticed the responsibility of man in the evils that the world will experience in the following words: "the earth is defiled by its people; they have disobeyed my laws, violated the statutes, and broken the everlasting covenant" (Isaiah 23:5).

What we can draw from the above information is that we cannot take Covid-19 as a premeditated evil to control the world since there is no accurate information. But this does not negate the possibility. We also do not have a strong argument to repudiate the hypothesis that covid-19 will be a means to lead to the biblical new world order.

The Nature of the Prophetical/Biblical New World Order:

According to Ellen G White, the new world that is awaiting the human race is **godless, unsecured,** wicked, and **a place where religious liberty is denied.** In his sermon entitled Coronavirus: Dress Rehearsal for the new world order, Pastor John Hagee (2020), the founder of the Cornerstone Church, refers to the political system that seems to settle itself in America: "If we do not use our freedom to defend our freedom, we will lose our freedom." The freedom of worship will be lost in the envisaged new world order according to that Pastor. Though White does not refer to covid-19 as a way to end the freedom of worship, she only submits that the time will come where the whole world will unite to abolish the religious liberty in a way that people will be forced to believe and practice according to the will of the superior. "Religion, like all other things else, will be a matter of authority. The people will be forced to believe and practice as their superior will direct; the right of a man to think and act for himself will not be recognized" (White 1898: 333).

The suppression of the religious liberty in the new world order will not be done in a vacuum. The legislative power will establish laws to make a way for the executive power that strives to control the conscience of the people. "Men in authority will enact laws controlling the conscience, after the example of the papacy" (White 1992). Such practice will not be limited to one or same countries rather it will be a worldwide concern. "The authorities in the United States and in other countries will rise up in their pride and power and make laws to restrict religious liberty" (White 1992).

All nations will follow the example of the initiating nation in its wickedness. "Babylon will make all nations drink of the wine of the wrath of her fornication. Every nation will be involved. Of this time, John declares: (Revelation 18:3-7; 17:13, 14). "These have one mind." There will be a universal bond of union, one great harmony, a confederacy of Satan's forces. According to Wieland (2014), such situation coincides with the repudiation by Americans for the constitution principles that guarantee the complete separation of church and state and inducing other nations to follow that example. This decision will subdue the civil governments to the religious control and church supremacy.

The civil governments shall give their power and strength unto the beast. "Thus is manifested in the same arbitrary, oppressive power against religious liberty or freedom to worship God according to the dictates of conscience as was manifested by the papacy, when in the past it persecuted those who dared to refuse to conform with the religious rites and ceremonies of Romanism' (White 1992: 137).

According to White, the new world order in its externalities, the denial of religious liberty will be based mainly on the days of worship, between Sabbath and Sunday. "A great crisis awaits the people of God. Very soon our nation will attempt to enforce upon all the observance of the first day of the week as a sacred day. In doing this, they will not scruple to compel men against the voice of their own conscience to observe the day the nation declares to be the Sabbath (White 1992). As the Sabbath has become the special point of controversy throughout Christendom and religious and secular authorities have combined to enforce the observance of Sunday, the persistent refusal of a small minority to yield to the popular demand will make them objects of universal execration (White 1911: 450).

All Christendom will be divided into two great classes, those who keep the commandments of God and the faith of Jesus, and those who worship the beast and his image and receive his mark (White 1980).

Unsecured World

The coming new world order will rule the world with fear (Hagee 2020). Protection will be denied to those that do not fit with the expectations of the ruling powers. White said: 'As the decree issued by the various rulers of Christendom against commandment keepers shall withdraw the protection of government, and abandon them to those who desire their destruction, the people of God will flee from the cities and villages and associate together in companies, dwelling in the most desolate and solitary places' (White 1911:626). All, godly people, men, women, and children will be forced to give up their faith or suffer the penalty of confiscation of property, torture, and death.

> "Then I saw the leading men of the earth consulting together, and Satan and his angels busy around them. I saw a writing, copies of which were scattered in different parts of the land, giving orders that unless the saints should yield their peculiar faith, give up the Sabbath, and observe the first day of the week; the people were at liberty after a certain time to put them to death. In some places, before the time for the decree to be executed, the wicked rushed upon the saints to slay them; but angels in the form of men of war fought for them" (White 1945)

The Wicked World

Pastor Hagee (2020: np) notices that the objective of every new world order is to cast God off the face of the earth and human societies. The world that we are waiting for is a world of lawlessness, a world that will rise against God, the Creator of the universe. White too emphasizes that the rejection of the law of God will be the cornerstone of the new world order:

> The wicked… declared that they had the truth, that miracles were among them, that angels from heaven talked with them and walked with them, that great power and signs and wonders were performed among them, and that this was the temporal millennium that they had been expecting so long. The whole world was converted and in harmony with the Sunday law (White 1980).

The whole world is to be stirred with enmity against Seventh-day Adventists because they will not yield homage to the papacy by honoring Sunday, the institution of this antichristian power (White 1992). The religious powers will unite with secular powers to set up rules that will force Sabbath keepers to keep Sunday as a day of worship.

> Those who trample upon God's law make human laws which they will force the people to accept. Men will devise and counsel and plan what they will do. The whole world keeps Sunday, they say, and why should not this people, who are so few in number, do according to the laws of the land? (White 1980).

A World of Fatal Disease

As wickedness increases, diseases increase too, for there is a close relationship between sin and disease. "If you do not obey the Lord your God and do not carefully follow his commands and decrees … The Lord will plague you with diseases … which will plague you until you perish." (Deut.28:15-22) If you listen carefully to the voice of the Lord your God and do what is right in his eyes … I will not bring you any of the diseases I brought on the Egyptians…" (Ex.15:26). Once, God complaining against the wickedness of the Israelites said unto Moses "How long will this people provoke Me? And how long will it be ere they believe me, for all the signs which I have showed among them. I will smite them with the pestilence..." (White 1911).

The coming new world order will be marked by confusion coming from fatal diseases that will be spread all over the world sweeping away thousands of thousands of people. World governments with their entire arsenal will try their best to heal or prevent such diseases but without success. Why? Simply because God will restrain little by little "the powers of darkness from carrying forward their deadly work of vitiating the air, one of the sources of life and nutrition, with a deadly miasma. Not only is nature affected but man suffers from pestilence… These things are the result of drops from the vials of God's wrath being sprinkled on the earth, and are but faint representations of what will be in the near future" (White 1980).

In one of her visions White was shown the inhabitants of the earth in the utmost confusion. She said that war, bloodshed, deprivation, want, famine, and pestilence were abroad in the land.

> "My attention was then called from the scene. There seemed to be a little time of peace. Once more the inhabitants of the earth were presented before me; and again, everything was in the utmost confusion. Strife, war, and bloodshed, with famine and pestilence, raged everywhere. Other nations were engaged in this war and confusion. War caused famine. Want and bloodshed caused pestilence. And then men's hearts failed them for fear, and for looking after those things which are coming on the earth." (White 1855)

Covid-19 and the New World Order

The covid-19 pandemic presented itself as a unique pandemic. "With sweeping speed and global dimensions of unprecedented proportions, it has forced into social distancing…It poses tremendous challenges…The new experience of social distancing that we are forced to endure has brought amazing restriction on our freedom. The restrictions of personal freedom and the right of free assembly and worship have raised important questions about the power of the state, religious freedom, and our human responsibility in all this" (Hasel, 2020: 10). The ability that this pandemic has to instill panic and a feeling of angst in many of us (Hasel, 2020:10) led to different interpretations of what is going on as far as the new world order is concerned.

Though many people may see the similarities with other historical pandemics, they also accept that covid-19 is somehow different. Covid-19 is believed to lead human kind to the new world. According to Manyika (IMF F&D 2020: 27), "The world after COVID-19 is unlikely to return to the world that it was". This is a shared idea among different scholars. In the same thought, Saldhana (IMF F&D 2020: 27) says: "pandemics have forced humans to break with the past and imagine their world anew. This one is no different. It is a portal, a gateway between one world and the next."

Basing on the above quotation, Covid-19 is now to become one of the points of references. One, while referring to the impact of this pandemic says that we will no longer be referring to Jesus Christ, but to the covid-19 to locate historical events, we will be saying before and after covid-19. Daniel Susskind referring to the changes that are to occur says:

> "Many of the problems we will face in the next decade will simply be more extreme versions of those that we already confront today. The world will only look significantly different this time if, as we emerge from this crisis, decide to take action to resolve these problems and bring about fundamental change" (IMF F&D, 2020:26).

From what he says, it can be deduced that changes will be coming as a result of human decisions. Unless we, human beings take decisions to cope with the existing problems, no fundamental change will be experienced. In the same line, some authors suspect that the changes that are to be undertaken in the political, social, and economic domain match with the stressing crisis left behind by the covid-19 especially on the international affairs.

> "International trade, we assert, is merely symptomatic of larger, highly complex, and more profound global

> forces, which in turn require a broader canvas if one desires to competently understand what is transpiring in our world system at this time." (Jannace, Tiffany 2019)

From the above quote, what we see is not what is ongoing. And this may support the claims of conspiracy that:

> "Many influential historical and contemporary figures have therefore been alleged to be part of a cabal that operates through many front organizations to orchestrate significant political and financial events, ranging from causing systemic crises to pushing through controversial policies, at both national and international levels, as steps in an ongoing plot to achieve world domination" (Wikipedia 2020)

With such concerns, many questions flow out of a Christian mind: In which ways will the change be operated? What are the agents of the change? Will it be a natural change or human made change? What are the indicators of the change? For many and different Christians, the question is the meaning of Covid-19 in the biblical prophecies. Below are some examples of these different views:

Since the biblical prophecies relating to the pestilences to come before the coming of Jesus Christ are not specific, the majority of Christians do not doubt that covid-19 is one of them. They are reluctant to say that Covid-19 will lead to the new world order but that the possibility is there.

> "There is a possibility that Covid-19 may lead to the new world order. The main indicator is the covid-19 vaccine that the world is waiting for impatiently. All inhabitants of the world will be required to be injected and in case one refused to be injected, the possibility is there for him/her to be cast out from the public. The services like market services, school services, church services and other public services will be denied him /her.

The example is not far, see how the Tanzanians are not

allowed to move from their country to other countries, simply because the government did not comply with the worldwide agreed measures to fight against the spread of the pandemic. But see how Rwandans are allowed to move all over the world without any problem. This will be the fulfillment of what is written in the Bible, Revelation 13: 17" (Gatsinzi)

According to some Christians, covid-19 does not exist. "I don't believe that there is covid-19. People are just cheating others that there is covid-19. They cheat to fulfill their plans which people don't know. Perhaps they are trying to unite people and control them. Covid-19 does not exist. Can you give me at least one name of the people you know being contaminated by the virus, or who died of covid-19? How many people are dying of malaria? Are they made public? Those numbers are cooked numbers" (Muthuri).

Another group of Christians embrace the idea that covid-19 is a man-made virus. "Covid-19 is a man-made virus which I think is made to bring the new world order…Covid-19 is one of the fulfillment of biblical prophecies relating to the last days events…Covid-19 has brought restriction on how people worship from the whole Sabbath to two hours…I think world leaders are going to unite and say that covid-19 is a curse from God; let us be united in worship, we will worship the same day which will be Sunday to avoid God's curses…World economy is collapsing, people will be forced to work for six days to build their economy back, which will lead to the new world order." This idea is not different from what Isiko (2020) says "In some circumstances, theological conspirators denied the existence of COVID-19 as a natural disease caused by either God or Satan but a biological warfare between China and America" (Kang'entus, np).

For others, covid-19 is a pandemic which has been exaggerated by powerful countries with a hidden agenda. Covid-19 exists in a 'given form' not in its 'real form'. "The covid-19 declared by politicians is totally different from its real existence. Jesus talked about wars and rumors of war. And these will be done to deceive many (Mat.24:6). Paul also said that there will be terrible times in last days. In Rwanda and other African countries, people travel seating together in cars all over the county and this does not matter to leaders, but seating together in churches seem problematic to them. Yes, one can guess that Covid-19 is leading to the new world order. According to the biblical prophecies, the new world order will be settled after the realization that the world is economically declining in order to uphold it. Looking at how many countries are burdened by the effects of Covid-19, for sure the world will be in crisis, thus the new world order will be the solution" (Dusengimana, n.d).

There are also Christians who accept that covid-19 exists as a natural disease. For them, the issue is that world leaders may use it as an opportunity to unite the whole world and embark on suppressing religious liberty. "Even though covid-19 is a natural disease, world leaders and ecumenical movement through the World Council of Churches (WCC) pretending to deal with social and economic consequences left behind by the pandemic, will unite the whole world and churches to suppress religious liberty for them to reach their goal which is the abolition of the Law of God" (Ruzindana)

"Covid-19 exists but it is totally different from the way it is referred to by decision makers. And this is a systematic way that some powerful countries are using to reach their political, social, and business goals that they alone know. They are lying to fulfill their hidden plans. See, the way leaders are traumatizing people through unreasonable decisions!" (Ntakirutimana, 2020:n.p)

"Covid-19 is a mysterious pandemic. It is possible that secular leaders and the papacy use it to unite the world under one and same leadership" (Niyigena)

"The virus is a human made virus. It is coming from industries. It was made to help the secretive power elite to rule the world. The vaccine will be used to transfer the microchip to the human body. And this

will help them to enslave the entire world"
(Anonymous, n.d))

The denial of public worship due to measures to fight against Covid-19 was interpreted by some believers as a denial of religious liberty. Such view was given power by the fact that the same activities that are more risky than public worship like, public transportation was allowed, in some countries, to continue. Thus, seeing covid-19 as a way to the new world order was given credit. But what is to be considered in this case is that all religions not only Christian denominations or let us say not only the remnants were denied the right to continue with public worship and given a go ahead with family worship. (Sermon of Pr. Lebalele, 2020)

According to these different views, the following hypotheses may be drawn: Covid-19 is a natural disease which is intentionally presented as dangerous by worldly powers to achieve their agenda; Covid-19 is a natural disease that worldly powers took as an opportunity to achieve their agenda; Covid-19 is a man-made virus purposefully created in a laboratory to help secretive powers to rule the world; Covid-19 does not exist, it is a phantom. Worldly powers are cheating people to achieve their plans.

Politics, conspiracy theories, and Christians agree on the fact that things will not continue to go the way they do today. Changes are bound to occur and to be initiated, using different means by human beings whether it is for the interest of human race (politics), or for the interest of a secretive power elite (conspiracy), or for the interest of the antichrist (Christians). From the exploration of the biblical prophecy relating to the new world order, the following points were noticed:

I. Taking the suspension of public worship as an argument to suspect Covid-19 as a way to the new world order is incorrect because Christians are not the only ones affected but all religions.

II. The vaccine that is suspected to carry the device that will make humans to act according to the will of the authorities is not supported by the free will that determines the choice to obey or to disobey God's commands.

III. Yes, we are experiencing the end time period, but we are not to isolate the Covid-19 as we gaze on the signs of the Second Coming.

For these reasons, there are no tangible evidences that prove that covid-19 is being used by politicians or secret elite to achieve the new world order. But also, we have to be careful because there is also no strong argument to refute this idea. As White said there is a time of trouble coming to the people of God, but we are not to keep that constantly before the people and rein them up to have a time of trouble beforehand. There is going to be a shaking among God's people, but this is not the present truth to carry to the churches (White 1992: 17).

CHAPTER TEN

The Phenomenology of Peace and the Prince of Peace

Nehemiah M. Nyaundi

The current state of peace in the world is extremely unpleasant. Due to various reasons, peoples of the world are honestly not sitting pretty, eating and drinking. At the national level, negative ethnicity continues to gnaw into the 'ties that bind' communities together. Political innuendos remain the reason heads of house-holds die early, leaving families without sources of livelihoods. In many urban areas, violence remains the norm, rather than peace. Economic malpractices including the misappropriation of budgetary allocation are still the cause of undue suffering to the economically disadvantaged. Where this is the case, the net result is unrest and instability; thus, inflicting a serious threat to sustainable peace.

Nations of the world continue to sign bilateral, continental and international treaties with the aim of achieving mutual peace. In some cases, the treaties have continued to hold, resulting to peaceful co-existence while in other cases, the treaties have embarrassingly

Prof Nehemiah M. Nyaundi (nenyaundi@ueab.ac.ke) is a professor of religion teaching at the University of Eastern Africa, Baraton, Kenya. Prof Nyaundi is a graduate of Lund University, Sweden where he studied religion and social sciences. Prof Nyaundi is the author of Introduction to the Study of Religion: A Study of the Phenomenon of Religion, 2004, including journal and periodical publications, all in the field of religion.

failed from the moment they were signed due to suspicion, mistrust and lack of sufficient conviction among the parties. Regardless of this, the search for sustainable peace must be the priority among progressive nations of the world.

At the international level, many countries are at logger-heads and in tension with one another. Historical and contemporary causes appear to be threatening international relations relentlessly. Countries that experience misdirected nationalism continue to make decisions which dangerously compromise the cause of peace. In many regions of the world, the hope for sustainable peace seems to be a pipe dream as peace continues to be affected. The question worth asking is how long will the quest for global peace remain and whether or not that quest will come to fruition.

The objective of this chapter is to demonstrate that the quest for sustainable peace is viable when a divine component is injected into the pursuit, while that pursuit can be expected to come a cropper if it is hinged on mundane ambition and desire. The search for peace in the world is often pivoted on self-interest and therefore driven by selfish motives. The chapter shows that genuine and lasting peace comes from God through Jesus Christ. The need to produce a monograph on this subject evolved out of the concern for what can be done towards making the world a safe place. In many regions of the world there is strife, conflict, tension, hostility, skirmishes, et cetera. Is there something that can be done to mitigate the never-ending tension? Contributions such as the production of this volume are a modest way towards that provision.

The Phenomenology of Peace

The phenomenology of peace is not a straightforward location to allocate a map to. The phenomenology of peace is best described with a hope that the description will succeed in drawing a map which accurately locates that phenomenon. Hence, it is precise to start its semantics. The condition of peace is multi-pronged and multi-dimensional. It is not certain whether the phenomenon of peace can be sufficiently unpackaged in order to clarify what one is discussing. The word peace is a popular notion in both the Old and the New Testaments. In the NIV Concordance, the root word of peace appears nearly 250 times (1990:864-865). Bible writers write copiously about peace and Jesus too, unambiguously spoke about peace. At the Dictionary, 'peace' is defined as 'a situation or a period of time in which there is no war or violence in a country or an area' (2001:857). According to a Dictionary of the Bible, the word peace as used in the Old Testament is translated from the Hebrew word *Shalom*. In the Hebrew context, *Shalom* means 'wholeness, soundness, health, prosperity and general well-being' (1911:732). In a broader sense therefore, *shalom* embodies peace as opposed to war, and concord as opposed to strife (1911:732).

The common Hebrew greeting of *'Shalom,'* is a popular salutation where the speaker wishes the respondent peace, calmness and harmony. It expresses completeness, totality, wholeness and well-being. In the Septuagint, the Greek equivalent of *Shalom* is *'Eirene.'* The Analytical Greek Lexicon (1978:119) expresses the conception of Eirene as that of tranquillity, wholeness and well-being. The similarity between *Shalom* and *Eirene* indicates that 'peace' is a broad perception whose root is found in 'completeness' and 'well-being'; expressing a calm state of mind. Notice further that from the Greek language, the substance contained in *Eirene,* which in the Septuagint is translated from *Shalom,* carries the meaning of quietness, security, safety, prosperity, et cetera. Hence, the fundamental meaning of *Shalom* (and *Eirene*) is well-being, as in Psalms 122:7, Is. 52:7, Jer. 29:7 carrying the element of peace as opposed to evil. It is in this sense that *Shalom* is used in greetings with the sense of: 'Is it peaceful with you?' This notion is found in the Bible (Gen. 29:6, 37:14, Num. 6:26 and Luke 24:36). The word *Shalom* is also used when sending away a friend; it is done in good faith as in a benediction. When Eli, the High Priest at Shiloh, finished speaking with Anna wife of Elkanah, who eventually bore Prophet Samuel, Eli tells her, 'Go in peace, and may the God of Israel grant to you what you have asked of him,' (1 Samuel 1:17).

In the Islamic community, peace is always held at a premium. The Arabic greeting '*As-salaam Alaikum*' (may peace be unto you) is a standard greeting which is used for wishing peace, and whose answer '*Wallaikum Salaam*' (And unto you, peace) is also entirely about peace. Notice also that among Muslims, any time the name of Prophet Mohamed is mentioned, the expression '*Sallallahu Alaihi Wasallam*) (may peace be upon him) is uttered. On Tuesday September 15, 2020, the Prime Minister of Israel and the Foreign Ministers of the United Arab Emirates and Bahrain signed a diplomatic peace pact at the White House in the US. The New York Times (Online edition) reported that having articulated the dividends of the deal, the Israel Prime Minister, Benjamin Netanyahu greeted the people of his new-found friendly nations with a hearty '*As-salaam Alaikum*.' It was easy to discern that the Israel leader used the Arabic language gesture for peace, hoping that by so doing, he would resonate with the people whose language he used. In seeking to unravel the concept of peace, it is appropriate to observe that there are languages which have the word peace featuring prominently in their greetings. In some communities, the word peace forms the critical component in common greeting. Among the Luhya people of Kenya, with a population of over six million people (Kenya Bureau of Statistics, 2019), the word '*Mulembe*' (peace) is a common greeting which forms the opening expression in common greetings' protocol. With this in mind, we are left with one thing that is a common denominator, namely that peace in any name is still peace. It is known in many languages as *amani* (Kiswahili), *salaam* (Arabic), *la paix* (French), *la paz* (Spanish), *frieden* (German), peace is a much sought after component in the living experience.

Furthermore, let us proceed from the acknowledgement that peace is a generic concept which can be spread into more than one meaning. The concept accommodates both a narrow and a broad definition. In a report of the World Council of Churches, Deenabandhu Manchala (2005:61) takes the liberty to define peace as 'a condition of belonging and a state of longing.' The definition is similar to the one attributed to Emperor Haile Selassie (1892-1975) wherein he said that 'peace is a day to day problem, the product of a multitude of events and judgments. Peace is not an 'is,' it is a becoming,' (web page); in this way, peace is a dynamic consciousness; a type of 'being-ness.' Malcom X was an African-American human rights activist during the American civil rights movement. According to Malcom and Haley (1992), peace was a constantly evolving condition which he argued, 'you can't separate peace from freedom because no one can be at peace unless he has his freedom, (web page). It is widely acknowledged that there is a challenge when defining what peace means. There are many international associations that engage in the search for peace. The International Peace Studies Association is one of such outfits. In an article by Yuval Katz (2020), it asserted unambiguously that peace is one phenomenon which presents a conceptual problem. This is so because of what the ontology of peace is. Katz defined peace as 'what is found in the everyday lives of people' (2020: I-II).

With what we have observed thus far about peace, it is fitting to state that there is so much that can be averred about what peace is. For instance, peace is commonly understood as the absence of war. This is to say that 'peace' is equal to harmony, tranquillity, and serenity; where there is conflict or war, then peace is lacking. Notice that in the Dictionary of the Bible, peace is defined as 'the tranquil state of the soul assured of its salvation through Christ and so fearing nothing from God and content with its early lot, of whatever sort it be' (1911:733).

Perceiving peace from another dimension it is correct to state that peace is how we regard our fellow human beings; whether we see them as a valuable creation of God or as creatures we can trample and crush underfoot, whether at the individual or national level. Peace is a state of concurrence and concord; a state where there is a reciprocal acceptance, agreement and mutual consonance. Peace is the absence of hostility and the freedom from the fear of violence; this confirms that peace is a critical component. The element of community features in a discussion by Alastair McIntosh, who asserted that peace, is the building of a community, where community means belonging in a consciousness of interconnection (2004:215).

Some twenty years ago, a group of academicians belonging to the Ecumenical Symposium of Eastern Africa Theologians did a study on the prevalence of violence in Eastern Africa at the time. The report of the study came out in book form (Getui and Kanyandago 1999). In the book, two chapters are of notes. In the chapter about the Christian ideal of peace, Jesse Mugambi raised the issue of conceptualization surrounding the theory of peace. Mugambi observed that for peace to thrive, the threat of war must prevail, such that the two must co-exist in order that peace may abound (1999:81-82). In his conceptual clarification, Mugambi declared that peace must always be associated with divine providence as in the prayer; 'We beseech thee O Lord our God, to set the peace of heaven with the hearts of men (Getui and Kanyandago, 1999:78). The idea Mugambi is advancing is similar to what Alastair McIntosh promoted in the chapter, 'Peace in the Tiger's Mouth' wherein, he contended that peace is best maintained in an environment of austerity, such as the imminent danger prevailing if one were in a tiger's mouth (2004:215). The other chapter offering a considerable dimension is by Nehemiah M. Nyaundi who discussed the forms of deprivations which hinder the operationalization of peace. Nyaundi contended that for peace to prevail, it is necessary to take a society through the deliberate bouts of re-education, observing that a 'peaceful society obtains where all forms of individual deprivations are tackled and removed (Getui and Kanyandago, 1999:51).

Peace in the Bible: Views in the Old Testament

There are many references to peace in the Bible. The references may be given various interpretations which range from the Old Testament proclamations, to the New Testament utterances by Jesus Christ, to the declarations by Apostle Paul, among others. The concept of 'peace' is a household perception in the Old Testament. Starting from the Pentateuch, the Judges, the Psalms, and right through to the prophets; the notion of peace is unmistakable. One of the earliest occasions where peace features shows was when God instructs Moses on how Aaron, the High Priest should bequeath blessings onto the children of Israel.

> And the Lord spoke to Moses, saying: 'speak to Aaron and his sons, saying. This is the way you shall bless the children of Israel. Say to them: The Lord bless you and keep you; The Lord make his face shine upon you. And be gracious to you; The Lord lift up His countenance upon you. And give you peace' (Num. 6:22-26).

According to the Aaronic blessing, peace is the synopsis of all that is good from God to His people. The synopsis also means that peace is a God-given provision which He endears to His people. The covenant which God made with the people of Israel was a covenant of peace (Num. 25:12).

The prophets spoke about peace liberally. In the writings of Prophet Isaiah for instance, the word peace features prominently in the Messianic prophecy. Among the blessings which Israel expected upon the arrival of the Messiah was peace. Peace is such a phenomenon to the extent that prophet Isaiah passionately commends a herald of peace; 'How beautiful upon the mountains are the feet of him who brings good news, who proclaims peace; who brings glad tidings of good things,' (Is 52:7). A messenger who brings the good news of the coming salvation is regarded as a worthy harbinger of peace. Prophet Isaiah got it right when he prophesied about the coming Messiah;

> For unto us a child is born, unto us a Son is given; and the government shall be upon his shoulder. And his

name shall be called Wonderful, Counsellor, Mighty
God, Everlasting Father, Prince of peace. (Is 9:6).

According to prophet Isaiah, the promise of the coming
Messiah benefits those who love God, to whom God promises to
bequeath peace which flows like a river 'I will extend peace to her
like a river' (Isa. 66:12). The symbolic use of 'a river' denotes the
abundance and perpetuity of the peace in the same way a river is
always flowing. Be that as it may, the prophet is cognizant with the
caution that peace benefits those who love God while to
transgressors there can be no promise to that benefit; 'There is no
peace, says the Lord, to the wicked' (Isa. 48:22). The prophet
expresses caution to the effect that God's goodness has limits,
especially to those who do not conform to His commands.

Prophet Jeremiah in his letter to the exiles in Babylon
conveyed God's blueprint to His people. God's strategy was to
bequeath the exiles with peace and prosperity. In that plan, the
promise to impart peace towers prominently 'For I know the
thoughts that I think toward you, says the Lord, thoughts of peace
and not of evil, to give you a future and a hope,' (Jer 29:11). And
when God continued to assure the people of their certain return to
their homeland, He through the prophet pledges; 'Behold, I will
bring it health and healing; I will heal them and reveal to them the
abundance of peace and truth,' (Jer 33:6). In this text, peace
constitutes healing and health. The prophecy of deliverance,
restoration and the return of the exiles from Babylon to their
homeland are expressed in the terms of healing, health and peace.
In prophet Jeremiah's writing, peace is a healing balm 'Is there no
balm in Gilead? Is there no physician there? (Jer. 8:22).

King David in the Bible is referred to as 'a man after God's
own heart' (1 Sam 13:14). David spoke about peace; he confirmed
that the enjoyment of peace comes as a result of the observance of
God's law 'Great peace have those who love your law,'
(Psalm119:16). David's son Solomon as a king also, puts a premium

to what constitutes peace, 'Righteousness exalts a nation, but sin is a reproach to any people' (Prov. 14:34). It is doubtless that peace is a critical component in the wellness of a people. The fact that it is God who says it means the fact cannot be overstated or gainsaid.

Jesus, the Prince of Peace in the New Testament

The title, 'Prince of Peace' is in theology used to refer to Jesus Christ who was born a Prince of Peace; (Is 9:6, Micah 5:5). The title is commonly popular during the Christmas season when the birth of Christ is a fashionable celebration. During Christmas, the theme in many communications is peace and goodwill to family, relatives and friends.

Early during His ministry, Jesus called the twelve disciples and sent them off to an evangelistic tour with the charge; 'if the home is deserving, let your peace rest on it; if it is not, let your peace return to you,' (Matt 10:13). In the same way, when Jesus sent out a team of seventy evangelists, He similarly charged them, 'when you enter a house, first say, peace to this house' (Luke 10:5). After His resurrection, Jesus visited were His disciples ere gathered fearing for their lives, 'behind locked doors' and He greeted them using the expression 'peace be with you,' (John 20:19). During Jesus' farewell bidding to His disciples, His parting words to them were, 'peace I leave with you: my peace I give you. I do not give to you as the world gives.' (John 14:27). He also told them, 'I have told you these things, so that in me you may have peace' (John 16:33).

The theme of peace permeates the two Testaments. Many centuries after the completion of the writing of the Old Testament to the birth of the New Testament, the theme of peace still reverberated, remaining a critical component. When an angel announced to the shepherds about the birth of Christ, accompanying the angel was a choir which praised God saying; 'Glory to God in the highest, and on earth peace, goodwill toward men' (Luke 2:14). Jesus was constantly conscious of His birth-right and He did not disappoint in publicising it, 'Everything must be fulfilled that is written about me in the law of Moses, the prophets and the Psalms,' (Luke 24:44). Jesus is Himself peace, becoming the catalyst through which God has reconciled Himself with humanity, (2Cor 5:18 and Eph 2:14). Jesus is reckoned as the Prince of Peace because He is a role-model and consummate instrument of reconciliation. The mission of the Prince of Peace is to bring peace to a troubled world and to restore the broken relationship between God and humanity, (Rom 5:10). In the commonwealth of Christ, the old dispensation is made new, and the old correlation between God and humanity is restored. The world without the Prince of Peace is chaotic and anarchic. The mission of Jesus Christ was to bring peace to a troubled world. This fact comes out clearly when Jesus cautioned, *'These things I have spoken to you, that in me you may have peace.'* (John 16:13).

In Jesus Christ's teaching about peace, a new template is introduced. What Jesus said about peace plainly communicated a paradigm shift. According to Barclay M. Newman (1980:474) Jesus presented a new model of peace, which He conveyed unmistakably, *'Peace I leave with you. My peace I give you, not as the world gives do I give to you* (John 14:27). In the field of peace studies, there is a notion of *Pax Christi* (van Lersel, 1995). According to Claus Wengst (1987), *Pax Christi* (Peace of Christ) differs from *Pax Romana* (Roman Peace). The Peace of Christ is genuine while the peace of the world is selfish and conditional. It is no wonder that Jesus stated the difference unequivocally when He said; 'My peace I give you, not as the world gives do I give to you' (John 14:27). The peace of Christ is eternal while the peace of the world is temporal. The mission of Christ was to bring peace to a troubled world. This fact comes out clearly when Jesus himself proclaimed what the New Testament scholars view as the Gospel Charter in (Luke 4:16f).

Two things are worth mentioning concerning Jesus' new template of peace. In the beatitudes, Jesus declared, 'Blessed are the peacemakers,' (Matt 5:9). Notice the high status that peacemakers occupy in the commonwealth of Christ. Jesus the Prince of Peace authenticated the vocation of peace-making. Similarly, in the Lord's Prayer, the wish; 'Our Father in heaven, hallowed be your name, your kingdom come, your will be done on earth as it is in heaven' (Matt 6:9-10); remember, that the Kingdom of God is the one of peace. Manchala (2005) prompted that in praying for the Kingdom of God to come, we are thereby longing for peace, because it is a conspicuous characteristic of God's Kingdom. Peacemakers are people who put their own lives at risk in order to improve the lives of others, many times through risky conflict resolution initiatives, all in the quest for peace. Take for instance the contributions of legendary peace crusaders such as Mahatma Gandhi, Martin Luther King Jr., Nelson Mandela, the Dalai Lama of Tibet, et cetera. These are people who are known to have put their own interests aside and decided to give a voice to a voiceless majority in the cause of peace. In addition, it is in order to remind that God rewards those who espouse peace; something that has a biblical mandate, 'peacemakers who sow in peace raise a harvest of righteousness' (James 3:18). In a similar version, it is insightful to beware that God sulks on those who neglect peace, 'the way of peace they do not know … justice is far from us, and righteousness does not reach us' (Is 59:8-9). Jesus is the Prince of Peace. A great number of His conversations with His disciples were themed on peace. He did that consistently, before and after the crucifixion event. After His resurrection, and immediately after the 'road to Emmaus' episode, Jesus appeared to His disciples and saluted them; 'peace be with you' (Luke 24:36).

The Apostle Paul speaks widely about Jesus as the Prince of Peace. Paul made outstanding statements concerning Jesus as the Prince of Peace, 'For he himself is our peace,' (Eph 2:14). In Paul's proclamations, the attraction to peace is a clarion call; 'and let the peace of God rule in your hearts,' (Col 3:15). Notice for instance that according to Paul, peace is so critical that he admonishes Christians to harness the 'peace that passes understanding' (Phil 4:7).

The Quest for Peace-building in the New World Order

The expression, the New World Order is an old phenomenon which dates as far back as during the end of World War 1. After the war, nations of the world came together and crafted an agreement which created the League of Nations and the precursor of the current United Nations. In the on-going geo-politics, the New World Order is supposedly a new governance structure where nations of the world agree to co-exist amidst the diverse differences that abound.

The prevailing aura in the contemporary New World Order is the feelings which were mostly in the air when Mikhail Gorbachev and George H. Bush were in power in the USSR and the United States respectively. President Gorbachev popularized the concepts of *Perestroika and Glasnost* which meant 'openness' in political affairs (Babatunde Adeyemi, 2015:119). According to Adeyemi (2015:128), the New World Order was meant to capture the emerging cooperation between the two political systems which for nearly seventy years there had been a 'cold' war between Eastern Europe and its allies against Western Europe, the United States and their allies.

Today, the New World order wishes to be characterized by a flagrant show of peace and tranquillity. One of the ways of moving towards sustainable peace is to secure the freedom of religion. It is believed that where there is freedom of religion, peace thrives therein because inherent in religious teaching is the preservation of the *status quo*. Ingrained in the UN Human Freedoms Charter 1948 (Article 18), is the right of each person to access religion. According to the UN Charter article 18, freedom of religion is an inalienable right accorded to all by virtue of one being human. Many countries take over directly from the UN's Charter into national Constitutions. One of such nations is the Kenyan Constitution, 2010 (Chapter 4 Article 32). In the UN's Universal Declaration of Human Rights, several articles dwell on 'rights' which sought to foster individual and national peace. The component which comes out here is that religion as a prominent phenomenon in a society plays an unmistakable role in fostering peace in the nations of the earth. eace is a critical equilibrium. This has been the case since time immemorial. At the present time, there are many organizations at local, national and international levels which pursue the cause of peace in the world. In a study by Denis J.D. Sandole (2007), peace-building organizations work towards the peaceful co-existence and attainment of unreserved respect for human rights and believing that achieving peace in the world is possible (2007:1). Some of the organizations which engage in the search for peace are: the International Commission of the Red Cross, the Coalition for Peace in Africa, the Africa Peace Forum, Amnesty International, the Greenpeace Movement, *Pax Christi* International, World Vision, African Union, among others.

In an article which discussed the politics of keeping peace among nations, Mulugeta G. Berle (2017) identified a raft of peace protocols, declarations and memorandums of understanding which work towards safeguarding the peace among nations at the United Nations and also at the African Union. The UN Security Council is tasked to oversee matters concerning conflict prevention, management and resolution. At the African Union, the African Peace and Security Architecture is a set of norms that guide African actions to peace and serve as an instrument to implement the policies regulating the sustenance of peace among the African nations (2017:671). The African Peace and Security Architecture works alongside the African Union Peace and Security Council to police member-states in respect to peace. The article traces the evolution of the OAU from a nascent and docile organization to the dynamic organization it is today in its quest to build sustainable peace in the African Continent.

The attempts to procure peace are many and vary. In South Africa, the attempt took the form of Truth and Reconciliation Commission which was inaugurated in 1995 as a recommended panacea to reconcile the formerly racially segregated society. The activities of the TRC were touted as measures which would enhance what the South African society viewed as a 'rain-bow' nation. It is appropriate to observe that Bishop Desmond Tutu, a well-known clergyman and human rights activist earned the coveted Nobel Peace prize in 1984, an award which according to its founder, a Swedish industrialist, Alfred Nobel is awarded to a person who, 'has done the most or the best work for the fraternity between nations, for the abolition or reduction of standing armies and for the holding and promoting of peace.' As a Nobel peace prize laureate in 1984, Bishop Tutu is remembered for his peace-building publication (1999).

In the search for peace and reconciliation such as the South African one was initiated in Kenya after the infamous 2007/2008 events of post-election violence where more than one thousand people died and many more were driven into internal refugee camps. The Kenyan attempt was given the name, the Truth, Justice and Reconciliation Commission of Kenya. The purpose of the commission was to find ways of reconciling Kenyan communities which had killed fellow Kenyans and destroyed property amongst themselves. It took many man-hours of the so-called eminent persons of Africa, including Ghanaian John Kufuor [ruled 2001-2009] to negotiate a peace deal that settled the wrangle between the warring political parties. Efforts such as the South African and the Kenyan scenarios augur well for the welfare of national peace in a social and political world where diverse interests are constantly at variance with one another. Nehemiah M. Nyaundi (2015) study traced the events of the Kenyan conflict and found reason to indict the Christian community for the failure to offer leadership at that critical time in the history of the Kenyan nation.

There are a number of peace drives here and there throughout the globe, all in the hope that peace would be the result. Bilateral agreements are concluded because nations espouse peace. It is broadly consented that peace is cheaper in respect to human lives and property than conflict. As at the time of writing this chapter, there is a looming disagreement between Egypt and Ethiopia regarding the use of the water of the River Nile (web page). If the dispute is not handled with diplomatic finesse, the result can be expected to impact negatively on peace in the region.

In the address on the phenomenology of peace, it is appropriate to include the contribution of the Christian church in its capacity as a mass movement in whose home peace commands a strong appeal. Further, it is equally applicable to take into account the fact that the Christian doctrine puts a premium to peace. Irrespective of how that contribution is viewed, the fact stands on its own right. In an analysis of the contemporary politics and politicking that is commonly rife among Christian churches, Emmanuel O. Eregare (2018) alluded to the perception that politicking is about governance which itself directly influences the presence or absence of peace in a nation. In sum, this is to verbalize that the life of the Christian church is encapsulated in a quest for peace which in this discussion has been identified as a prominent characteristic of the Kingdom of God.

Furthermore, there are many non-governmental institutions which engage in peace-building within the limits of the New World Order. The ecumenical movements found among Christian churches are one of such institutions which has done splendidly well in the search for peace, justice, fairness and lawfulness in the world. The World Council of Churches (WCC) to be specific can be credited to have played, and continues to play a distinguished role in originating viable peace initiatives at the regions of conflict. The WCC played a leading role of pacifying the tension which existed between Christians and political authorities in the former socialist governments in Eastern Europe. The WCC's contributions in undermining and emasculating the apartheid regime in South Africa cannot be forgotten nor ignored, and so forth. Considering the foregoing discussion, it can be affirmed that peace is a critical harness which is commendable towards reconciliation, transformation, emancipation and human relations.

The world we live in is not peaceful; there is conflict, war and rumours of war. In diverse places in the world, there are social, economic and political disagreements which at times end in hostile aggression. It is therefore repeated that a peaceful mind is a healthy mind. Similarly, a peaceful nation is a healthy nation. The promises of the Bible relating to peace are assuring, 'You will keep him in perfect peace, whose mind is stayed on you' (Isaiah 26:3).

It seems modest to propose that for humanity to enjoy peace the prerequisite is reconciliation with God. The consideration is a great lesson to learn and a lesson to be impressed to nations of the world. Perhaps it may not be far-fetched to claim that the reason why many peace agreements do not last is the lack of the divine component. The apostle Paul caught it right when he commended Jesus to the Christians in Rome, 'since we have been justified through faith, we have peace with God' Rom. 5:1. The same thing he told the Ephesian Christians, 'For he himself is our peace' (Eph. 2:14). Nations of the world crave peaceful co-existence, but it is doubtful if that ambition can be brought to fruition. The search for peace needs to be a relentless quest for individuals and nations. In the words of the 1969 pop song by the British rock musician John Lennon (1940-1980), 'All we are saying; give peace a chance' (web page). The words of the song are an unmistakeable call to the peoples of the world to rise to the occasion and to rally behind the banner of peace.

The search for peace is a perennial pursuit which goes back into the history of the formation of the nations of the world. The formation of the world-wide United Nations Organization was a conspicuous quest to create and preserve peace. During the 2020 Annual Summit of the UN General Assembly meeting, the Secretary-General, Antonio Guterres, in his address made a noteworthy remark in respect to the quest for global peace: 'Now is the time for a collective new push for peace and reconciliation' (Fox TV News Sept 22, 2020). It is in order to remind that the UN Human Freedoms Charter is an unequivocal document whose aim is to foster international peace.

Peace is an eminent prerequisite in any society. A society that has peace flourishes and progresses unlike the one that is undergoing conflict and war. Throughout the history of the world, the quest to access peace has been a perennial search. In a similar manner, there have been concerted efforts to create and maintain peace. As to whether the global community has succeeded in peace-building, is a matter best described as being neither here nor there

CHAPTER ELEVEN

An Insight on the Role of America in the New World Order

Emmanuel Orihentare Eregare

September 11 marked the end of the age of geopolitics and the beginning of global politics in America. The age of global politics has been characterized by the "the combination of America's unrivaled power in world affairs, and the extensive and growing globalization of world politics" (Daalder & Lindsay (2003:1,2). The New World Order, on the other hand, is a movement towards global authority. The New World Order is a new age that features change not just world politics but also religious thoughts through conspiracy. This projects the New World Order as a Politico-religious affair. The New World Order is a situation when all the countries of the world will no longer be divided but will work together to solve international problems by achieving peace and safety on earth (Wikipedia, 2021: n.p; Cambridge Dictionary, 2021.n.p; See also Newmann, 2003: 1-100). Both the event of September 11 in the United States and the New World Order form the beginning of the change in global politics. Based on this backdrop, it means that the fulfilment of the New World Order

Emmanuel Orihentare Eregare (eregaree@babcock.edu.ng) is a Senior Lecturer in the Department of History and International Studies. He has been teaching the History of the United States of America for about a decade. He had once visited the Vatican City and regularly the city of Rome on field trips. Dr. Eregare has many articles, books

became palpable on September 11 (Daalder & Lindsay (2003:1,2). Nonetheless, the New World grows through the wings of the conspiracy theory.

The Conspiracy Theory

This theory has not been given much attention by philosophers; however, the definition of its operations is explicit. Hegel as cited in the work of Keeley, (1999:109-126) states that philosophers, through the philosophy of History, have only brought into the conspiracy theory the simple thought of Reason. This is to say that the thought of reason rules the world. So, 'reason' makes up the ideology to rule the world through conspiracy.

Conspiracy theory is a belief or idea that rejects standard explanation to any subject which is usually carried out by a covert group or organization mainly through deceptive plot unknown to the public. On the other words, a conspiracy theory is a theory that has "an effort to explain some events or practices by reference to the machinations of powerful people, who have also managed to conceal their role". Conspiracy theories have been generally described to have the attribute of certain agents with extraordinary powers planning, controlling and maintaining secrets (Sunstein, 2008: 3,4).

The Root of the Conspiracy Theory

God in Heaven had a standard rule that governed the inhabitants of Heaven before the creation of man. Lucifer was an anointed cherub, perfect or holy in his ways until sin was found in him. Lucifer corrupted his mind by the simple thought of reason when the Book of Ezekiel said that Lucifer lifted up his heart because of his beauty. Ezekiel added that by that act, "…thou hath corrupted thy wisdom by the reason of thy brightness…." (28:17). This shows a need to be cautious about our thoughts. Thereafter, Lucifer by the simple thought of reason sinned (28:18) against God. The Bible explains further that:

> How art thou fallen from heaven, O Lucifer, son of the morning! How art thou cut down to the ground, which didst weaken the nations. For thou hast said in thine heart, I will ascend into heaven, I will exalt my throne above the stars of God: I will sit also upon the mount of the congregation, in the sides of the north: I will ascend above the heights of the clouds; I will be like the Most High" (Isaiah 14:12-14, KJV)

Revelation 5;14; 19:4; 7:1 give an insight into what happens in Heaven. These passages are evidences that all the inhabitants in Heaven worshiped God. Lucifer sinned against God by the simple thought of his reason to take over God's position, seat, authority and especially worship (Mat. 4:10). Lucifer, thereby, sinned against God in Heaven by his reason to take the place of God. This is the beginning of philosophy. 1 John 3:4b declares "…sin is the transgression of the law." The Law here is the Ten Commandments. The sin of Lucifer was chiefly covetousness, among others. Covetousness is the 10th commandment. Consequently, the Ten Commandments are deciphered as the standard of God's government (Exo. 20:3-17). In addition to this abysmal act of Lucifer in Heaven, he succeeded in deceiving one third of the angels in Heaven through conspiracy (Rev. 12:4). God caught him and sent Lucifer away from Heaven to the earth. In Heaven, God does not cohabit with sin.

Lucifer, further, brought the same crafty art into earth when he deceived Adam and Eve in the Garden of Eden. The Bible further confirms that he seeks to steal, kill and destroy all that is of God including worship right from the Garden of Eden (See John 10:10; Genesis 3: 4, 5). Lucifer also applied the conspiracy theory on Jesus when He was led into the wilderness after fasting for forty days and forty nights (Mat. 4:1-10). Lucifer failed before God and His son, Jesus Christ on earth.

The brief biblical exposition above shows that there are four major similarities between the Luciferian theory and the New

World Order, probably among others. Firstly, there was a standard order or explanation (the Ten Commandments) established by God as the principle of His government in Heaven. Secondly, Lucifer rejected the standard principles of God's government. Thirdly, Lucifer through conspiracy or deception took one third of the angels from Heaven. Fourthly, Lucifer sought to take the position of God in Heaven especially in the aspect of His worship, to mention a few as considered for this study.

Consequently, the New World Order is a movement that is made up of cabal and secret power. It is said to be a powerful movement that seeks to control the globe through the conspiracy between Lucifer and human organizations (See also Newmann, 2003: 1-100). According to Newmann (2003: 1-260), the ones behind this robot system of the one-world system of government and religious bigotry have been seemingly perceived as secret organizations such as Freemasonry, Illuminati, the Society of Jesus and the likes through the Church of Rome (Newmann, 2003:171; See also Cusack, 1896: n.p).

Long Term Plans of the New World Order

The long-term plans for the world government are : (1) to establish a one-system world power, (2) through secret and duplicity of faith and practices, (3) establishment of one-system of government, a revolution and class warfare destabilizing the opponents, (4) influencing the great and powerful to abolish Protestantism which has been purported as the cause of evil on earth to secure the minds of the modern thinkers in the campaign, (5) using writers and authors for the propaganda of the New World Order, (6) using Catholic Irish-Jesuit Champions, (7) Catholics claiming to be the modern-day Israel that will use extermination against those that may not believe, (8) there will be hatred for the heretics against the one-system of government, (9) Destruction of Protestantism and (10) hatred of the Bible as the last shocker (Riplinger, n.d).

The United States of America as a Superpower

From History, the United States of America has always cherished liberty especially from the British. It is a throttlehold of global democracy. It is dominant in global power. (Finley,2021, n.p). America is presently recognized as the sole global power. Its military can be compared with none on the global arena whether on the sea, air or land. It extends to every part of the globe. Economically, America fuels the world trade and industry. The U.S economy is as proficient as its major competitors across the globe. The population growth of Japan and Europe became rapid which created shortage in labour and severe budgetary pressures. China is developing rapidly (Daalder & Lindsay (2003:1,2), and Russia may have not been progressing but their economies today can also be compared to that of Italy and Belgium (Burns, 2019: n.p). None of these powerful nations has the political infrastructure that can match the economic growth of the United States of America (Daalder & Lindsay (2003:1,2).

The cultural and political appeal of America has been described as soft power. This is evident as most international institutions reflect American interest. The position America is placed in history is unique because no country within the globe has ever come close. The U.S defense is growing while that of other nations is falling. The United States defense budget is greater than the Chinese budget which further confirms the might of its power as a nation (Daalder & Lindsay (2003:1,2).

Based on the evidences above, America can be decoded as the superpower. It is a superpower because of its exceptional prowess and control, which can be compared to none, especially in the aspects of global political, military, security, economic and cultural which are the basic bedrocks of a nation's sovereignty.

The Root of American History

America is a very vast nation from a few settlements of men in the 15th century. Red Indians were the first settlers as discovered by Christopher Columbus which is now described as the most powerful nation on earth. American territory expands from ocean to ocean. From its existence, it holds the power of independence and glory among the nations of the earth. Smith (1874) added that,

> No nation ever acquired so vast a territory in so quiet a manner. (2) No nation ever rose to such greatness by so peaceable means. (3.) No nation ever advanced so rapidly in all that constitutes national strength and capital. (4.) No nation ever rose to such a pinnacle of power in a space of time so incredibly short. (5.) No nation in so limited a time has developed such unlimited resources. (6.) No nation has ever existed founded on principles of justice so pure and undefiled. (7.) No nation has ever existed in which the conscience of men has been left so untrammeled and free. (8.) In no nation and in no age of the world, have the arts and sciences so flourished, so many improvements been made, and so great successes been achieved, as in our own country during the last fifty years. (9.) In no nation and in no age has the gospel found such freedom, and the churches of Christ had such liberty to spread abroad their principles and develop their strength. (10.) No age of the world has seen such an immigration as that which is now pouring into our borders from all lands the millions who have long groaned under despotic governments, and who now turn to this broad territory of freedom as the avenue of hope, the Utopia of the nations (1874: 3-8; See White also 2002).

Sumner (1807: n.p) added that the establishment of America was not accidental. Aside the biblical prophecies, some personalities had envisaged the nature America would grow into. One Sir Thomas in 1682, after a century from the European discovery in the late 16th Century predicted that America would be greater than Europe in strength and prowess. While in 1776, Adam Smith and Gilani, a

Neapolitan, foretold the fall of Europe, among others.

The United States of America in Biblical Prophecy

America has a fascinating history that has had no parallel since the distinction of nations among men (Burns, 2009: n.p; Smith, 1874: 1). It is also rooted in Christian heritage mainly Protestantism. The understanding of the United States in prophecy can be gleaned from two basic concepts which refer to America in the Bible. They are classified as the specific and symbolic theories, in this study.

The first school of thought claims that America is found in the book of Ezekiel 38:13. The key phrase in the text that identifies the American nation is the "merchant of Tarshish with all his villages" (38:13). The Hebrew text signifies that the term 'villages' refer to 'the young lions' as well. According to the modern Tarshish, the interpretation refers to the Phoenician maritime which is also a trading community. Tarshish is located in the Western Europe like Spain, Holand and Britain. However, America is therefore identified to be among the 'villages or young lion' of Tarshish because it is the most dominant among the Western nations (Steuart McBirnie,1978:89). According to a write up on Christipher Columbus (2009) and John Cabot, (2021), October 12, 1492 marked the opening of the way for the widespread of European exploration and colonization of America by Christopher Columbus. Britain through the voyage of John Cabot got land for the British and exploration goes on and on though there are various version of theories on this subject (See Fargher et al, 2000:1-150; Nash et al, 1996:25-95). Based on the Ice theory, Steuart McBirnie (1978:89) concluded that 'Tarshish and the young lions or villages' refer to the Western Europe and America specifically the United States of America (See Hitchcock, 1994: 90-100). Ice (2009: 4,5) asserted further that America will be one of the Revived Roman Empire of the Antichrist because it is a colony established by Europe.

The second theory is classified as the symbolic theory. The

background is found in the book of Daniel and has its fulfillments in the book of Revelation. This school of thought claims that the United States in prophecy is not a mere theory but a revelation from God as it is signified with signs and symbols as stated in the Book of Revelation written by Apostle John, the Zebedee. Though scholars over the years have always had negative attitude towards the Book of Revelation; they thereby view them, generally, as speculative and sensationalistic.

The Book of Revelation chapter 17:15 shows a Beast coming out of the sea representing peoples, nations and tongues; as an apocalyptic book, it has a negative connotation. The people that came from there oppose God and His chosen people while Revelation 13:1,11 which represents the nation from the earth has a positive connotation as it opposes the Beast from the sea. Eventually, Revelation 12:16 discloses how the nation representing the earth persecuted God's people through Satan's intervention and control.

The first Beast (sea or Kingdoms) is the Papacy (Papal Rome) and the second Beast is the United States of America, Letting the Bible be the interpreter of itself, the Beast from the sea represents kingdoms and nations while the Beast from the earth represents a nation (Daniel 7:17; Rev. 13). Rev. 13:10 reveals the rise of the second Beast (nation) was at the same time when the first Beast went into captivity (verse 3). In 1798, the United States became a nation to reckon with as a supernation globally and the first Beast (Kingdoms) received a deadly wound. By this, it represents the collapse of the Papal Roman when the French took the Pope prisoner which ended the supremacy of the Papacy (Finley, 2021). Rev. 13:11 shows that the second Beast had two horns like a lamb. The two horns signify authority, religion and politics by the Scriptures. The use of lamb to describe the United States of America in the Bible shows that the United States is not by any means the enemy of God and His people.

Stefanovic (2017) asserted, nonetheless, that the Book of Revelation pronounces blessings on those who read, hear and understand the teachings therein from the prologue. The Book of Revelation encompasses the past, present and future events. Any interpretation that denies the nature of the prophecies of the Book of Revelation does not do justice to its intention. This sets historicism aside as the adequate approach to prophetic interpretation. Stefanovic added that historicism:

> Recognizes that Revelation contains the movement and events in Christian history from the first century and the end of time. This method also recognizes the spiritual relevance of the book to all Christians regardless of time and space (n.p).

The biblical prophecy can be well understood and traced to the book of Revelation chapter 13 from the backdrop prophecies found in the book of Daniel chapters 2,7 and 8 which show the Roman Empire as the Beast power which will cease the control of power through America though once lost its power to French. The Book of Revelation posits that

> And I beheld another beast coming up out of the earth; and he had two horns like a lamb, and he spake as a dragon. And he exerciseth all the power of the first beast before him, and them which dwell therein to worship the first beast, whose deadly wound was healed. (11,12).

The Papal Rome will rise again through the United States of America. Papal Rome will not only exercise its present political power but also through religious global affairs based solely worship. Based on these evidences, the United States of America in the present-day global politics stands out as a pivotal center for international political. Therefore, America will play a major role in the implementation of the New World Order instead of the Roman Empire where the Papal seat is situated.

Papacy and its Role in the New World Order

The Roman Catholic or the Church of Rome does not believe solely on the authority of the Bible but on the authority of the Bible and tradition (human commandments). Tradition is rather equated with the Scriptures (Holy Bible) as sources of revelation. The Roman Catholic has biblical and paganistic beliefs by implication. (Eregare, 2013:208). The Roman Catholic Church has absorbed the ancient pagan beliefs into Christianity, especially in relations to God and His worship. This is blasphemy, if critically analysed. A few of their beliefs and practices are:

(1.) The concept of celibacy in the monastery was common to Buddhism about a century before the Roman Catholic adopted the usage;

(2.) The two-pointed mitre which represents the fish-god, Dagon is the headdress of the Catholic Bishop;

(3.) The solar disc or sun symbol and the crescent moon represent the element of deity; crescent moon and mother god respectively or her womb as a symbol of the host and demonstration in the Catholic mass;

(4.) The adornment of pinecone, which is a symbol relating to pagan gods in Babylon, Egypt, Greece and Rome as the staff of popes and worship rites;

(5.) The rising phoenix which represents the sun god placed in the Catholic church,

(6.) The mother and child replacing the Isis and Horus;

(7.) The concept of Mary playing the role of a mediator for man between heaven and earth;

(8.) The use of relics and saints gotten from the pagan ideology of worship and the power to communicate with the saints or ancestors;

(9.) Isis Huros is the inscription of the Roman Catholic Church;

(10) The Tripple Crown of the pagan hierarchy becoming the crown of the popes, and

(11) The Society of Jesus that is otherwise known as the Jesuits with the symbols of Lucifer sexagesimal triangle (Neumann,

2003:159-160).

This system possesses the most intelligent networks across the globe. The intelligence is widespread and far-reaching than any organization around the globe. They are pursuing the total take over or the control of the earth because they seemingly possess the power that no one on earth can repel. The Roman Church once claimed that "the power of the church exercised over sovereigns …is held by divine right and whoso resist it rebels against the King of Kings and Lord of Lords" (Ecclesiastical megalomania: n.d). Is this not blasphemy? Can the church on earth ever equate her power or thought with the thought of the Creator of heaven and earth as the sources of divinity? Never!

According to Bailey as cited in Neumann's work, the strategy of the unification of the whole political institutions or global religions will be making affiliation to Christ without being a Christian. You could be a Buddhist or Mohammedan or of any other faith. This is the trend in which the current ecumenical initiatives toll. The ecumenical missiological concept is tagged on love your neighbour as yourself, maintain a disciplined life, and recognize the divinity of all faiths and beings (Neumann, 2003:43, 265). According to Newmann, in his narration, the papal Rome would work through America by the mission of the Jesuits. The New World order would take a shift from global politics to religious affairs (Epperson, 2016: xvi-xvii). The Jesuits have always been Rome's militants against all those that oppose her. The present Protestant America would be bought over. In view of the latter, in 2017, there was a recent reconciliatory movement between the Protestants and the Roman Catholic Church in England and Castle Church (where Luther pasted his 95 Thesis) in Wittenburg, after 500 years of division from 1517. This true 'fraternity' as posited by Pope Francis was basically premised those past errors are recognized, injuries can be forgiven and wounds healed. A spokesman for the Catholic Church in England and Wales added that:

> We give thanks to the joy of the gospel we share as
> Christians, express repentance for the sadness of our
> divisions and renew our commitment to common
> witness and service to the world (n.p)

One would have thought that the basis for the reconciliation should
have been driven by the acceptance and correction of the errors
(separation of sacred from the mundane) committed by the church,
forgiveness from those who were hurts and wounded (division).
Since the latter was not the case, Sherwood, (2017), submitted that
the Roman Catholic has not changed her positions (See also
Reformation, 2021: n.p.).

The Rome and the rest of the Political world will combine
forces. The three secret societies are the Free Mansons, Zionists and
the Catholic Order (Opus Dei and Jesuits). The movement will
condemn anything that dares to claim that their faith is based on the
Bible alone for understanding and interpretation of the words of
God (Newmann, 2003:100-180 Encyclical letter, June 20,
1894:304).

The Key Changes by the New World Order

Finley (2021:1) revealed that the issues of liberty and
human conscience though loom during the end time according to
the Book of Revelation; will it continue to the last days? In
Newmann's narration (2003: 1-125), The strive of the New World
Order would tamper with the freedom of the press or the freedom
of expression, which applies to all ideas of all kinds in the last days
that should be enjoyed seamlessly under the international law.

Since September 11, some of the significant changes that
are coming with the New World Order are: freedom on family
(gender pluralism as against the biblical tradition on family life),
workplace and religion (control of economy and religion). There
had also been cases of suicide bombings, mass, 2003: 138-202; See
also Kamran (2014: 1-300). For example, the Covid-19 pandemic
killings, natural disasters, rumours of global uncertainties, the

splenic fever scares and flaring Israeli-Palestinian animosity which creates a severe sense of global fear and instability as a very disastrous calamity on humans among others which invariably may promote a new world order. It has virtually caused a failure of the prior world and opened up another world. The wish of humans to go back to their normal life even scares so many people so there is a need for a new normal. Also, the risks that are presently found in the climate change will continuously lead to the emergence of new viruses. There is also a high risk in environmental change on deforestation which is increasing the potential for zoonotic viruses. Based on these among others, create a platform that there should be the establishment of a new world order (The Club of Rome, 2021: n.p). It is worth noting that some freedoms of expression have been either publicly or privately criminalized by a few political leaders especially when it upsets their governance. Such people alleged to be terrorist groups which caused the restrictions on the expression of personal convictions or opinions. This implies that freedom of expression could be withdrawn by political powers.

Profound evidence is the development of the scientific revolution through artificial intelligence. Information on everyone on earth is being computed and can be monitored systematically through intelligent machines also known as artificial intelligence (AI) that are capable of solving problems, speech recognition and planning. Various governments have started employing this intelligent machine for governance as it implies. In short, computers have turned the globe into a connected village and can easily be governed (Artificial Intelligence, 2021: n.p). By this, the world is fast becoming governable.

Eregare, (2013: 207) wrote that the establishment of the ecumenical initiatives promote the union of all religions on earth. But under this movement for peace among all religious group stampedes freedom by glossing over or accommodating or cohabitating the flexibility of beliefs and practices which rather destroys the law of love (the Ten Commandments) or biblical truth.

The latter signifies "come let us work together with our differences in beliefs and practices".

In addition to the ecumenical initiatives, the introduction of the indigenization of Christianity to assimilate the tradition of the host community is raised higher through scholarship and otherwise (Eregare, 2013:207 See Cohen, 1995:46 as cited in Scruggs, 2005: 91-123). Based on this, the expression of biblical truth becomes relative and thereby reviving the societal ills. If adequate caution is not taken, it will leave people discontented, unconverted and worldly which, by implication, does not encourage righteousness by faith in Christ Jesus (Matthew 4:23; 28:19).

Righteousness by Faith in Christ and True Peace Response

The concept of the just shall live by faith in Christ Jesus centers on righteousness (Romans 1:17; Gal. 3:11; Hab. 2:4; Heb. 10:28). What rules mirror righteousness? It is the Ten Commandments. It is through the Ten Commandments come the Knowledge of sin. The Ten Commandments are the laws of God which either shows humans as under its condemnation or jurisdiction. They are clear and not burdensome because it reveals clearly what sin is and God's divine character (See Romans 7:7-12, 14; Psalm 19:7-9). According to Knight (2013:75,76), the law was burdensome because the Pharisees were excellent on the letters of the law but poor in its spirit. They were perfectionists. Perfectionists will always have a list of do's and dont's. This led to, for example, the creation of 1,521 laws under the Sabbath commandment. Based on this burdensome approach, Jesus came to fill up the gaps that were created on how to keep the Sabbath. Jesus did not change the Sabbath from Saturday (7th Day of the week) but filled up instances on how to keep it without it being burdensome (Matthew 5:17-19).

The Ten commandments are rather a letter of love to humanity (See Deuteronomy 7:9; 11:1; 11:22; 1 John 4:16). They form the foundation of God's kingdom where God's injunctions are categorically spelt out. Therefore, to live under the jurisdiction of the law of God is expedient. Everyone should endeavour, through dependence on God's strength, not to be under the condemnation of the laws of God because of the blessings (rights and privileges) attached to those who obey God and His words (See John 5:24; Romans 8:1; Exodus 31:18). This should devoid any form of tradition or philosophy of men because God grimaces it (Matt 15: 3; Mark 7:8; Mark 7:9; Matthew 15: 6). This study submits that it is Luciferian if its aims are to make less important the character of God; the Bible states that for such will be called the least in the Kingdom of God (Matthew 5:20). The laws of God are like a mirror which gives evidences of whose power human beings give their allegiance. It also shows clearly all that has to do with God, His worship and man in relation to fellow man. This is the true peace that God employs human beings to make reconciliation with God and man in preparation for the new earth planned by Christ at His advent (Rev. 21:1; Isa. 65:17; 2 Peter 3:13).

The Role of Papacy in the New World Order

Based on the claim that the Pope is all powerful, The Roman Catholic Church has made a lot of changes in the commandments of God. She has revealed the secret behind the Sunday worship when she claimed that:

> :..We observe Sunday instead of Saturday because the
> Catholic Church in the Council of Laodicea (A.D) 336)
> transferred the solemnity from Saturday to Sunday"
> (The Convert's Catechism of Catholic Doctrine, by
> Peter Geiremann).

The Roman Catholic and other Christian denominations share Sunday worship as a day of worship though not biblical; meanwhile the Sabbath (Saturday) symbolizes the seal of God (Ex. 20: 8-10). The fourth commandment has the name, title and domain of God which comprises God's official seal of authority when He stated that humanity should 'remember' to keep it holy. But the

Roman Catholic transferred the day of worship and images honouring it by the power of the church (The Church of God International, 2021: n.p). Sunday worship, from the above context, is a human tradition and a seal of Luciferian or mark of the Beast. It is not biblical and it implies an opposition 'reason' to reject the biblical standards on Sabbath Worship, which in other words is one of the characteristics of the New World Order. People would be enforced to follow suit in Sunday worship when fully established. The Freemason, Jesuit's order, Papal Rome, the CIA and other institutions are the ones behind the secret conspiracy in controlling the world from political to religious affairs. This platform would enable the enforcement of human tradition over and God's commandments (Newmann, 2013:244-265; See also Manuscript 34, 1897; Selected Messages, Book 3,423; Eregare E.O, et al, 2017: 51-69).

Roman Church and Islamic Religion

The ecumenical movement is based on the unity of Christian faiths though differ in doctrinal beliefs and practice. The union in its true sense is uniformity of all religions. In addition, the Roman Catholic Church and Islam since the 20th century has been having a notable change in relationship (Sydney, 2010) though Islam was described as a Christological heresy by John of Damascus in the 7th Century text. Ferguson (2005: n.p) added the claims of the apologists:

> (1) Islam was a Christian heresy because of their points of similarities as monotheism, prophetic revelation, judgment, and afterlife, (2) Islam was God's judgment on the shortcomings of the church, (3) Islam is pagan related (p.336).

The relationship between the Roman Catholic and Islam is further built on the declaration by the Vatican Council that Islam is the plan of human salvation (Lumen Gentium, 2014: n.p). Though Islam claims that its adherents should live peacefully with non-Muslims especially Christians by being patient with "what they say and part with them courteously", it however claims that "kill them wherever you find them" (Sura 73:10; Sura 2:256). Basically, Islam connotes to force the 'unbeliever' to convert or die.

Despite the seeming inconsistencies in the Quran, the relationship between Christianity and Islam has been strengthened by the narration of three shepherd children, Lucia Santos and her cousins Jacinta and Francisco Marto who reported visions of a shining lady believed to be the Virgin Mary. They claimed that Mary appeared to the children in the Cova da Iria fields outside the hamlet of Aljustrel near Fatima, Portugal. The relationship has also grown based on the claim that Muhammed and Kadijah were said to have had a close relationship with the Catholic monastery in Rome (Our Lady of Fatima, 2017). The Roman Catholic Church through the doctrine of indigenization of Christianity and reorganization of images honouring, among others form her relationship with paganism (Eregare, 2013:207 See Cohen, 1995:46 as cited in Scruggs, 2005: 91-123). So far, it is clear that the Roman Catholic Church and Islam are monotheistic, their practices are not completely on 'thus says the Lord' while the basic Protestantism hold on to the Bible and the Bible alone as the source of God's revelation to man. This properly situates the course to separate the sacred from the mundane.

Responses on the United States of America and the New World Order

The New World Order began from the United States of America which predominantly has protestant heritage. The reverse side of the great seal of the United States of America, at the bottom, has in Latin "Novus Ordo Seclorum", meaning "The New World Order". Papal Rome and the United States of America by the secret powers would form the basis upon which the unification of all religions and global powers would be formed into the one system of government. (See also Epperson, 2016: iii). Upon these backgrounds, peace would be sought to solve global problems. They are: (1.) the unification of global powers dealing with peace issues and disarmament, (2.) the second lays emphasis on dealing with the environmental issues and to the new international economic order and (3.) the alleged need for a change in the way things are done to Karl Marx's theory of communism which is in consonance with thinking globally and acting locally (See also Epperson, 2016: xv-xvi). This drive for the global Empire of peace rather distorts the biblical teaching of the coming of Jesus Christ to establish the true kingdom where true perfect peace, health and wholesome security will be established. It is, nonetheless, a distraction negating the teaching in the prophecy in the Book of Daniel about the historic breakdown on the panoramas on one-system government over the ages especially from the Babylonian Empire during the reign of Nebuchadnezzar. It is also inimical to the biblical teaching that the Roman Empire would be the last global empire before the coming of Jesus Christ-Jesus at His advent, will establish the eternal kingdom of God (Daniel 2:44,45).

In conclusion, the New World Order has begun from September 11 and the end is looming. The New World Order will shift from global politics to religious dogma. The ongoing earth's human peace mission is a deceptive scheme against the standards of the Bible. It aims at aiding God to solve global problems. It flies on the wing of secrecy. It aims at uniting the global political and religious leaders for a one system of government. More so, it is based on 'reasoning' to reject basic standards, put in the biblical context. This is nothing but Luciferian as it cruxes under the mixture of the Bible and human traditions. It seeks to make less the commandments of God or make alternatives by the philosophy of reason outside God's standards of His image in one voice. This can be described as nothing but the infiltration of the global moral relativism through the United States of America. Newmann, (2013: 1-133) admitted that the plan is set; decrees would be issued; constitutions would be changed to suit the new world agenda before the second advent of Jesus Christ.

CHAPTER TWELVE

Epilogue

Emmanuel Orihentare Eregare

Similar to the case of prophet Ezekiel, the 'cry' for peace, safety and unity is rapidly growing among contemporary political and religious leaders especially after the September 11 event in the United States of America (13:10-16). From the Antiquity to the modern age, there have been over 5,000 Global or Regional peace treaties. This study reveals that the various strive for peace treaties by human beings have been so futile from the earliest recorded peace treaty around 1274BC between the Hittites and the Egyptians (that took over a century). The United Nations also has tried to make peace yet the more the drive for peace, the more the state of global anarchy.

This study shows that global desire for peace, safety and unity is more evident based on the high level of political instabilities, religious and moral pluralism, insecurity, climate change; the salvage of human beings from the irreparable effects caused by pestilences, wars, famine, rumours of wars, false prophets or the emergence of false saviours, worldliness, among others as they take the central stage of global affairs. Laws and policies are being sponsored and enacted by political leaders and a few notable elites who have concerted to push for the New World Order (1 Thess. 3: 5).

Another profound evidence to support the growth on the formation of the New World Order is technological advancement. Due to this technological advancement, among others, the globe is becoming smaller and reachable at a 'snap of the fingers' because information now spreads like wildfire. Information is now laid unembellished before human beings to access. Moments, events, communications and personal identities are captured consciously and unconsciously. The reality of the world as a global village is becoming more evident. The possibility of a one world system is secretly becoming real so, do not be deceived.

The basic objectives of the New World Order are establishing a global change in the political and religious thoughts. The framework of this change hinges on the formation of a global governance by reason (philosophy) other than that of God. The projected intention is to identify and understand the global challenges that nations or states cannot resolve.

What has Covid-19 got to do with the New World Order? Sequel to climate change, global human health has undergone irreparable loss of humans which depicts the sign that the end is near. Covid-19 virus has, firstly, been premeditated as a medium to bring the whole world to a point where human freedom will be totally sacrificed for the cruel one-world structure for the sake of peace on earth. Secondly, Covid-19 vaccination carrying a bio censor adds to the fear that it is up to something mysterious. Thirdly, Covid-19 leaves the globe with a devastating health condition of humans. Fourthly, Covid-19 creates a general awareness that the new world order has either begun or it is about to set in; it may not be far from the reality. Examining critically the covid-19 pandemic and its antecedents further, it is clear that the pestilence is not new. One thing is also clear, Covid-19 is a pestilence which shows, among others, that the end of the human race on earth is evident. This study adds that from the ancient to the modern, the ever-recorded pandemics in human history have shown that viruses are the most major sources of global pandemics, among others are bacterias and parasites. The devastating effects caused by the Covid-19 have global influence and needs a global attention. This is to say that the drive to salvage human health is beyond the confines of the nations-states which depicts the coming together of global leaders to tackle the issue of human safety and peace.

The peace-keeping mission by politico-religious leaders around the globe will shift from political to religious dogmas. The basis of the religious dogma, among others, will center on worship. The bone of contention will focus on taking a tall stand on submitting to Sunday worship (pagan day of worship or human tradition or philosophy) instead of the Sabbath biblical day of worship (Saturday) while the government protective power will be withdrawn from those who keep the commandment of God and have the faith of Jesus Christ (1 John 5:3; Rev. 14:12). For those that do not consent, by the time it will be more permanent globally, they will be dealt with severely. This shows the influence of paganism in Christianity.

The infiltration of this paganism crux around the top 20 global religions except for Christianity at their primary levels of founding, history posits, however, that Christianity at some point, allowed some pagan connections especially in the Roman Empire which still lives on. In other to separate the mundane from the sacred then, Protestantism was birth through the missionary enterprise of Martin Luther. This connection informs their moral relativism which appears to have shifted from the biblical definitions of Christ's peace mission, among others.

Whatever is the case, it is imperative for everyone to go back to God, having in mind that the just shall live by faith in Christ Jesus and not by any human traditions or means. Furthermore, questions that should illuminate minds are: are we ready to accept Jesus as our lord and personal Saviour by forsaking the world and its lusts thereof? Are we also ready to say: 'I am done with low living (sin), "I die daily', 'For me to live is Christ and to die is gain', 'Not my will but

Thy will', 'I live by God's unfailing words in the Scriptures alone though the heaven falls and 'heaven is my goal' (Rom. 8:1;1 Cor. 15:31; Phil. 1:21; John 5: 31; Deut. 13:4; 2 Tim. 4:8)? Positive declaration to these questions would be the strength needed to withstand any persecutions against those who desire to stand for God rather than philosophy of men.

This discourse calls for everyone to stand firm for God and His righteousness. Worthy of note is the fact that the Bible remains the sole authority that distinguishes true Christians and it calls for everyone else regardless of the religion they may practice to join the reliable 'wagon' about human existence-believing Bible and Bible alone as the rule of faith and practice. To be a follower of Christ is to trust and simply obey Him without the consideration of any human philosophical and cultural beliefs or practices. This should be the anchor for Christians as the globe moves towards the great plan of the uniformity of all religions and the one-system of government on earth for the sake of peace and safety. True peace cannot be attained by any human efforts. Christ Jesus is the Prince of Peace; so, true peace and safety can only be obtained in Him alone. The banner of the Protestantism against false unbiblical teachings, beliefs and practices should be raised higher to enable separate the sacred from the mundane. It is also time to put forward and extend the banner of the ministry of human reconciliation back to God, His words and His righteousness alone. Every other 'ground is a sinking ground!'

James 3: 18 submits that, "Peacemakers who sow peace reap a harvest of righteousness." Every person is called to Christ to be a peacemaker. The fruit of peacemaking is righteousness not in the context of viewing the issue of Christian moralities as relative; it is rather upholding the morals as the Bible advocates. Righteousness is "right living or right standing or right relationship". To have peace is to have a right relationship with God and man; that is the summary of whoever is born again and lives by the dictates of God (Ex. 20:3-17). Righteousness alone can exalt global peace between God, His creation and man (Prov. 14:34). This shows that the peace Jesus offers is not as the world offers.

From this study, the context for global peace has been ongoing, relative and multiculturally sought. The human global peace and safety movement cannot resolve it except through the revelation made by God. God has promised that He is making a place of peace and safety for man in the New Heaven and Earth (Rev. 21). No matter the means or nature of global crisis, what should be the utmost desire of every Christian is developing God's image or character which is the true immune system that can withstand the forced and enacted religio-political laws and persecutions that may be attached to not cooperating with the developing human worldview on the New World Order.

REFERENCES

CHAPTER ONE- Loveday C. Onyezonwu, PhD.

Anderson, Paul N. "Jesus and Peace". *Faculty Publications - College of Christian Studies*, 1994

Arichea, Daniel C. "Peace in the New Testament" *United Bible Societies*, Vol. 38, No. 2, 1987.

Banda, Nicole. "The Peace Movement is Counterproductive" *The Peace Movement*. Edited by Harris, Nancy, Greenhaven Press, 2005.

Blackburn, Simon. *Oxford Dictionary of Philosophy*, Oxford University Press, 1994.

Bose, Sumantra. *Kashmir: Roots of Conflict, Paths to Peace*. Harvard University Press, 2003.

Brock, Lloyd "One on One with Jesus Personal Peace" from https://www.pekinfirstnaz.org, Accessed 24th, July, 2020.

Cortright, David. *Peace: A History of Movements and Ideas*, Cambridge University Press, 2008

Ekpoudom, N. P. "Ethics: Its Nature, Scope and Theories" *Summa Philsophica: An Introduction to Philosophy and Logic*. Edited by in Essien, Ephraim S., Lulu Press, U.S.A, 2011.

Fahey, Joseph J. "An Overview of Four Traditions on War and Peace in Christian History," *The Journal of Social Encounters*, Vol. 2, Iss. 1, 2013, pp 7-21.

Farneubun, Petrus K. "Understanding Christian's Perspective on Peace and War." *Ilmiah Hubungan International* Vol. 9, No.2, 2013, pp. 105-115.

Federal Bureau of Investigation (FBI) National Press Office, Washinton D.C (Sept. 2020). Available at https://www.fbi.gov/new.- Retrieved on 18th Dec., 2020.

Ferrell, Robert H. "Peace Movements", https://www.encyclopedia.com/social-sciences-and-law/political-science-and-government/military-affairs-nonnaval/peace-movements. Accessed on 15th July, 2020

Galtung, J. *Peace by Peaceful Means: Peace and Conflict, Development and Civilization*, SAGE Publications Ltd, 1996.

Gill, Cassandra (2016), "11 facts about the modern peace movement." Retrieved on July 16, 2020 from https://blog.oup.com/2016/08/11-facts-modern-peace-movement/

Healey, Joseph P. "Peace: Old Testament," *The Anchor Yale Bible 12 Dictionary*. Edited by Freedman, David N., New York: Doubleday, 1992.

Hornsby, A. S. *Oxford Advanced Learner's Dictionary*, 7th Edition. Oxford University Press, 2006.

Horst, Myron. "Building a Theology of Peace in the Old Testament" (2011), https://www.freehousechurchresources.com/peaceoldtestament.php. Accessed on 2nd July, 2020.

Howard, M. "Problems of a Disarmed World," *Studies in War and Peace*, New York: Viking Press, 1971.

Jamie Doward, 'One in five older people in the UK have been abused, poll finds', *The Guardian*, 29th November, 2020, available at www.theguardian.com. Retrieved from https://www.msn.com/en-gb/news/uknews/one-in-five-older-people-in-the-uk-have-been-abused-poll-finds/ar-BB1bsunf on 24th December, 2020.

Miller, J.R. "Jesus the Prophet of Peace: The Language of Peace in the Christian Scripture". *A Paper Presented at San Diego State University Symposium on Scripture, Hermeneutics and Language*, 2015.

Kalin, I. "Islam and Peace: A Survey of the Sources of Peace in the Islamic Tradition." *War and Peace in Islam: The Uses and Abuses of Jihad*. Edited by Muhammad, Ghazi B., Kalin, Ibrahim & Kamali, Mohammad H., The Islamic Texts Society, Cambridge, 2013.

Lysaught, Therese. "Christian Traditions of Peace: Just War and Pacifism." Institute of Pastoral Studies: Faculty

Publications and Other Works, 2003, pp 50-54.

Miller, Joseph R. "Jesus the Prophet of Peace: The Language of Peace in the Christian Literature" A Paper Presented at San Diego University Symposium, on Scripture, Hermeneutics and Language, 2015.

National Conference of Catholic Bishops, "The Challenge of Peace: God's Promise and Our Response", *A Pastoral Letter on War and Peace*, 1983.

Ojumu, Busola. "Definition of Peace", https://passnownow.com/classwork-support/2016. Accessed on 16th July, 2020.

Olanrewaju, Iemobola P. "The Conceptual Analysis of Peace and Conflict". *Readings in Peace Studies and Conflict Resolution.* Edited by Soremekun, K., 2013, pp. 6-14

Omoregbe, Joseph. *Knowing Philosophy: A General Introduction*, Lagos: Educational Research and Publishers, 1990.

Opoku, J.K., Addai-Mensah, P, & Manu, E. (2017), "The Church, Justice and Peace: A Holistic View for a Prosperous Africa." Available on https://www.researchgate.net/publication/322550804.

Ozumba, G. O, *A. Course Text on Ethics*, Calabar: Jochrisam Publishers, 2008.

Padilla, Mariel, The New York Times, Jan. 4, 2020. Available on https://www.nytimes.com/2020/01/04/us/iran-anti-war-protests.html

Philpott, Daniel, *Just and Unjust Peace: An Ethic of Political Reconciliation*, Oxford University Press, 2012.

Press, Robert M. "Peaceful Resistance during a Civil War." In *Ripples of Hope: How Ordinary People Resist Repression Without Violence*, 175-202. Amsterdam: Amsterdam University Press, 2015. Accessed December 16, 2020. doi:10.2307/j.ctt1963121.10.

Radio Free Asia, *Antiwar protesters charged with violating Myanmar's peaceful assembly law,*

15 May 2018, available at: https://www.refworld.org/docid/5bb72da1a.html. [Accessed 24 December 2020].

Richie, Nivine, "God's Peace is different from the World's Peace". unlockingthebible.com/2018/08/gods-peace-different-worlds-peace/. Accessed on July 16, 2020.

Rummel, R. J. "Understanding Conflict and War: The Just Peace. https://www.hawaii.edu/powerkills/TJP.CHAP2.HTM. Accessed on 18th July, 2020.

Strangio, Sebastine. 'Myanmar Accelerates Arrests of Student Anti-war Protests', *The Diplomat*, October 2, 2020. Available on https://thediplomat.com/2020/10/myanmar-accelerates-arrests-of-student-anti-war-protesters/

Slote, Michael and Pettit, Philip, "Satisficing Consequentialism" *Proceedings of the Aristotelian Society*, Vol. 58 (1984), pp.139-163+165-176. Blackwell Publishing, 2008.

Taheri, Mohammad A. & Dehghan, Maryam, "Definition of Peace and its Different Types as Approached by Halqeh mysticism" *Procedia - Social and Behavioural Sciences*, Vol. 114, 2014, pp. 56 – 61.

Tanabe, Juichiro. "Exploring a Buddhist Peace Theory" *Cultural and Religious Studies*, Vol. 4, No. 10, 2016, pp. 633-644.

Webber, Robert "The Biblical Foundations of Christian Worship", *The Complete 53 Library of Christian Worship,* Nashville, TN: Star Song Pub. Group. Vol. 1, 1993.

Webel, Charles. "Toward a Philosophy and Metapsychology of Peace" (2007), *Handbook of Peace and Conflict Studies.* Edited by Webel, Charles and Galtung, Johan, USA: Routledge, (undated).

Wikner, Ben. "A Cost Analysis of Following Jesus," *Matthew: The Life and Words of Jesus, Part 43.* March 24, 2013, available on www.covlife.org/resources. Accessed 23rd July, 2020.

Woodley, Matt, "The Peace Jesus Brings". PreachingToday.com, 2009. Accessed on 20th July, 2020.

Young, Nigel J. "The Peace Movement, Peace Research, Peace Education and Peace Building: The Globalization of the Species Problem" *Bulletin of Peace Proposals*, Vol. 18, No. 3, 1987.

Youssef, Michael. *Jesus, Jihad and Peace: What Bible Prophecy Says About World Events Today.* Tennessee: Worthy Publishing Group, 2015.

Zimmerman, Bill, "The Four Stages of the Antiwar Movement". https://www.google.com/amp/s/www.nytimes.com/201 7/10/24/opinion/vietnam-antiwar-movement.amp.html. Accessed on 8th August, 2020.

CHAPTER TWO- Emmanuel G. M. Kollie, PhD., M.A., M. Ed

Abrams, Irwin. *The Noble Price and Laureates: An Illustrated Biographical History 1901-2001, Centennial Ed,* Science History Publications, 2001.

"Balkan War." www.history.com/this-day-in-history/the-first-balkan-war-ends. Accessed 20, July 2020.

Brown, Driver and Braggs. *Hebrew and English Lexicon,* Bible Works Version 8.

Carter, A. *Peace movements: International protest and world politics since 1945.* Routledge, 2014.Cold War. www.history.com/ topics/cold-war-history. Accessed 20, July 2020.

Chomsky, N. *Middle East illusions: including peace in the Middle East? Reflections on Justice and Nationhood.* Rowman & Littlefield, 2003.

Conti, Fulvio. "The Masonic International and the Peace Movement in the Nineteenth and Twentieth Centuries." *Reconsidering Peace and Patriotism during the First World War* Edited by Justin Quinn Olmstead. Springer International Publishing, 2017. pp15-30.

Costa Bona, Enrica. "The International Peace Bureau and the Universal Peace Congresses, 1899–1914." *Reconsidering Peace and Patriotism during the First World War.* Edited by Justin Quinn

Olmstead. Springer International Publishing, 2017, pp 3-14.

Detzler, Wayne A. *New Testament Words in Today's language,* Wheaton, Illinois: SP Publications, 1986.

Foster, Mary LeCrone. *Conclusion: Toward and Anthropology of Peace and War.* "Peace and War: Cross-Cultural Perspectives.". Edited by Foster LeCrone Mary and Robert A. Rubinstein. New Brunswick, NJ, 1986, P 353.

Fountain, Daniel E. *Health, the Bible, and the Church.* Billy Graham Center, 1989.

Fry, D. P. *Beyond war: The human potential for peace.* Oxford University Press, 2007.

Goedde, P. *The Politics of Peace: A Global Cold War History.* Oxford University Press, 2019.

Gultung. Johan. *Violence, Peace, and Peace Research , Essays on Peace: Paradigms for Global Order.* Edited. by Salla, Michael, et al. Central Queensland University press,1995.

Hartwig Richard. "Squaring the Circle: A Regional/Economic Proposal for Reform of the United Nations Security Council." *The Quest for Regional Representation Reforming the United Nations Security Council. Edited by Volker Weyel* Dag Hammarskjold Foundation Uppsala 2008, Pp 41-75.

Kollie, Emmanuel G M and Kollie, Erhuvwukorotu S. "A Need for a Broader Biblical Foundation for Healthcare Ministry in the Seventh-day Adventist Church in Liberia." *AUWA "Multidisciplinary Journal* Vol 1, 2021, pp 26-36.

Kollie, Emmanuel G M. "Christians in Contemporary Politics." *"A Survey of Church Politics in the Twenty-First Century: Re-Examining Religion-State Governance, Leadership and Laities.* Edited by Emmanuel Orihentare Eregare, 2018, pp. 49-63.

__________. "The Divine Plan of Redemption from the Point of View of Covenant Theology." *Valley View University Journal of Theology* vol 5, 2018, pp 61-70.

Kulkarni, S. *Health for Peace: Towards a Holistic Perspective.* Northern Book Centre, 1992.

League of Nations. https: www.britannica.com/topic/League-of

-Nations. Accessed 15 July 2020.

Leckman, James F., Catherine Panter-Brick, and Rima Salah, eds. *Pathways to peace: The transformative power of children and families.* Vol. 15. MIT Press, 2014.

Luke, Bethel Ulrich. *Hugies, Theological Dictionary of the New Testament (TDNT)*, Edied by. Kiel Gerhard Friedrich. WM B. Eerdmans Publishing Company, 1972, p 308.

Mbuende, Kaire M. *"Between* Enlargement and Reform the UN Security Council: Choices for Change." *The Quest for Regional Representation Reforming the United Nations Security Council.* Edited by Volker Weyel Dag Hammarskjold Foundation Uppsala 2008, pp 17-27

Meererk, Prayoon. *A Buddhist Approach to Peace.* Amrin Printing Group, 1989.

Millar, Willaim R. "Peace." *Mercer Dictionary of the Bible* (MDB). Edited by Mills, Watson E. Mercer University Press, 1990, p 665.

Paul, James & Nahory, Celine. "To contribute to the maintenance of international peace and security: The Case for Democratic Reform of the Security Council." *The Quest for Regional.*

Peace. https://news.un.org/en/story/2014/09/476992-peace-means-dignity-well-being-all-not-just-absence-war-un-officials. Accessed July 12, 2020.

Pilisuk, M. *Peace movements worldwide.* ABC-CLIO, 2011.

Prantl, Jochen. *The UN Security Council and Informal Groups of States: Complementing or Competing for Governance?* New York: Oxford University Press, 2006.

Representation Reforming the United Nations Security Council Edited by Volker Weyel Dag Hammarskjold Foundation Uppsala 2008, pp 29-38.

Scott Kin, Coretta. *The Words of Martin Luther King Jr.,* Newmarket Press, 2008.

Senehi, Jessica et al. "Introduction to the Special Issues: Peacebuilding, Reconciliation, and Transformation." *Peace and Conflict Studies* vol. 17, no. 1, 2010, pp 1-42.

Singh, Sohan. *Achieving Inner Peace.* I Universe, 2008.

Stendebach, "Peace." *Theological Dictionary of the Old Testament* (TDOT), Edited by. Johannes Butterwick, et al. William B. Eerdmans,1987.

St Peter, Anthony. *The Greatest Quotations of All-Time.* Xlibris Corporation, USA, 2010.

Swartley, William M. "Peace," *The New Interpreter's Dictionary of the Bible* (IDB) Edited by Sakenfeld, Katharine Doob. Abington, 2009, p 423.

Vesilind, Aarne. P. *Peace engineering: when personal values and engineering careers converge.* Lakeshore Press, 2005.

UNESCO. https://en.unesco.org/70years/building_peace Accessed July 12, 2020.

UN.org, "Organizations Formally Associated with the United Nations Department of Global Communications" November 2020, https://www.un.org/sites/un2.un.org/files/list_of_csos_associated_with_dgc_-_november_2020-1.pdf (Assessed December 6, 2020)

Weyel, Volker. "Beyond Extension: The UN Security Council: Insights into an Ongoing Debate." *The Quest for Regional Representation Reforming the United Nations Security Council. Edited by Volker Weyel* Dag Hammarskjold Foundation Uppsala 2008, pp 8-15.

Wilkinson, *John. Health and Healing: Studies in New Testament Principle and Practice.* Edinburgh: R & R Clark Ltd, 1980.

World War I. www.britannica.com/event/World-War-I/Killed-wounded-and-missing | Accessed 19, July 2020.

Vesilind, Aarne P, *Peace Engineering: When Personal Values and Engineering Careers Converge,* Lakeshore Press, 2005.

CHAPTER THREE- Oluwaseun Abel Akinpelu, M.A & Emmanuel O. Eregare, PhD.

Abdulaziz, S. *A New World Order*. New Jersey, USA: Princeton University Press, 2004, 15.

Abdulaziz, Sachedina.   "Religion, World Order, And Peace a Muslim Perspective", *Crosscurrents*, 332-338, September 2010, 333.

Abu-Nimer, M. *Nonviolence and Peace Building in Islam: Theory and Practice*, Florida, USA: University Press, 2003

Agarwal, R. *Hinduism*. In Athyal, J.M (ed). Religions in Southeast Asia: An Encyclopedia of Faiths and Cultures. ABC-CLIO, 2015.

Alan, Cooperman, ed. *The Future of World Religions: Population Growth Projections, 2010-2050*. Pew Research Center. April 2015, 5.

Alokan, P. O. "The Impact of Religion on The Promotion of Peace and Economic Integration in Yoruba Land", *Journal of Sociology, Psychology and Anthropology a Practice: Int'l Perspection* Vol. 2, Nos. 1-3, 2010, 4.

Anjum, A. *Concepts of Peace in World's Major religions: An Analysis*. International Journal of Scientific and Research Publications, Volume 7, Issue 4, April 2017, 248-259.

Annmarie, S. "The Real New World Order", *In Foreign Affairs*, Vol. 76, No. 5, Sep. - Oct., 1997, 183-197.

Arend, A.C. *The United Nations and the New World Order*, 81 Geo. L.J. 491 91992-1993), 491.

Baker, J.A. and DeFrank T.M. *The Politics of Diplomacy: Revolution, War, And Peace, 1989- 1992*, New York: G.P. Putnam's and Sons, 1995, xv.

Balakrishnan, S. "Sikhism Teachings on War and Peace". *Shanlax International Journal of Arts, Science & Humanities*, Vol. 2 No. 2 October 2014.

Brantmeier, E.J., Jing Lin, Miller, P. (ed). *Spirituality, Religion and Peace Education*, North Carolina, USA: Information Age Publishing, Inc., 2010. P.71

Chidester, D. "World Religions in The Journal for The Study of Religion", Vol. 31, No. 1, *Festschrift for Martin Prozesky,* Association for The Study of Religion in Southern Africa 2018, 41-53.

Conrad, H. and Grim, B.J. "The Global Religious Landscape", *2012 Pew Research Center,* 21. onrad, Hackett and David Mcclendon. Christians Remain World's Largest Religious Group, But They Are Declining in Europe, *Pew Research Center.* April 5, 2017.

Eastwest Ministries International. A Field Guide to Major World Religions. Plano, Texas, Us: 13-14.

Eric Gbotoe and Kgatla S.T. "The Role of Christianity In Mending Societal Fragility and Quelling Violence in Liberia". *Verbum Eccles.* (Online) Vol.38 N.1 Pretoria, 2017.

Esposito, J.L. and Yilmaz, I. *Islam and Peacebuilding: Gulen Movement Initiatives.* New York, USA: Blue Dome Press, 2010, 7.

Fozdar, F. "The Baha'i Faith: A Case Study in Globalization, Mobility and the Routinization of Charisma Australian". *Religion Studies Review* · September 2015 JASR 28.3, 2015: 274-292.

Frederick M.D. "Islamic Theology in The New World Some Issues and Prospects", *Journal of The American Academy of Religion.* Vol. Lxii, Issue 4, 1994, 1070.

G l o b a l   S e c u r i t y . https://www.globalsecurity.org/military/world/china/religion-traditional.htm. Retrieved January 6 2021.

Globalization. Procedia - Social and Behavioral Sciences 77, 2013, 205 – 209.

Graeme W. "Thinking Through Images: Kastom And the Coming of The Baha'is To Northern New Ireland and Papua New Guinea", *Journal of Royal Anthropological Institute.* Vol 11, Issue 4 December 2005.

Harper, Douglas. "Islam". Online Etymology Dictionary. Retrieved on 22/11/2007.

Hillerbrand, H.J. *A New History of Christianity*. Nashville, Abingdon Press, 2012, 2. Https://En.Wikipedia.Org/Wiki/Bah%C3%A1%Ca%Bc%C3%Ad_Faith.

Ian Markham. *Global Peace & Justice: The Christian Perspective*. Retrieved from https://Islamicmarkets.Com/Education/Global-Peace-Justice- on 2/11/ 2020.

Jinguang, L. *The Tolerance and Harmony of Chinese Religion in the Age, n.c.*

Joseph S. *What New World Order in* Foreign Affairs, Vol. 71, No. 2, Spring, 1992, pp. 83-96.

Jung, L. *Judaism And the New World Order: Human Equality and Social Reconstruction*, The American Journal of Economics and Sociology. Vol. 4, No. 3, April 1945, 388

Kamar, A. *Jain, Faith and Philosophy of Jainism*. Delhi, India: Kalpaz Publication, 2009, 3.

Kanu, I.A. *Igwebuike as an Igbo-African Modality of Peace and Conflict Resolution*, Journal of African Traditional Religion and Philosophy (Jatrep) Volume 1, Number 1, 2017, 32.

Kaur, I.N. *Sikhism*. In: Yaden D., Zhao Y., Peng K., Newberg A. (Eds) Rituals and Practices in World Religions. Religion, Spirituality and Health: A Social Scientific Approach, Vol 5. Springer.

Kettani, H. "World Muslim Population: 1950 – 2020", *International Journal of Environmental Science and Development (IJESD)*, Vol. 1, No. 2, June 2010, 143-153.

Khalili, E. "Sects in Islam: Sunnis and Shias". *International Academic Journal of Humanities*, Vol. 1, No. 1, 2014, p.41-47.

Lawrence F. and Karsh, E. *The Gulf Conflict, 1990-1991: Diplomacy and War in the New World Order*. New Jersey, USA: Princeton University Press, 1993, xxix

List of Religious Population. Https://En.M.Wikipedia.Org/Wiki/List_Of_Religious_Populations.

Lugira, A. M." African Traditional Religions". Christ Connection: How the World Religions Prepared the Way for The Phenomenon of Jesus. *Paraclete Press, 1935.*

Magonet, J. *Jewish contributions to interfaith dialogue and peaceful co-existence.* Accessed January 5, 2021.

Marcos A. F, and Karlberg, M. *Bahá'í Faith,* In the SAGE Encyclopedia of War: Social Science Perspectives. 2017 SAGE Publications, Inc., Thousand Oaks, CA, USA,

Mark, J. J. "Buddhism". *Ancient History Encyclopedia.* Retrieved from https://www.ancient.eu/buddhism/. January 5 2021.

Mcgrew, A. "Sustainable Globalization? The Global Politics of Development and Exclusion in The New World Order". *Poverty and Development in the 21ˢᵗ Century.* New York: Open University in association with Oxford University Press, 2000, 345-352.

Nasr, S.H. *Islam Religion, History, and Civilization,* San Francisco, USA: Happer Colins, 2003, 59-74.

Patti, J.A. "A World in Turmoil: Chaos, or A New World Order?" *Journal of American College of Radiology.* Volume 7, Issue 8, P551, August 01, 2010.

Peace in Islamic Philosophy, Wikipedia, 2021, np. Retrieved https://en.wikipedia.org/wiki/Peace_in_Islamic_philos ophyon the 7ᵗʰ February, 2021.
Print edition: pages: 131-133. Online edition: DOI http://dx.doi.org/10.4135/9781483359878.n57

Religion. Retrieved from Https://En.Wikipedia.Org/Wiki/Chinese_Folk_Religion, n.d.
Schroeder, P.W. *The New World Order: A Historical Perspective.* Pages 25-43 | Published Online: 05 Jan 2010. *The Washington Quarterly, Vol 17, 1994.*

Sikhism Promotes Peace Through Love, Compassion. Https://Www.Spokesman.Com/Stories/2008/Mar/01/Sikhism-Promotes-Peace-Through-Love-Compassion/ 12/3/2008.

Smith, P. .A. *Concise Encyclopedia Of The Bahá í Faith.* Oneworld Publications,

Stan Skreslet. *Emerging Trends in A Shifting Global Context Mission in The New World Order. Theology Today.* Stanley H. Source: Theology Today, 54 No 2 Jul 1997, P 150-164 150-164.

Stephen Juan. *What Are the Most Widely Practiced Religions of The World*, October 2006? Retrieved from Https://Www.Theregister.Com/2006/10/06/The_Odd_Body_Religion/ on the 22/3/2021.

Theresa Der-Ian Yen. "The Way to Peace: A Buddhist Perspective. International". *Journal of Peace Studies*, Volume 11, Number 1, Spring/Summer 2006. 91-112.

Thomas G. Walsh. *Religion., Peace and The Post-Secular Public Sphere*, International Journal on World Peace, Vol. 29, No. 2 (June 2012), 54

Todd M. Johnson And Brian J. Grim. *The World's Religions in Figures: An Introduction to International Religious Demography*. Chichester, Uk: John Wiley & Sons Ltd, 2013.

Ulrich Nitschke. *Religious Engagement in Humanitarian Crises.* (Berlin, Germany: International Partnership on Religion and Sustainable Development (PaRD), 2016). 5.

Varun Soni. *Religion, World Order, And Peace a Hindu Approach*, Crosscurrents, 310-313, September 2010, 310.

World Population. https://www.buddhisthumanitarianproject.org/about/about-bhp/. Accessed January 5 2021.

Zhignag, Z. "Chinese Cultural Resources in Building Harmonious World: A Review on the Exploring Achievements Made by the Chinese Senior Scholars Procedia" *Social and Behavioural Sciences* 77, 2013, 214 – 226.

CHAPTER FOUR- Alex Ugwukah, PhD.

Akinboye, S.O., Ottoh, F.O. *A Systematic Approach to International Relations-* Concept Publication   Lagos, 2005:251

Babatunde, I.O. *"International Journal of Business and Management Invention"*, ISSN (Online): 2319   – 8028, ISSN (Print): 2319 – 801X www.ijbmi.org Volume 3 Issue 3 March. 2014:07-18

Bell, Christine. On the Law of Peace: Peace Agreements and the lex Pacificatoria, Oxford   University Press, 2008.

Blainey as cited by Akinboye, S.O., Ottoh, F.O. *A Systematic Approach to*

International Relations- Concept Publication Lagos, 251

Brussels, E.E. Dictionary of Quotable Definitions, New Jersey: Prentice Hall Inc, 1970, 426.

Burton, J.W. World-Society, London: Cambridge University Press, 1972:138

Cain, P.J. J.A Hobson. "Cobdenism, and the Radical Theory of Economic Imperialism, 1898-1914 in *he New Economic History Review*, Willey

Fadeiye, J.E. Essays on Modern World History. From 1750 to the Present, Jumtom PrintingPress, Lagos 2016:139-143 see also Peacock,

H.L. A *History of Modern Europe, Heinemann* Educational Books - Secondary Division; 7th edition (1982:185-190). History.com/topics/korea/Korean-war. accessed 22/11/2020

Holsti, K.J. *International Politics London,* Prentice Hall Inc, 1967:141

Kleffner, J. Peace Treaties Oxford Public International Law Encyclopedia Centres March, 2011. See also, Naraghi-Anderlini, Sanam (2007) Peace Negotiations and Agreements

Lesaffer, R. Peace. "Treaties and the Formation of International Law" in the *Oxford Handbook of the History of International Law*. Oxford University Press, 2012:71-94.

__________*Too much History: from War as Sanction to the Sanctioning of* War, 37. Akinboye,

__________ Peace Treaties and International Law in European History from the Late Middle Ages to World War I.

Robertson, P., Will There Ever Be Lasting World Peace? www.1cbn.com accessed 21/11/2020. Please see also Isaiah 2:4

Rourke, J.T. *International Politics on the World Stage,* New York, McGraw-Hill, 2009:278

Ruppel, O.C et al, Climate Change: International Law and Global Governance. Vol. 2: Policy, Diplomacy and Governance in a Changing Environment, Nomos mbh, 2013

S.O., Ottoh, F.O. *A Systematic Approach to International Relations*-Concept Publication Lagos, 2005:235.

Trotsky, Leon. War and the International, *Marxists*, 1914.

Understanding Peace Treaties" *ABA Groups Division of Public Education Publications Teaching Legal* Docs-November 20, 2018, http://www.state.gov/s/l/treaty/

US Military History Companion/Peace www.answer.com accessed on 15/08/2020

Wilde, R. What is Mutually Assured Destruction, www.thoughtco.com http://www.beyondintractability.org/essay/structuringandpeace-agree www.merriam-webster.com

CHAPTER FIVE- John Apiah, PhD

Asafo, Dziedzorm R. *Research Methodology: Theories, Principles and Practices.* Advent Press, 2017.

Bernett, Michael N. "Bringing in the New World Order: Liberalism, Legitimacy, and the United Nations." *World Politics vol.49*, July 1997, pp. 526-551.

Boutros-Ghali, Boutros. *Agenda for Peace*, 2d ed. United Nations, 1995.

Brannen, S., et al. "World Order After Covid-19." *Center for Strategic and International Studies*, 28 May, 2020, pp. 1-3, https://www.csis.org/analysis/world-order-after-covid-19

Collins, Adela Y. "Introduction: Early Christian Apocalypticism." *Semeia, vol.36* (1986): 1-11.

Collins, Adela Y. "Apocalypse Now: The State of Apocalyptic Studies Near the End of The First Decade of the Twenty-First Century." *Harvard Theological Review, vol.104*, no.4, Oct 2011, 447-457.

Collins, John J., (ed.). "Apocalypse: The Morphology of a Genre." *Semeia vol.14*, 1997, 1-217.

Commission on Global Governance. *Our Global Neighborhood.* Oxford University Press, 1995.

Dahlheimer, Thoman I. "New Age Globalization and the Coming New World Order." *MilleLacs Messenger*, 3 Jun. 2011 (Updated 8 Aug. 2012), https://www.messagemedia.co/millelacs/opinion/blogs/new-age-globalization-and-the-coming-new-world-order/article_168bd527-9bd2-573e-90f2-f9b3a57aca4b.html

Douthat, Ross. "The End of the New World Order." *The New York Times*, 23 May, 2020, pp. 1-3.

Dussey, R. "The Covid-19 Crisis: Lessons for a New World Order." *New Africa*, 11 May 2020, pp. 1-5.

Evans, Craig A., & Porter, Stanley E. *Dictionary of New Testament Background.* InterVarsity Press, 2000.

Evans, Gareth. *Cooperating for Peace.* Unwin and Hyman, 1993.

Evans, Gareth. "Cooperative Security and Intrastate Conflict." *Foreign Policy*, no.96, Fall 1994, pp. 1-8.

Fowl, S. E. "Introduction." *The Theological Interpretation of Scripture: The Classical and Contemporary Reading.* Edited by Stephen E. Fowl, Blackwell, 1997, i-xxiv.

Freeman, Arthur. *Developments in New Testament Study.* MoraVian Theological Seminary, 1994.

Friberg, Barbara, et al. *Analytical Lexicon of the Greek New Testament.* Electronic Edition. Baker, 2000.

Gingrich, Felix Wilbur. *Lexicon of the Greek New Testament* (2nd ed.). Chicago: University of Chicago Press, 1992.

Gombis, Timothy G. Racial Reconciliation and the Christian Gospel. *ACT 3 Review vol.15*, no.3, 2006, pp. 117-128.

Harris, Stephen. *Understanding the Bible.* 6th ed. McGraw-Hill, 2003.

Jannace, William, and Paul Tiffany. "A New World Order: The Rule of Law, or the Law of Rulers?" *Fordham International Law Journal vol.42*, no.5, 2019, pp. 1379-1417.

Jemison, T. H. *Christian Beliefs.* Pacific Press Publishing Association, 1959.

Junk, Led. "Judaism and the New World Order: Human Equality and Social Reconstruction." *The American Journal of Economics and Sociology vol.4*, no.3, 1945, pp. 385-393.

Kelley, Earle M. "The Principles, Process, and Purpose of the Canon of Scripture." *Diligence: Journal of the Liberty University Online Religion Capstone in Research and Scholarship vol.5*, 2020, 1-27, https://digitalcommons.liberty.edu/djrc/vol5/iss1/4

Kotkin, J. "The New World Order: Mapping the Future." *The New*

World Order. Edited by Joel Kotkin, Legatus Institute, 2011, pp. 3-5.

Liddell, Henry Gearge and Scott, Robert. *Greek-English Lexicon With a Revised Supplement.* Clarendon Press, 1996.

Louw, Johannes and Nida, Eugene. *Greek-English Lexicon of the New Testament Based on Semantic Domains.* Second Edition. United Bible Societies, 1989.

McAlister, Melani. "Prophecy, Politics, and the Popular: The Left Behind Series and Christian Fundamentalism's New World Order." *The South Atlantic Quarterly vo.102*, no.4, 2003, pp. 773-798.

Paulien, J. "The End of Historicism? Reflections on the Adventist Approach to Biblical Apocalyptic-Part One. *Journal of the Adventist Theological Society vol.14*, no.2, Fall 2003, pp 15-43.

Peters, Prince E. "Understanding Persecution in Matthew 10:16-23 and Its Implication in the Nigerian Church. *"Historical Theological Studies vol.76*, no.4, 2020, pp. 1-9.

Piper, John. *Bloodlines: Race, Cross, and the Christian.* Crossway, 2011.

Punt, Jeremy. "The New Testament as Political Document." *Scriptura vol.116*, no.1. 2017, pp. 1-15.

Report of the Independent Working Group on the Future of the United Nations. *The United Nations in Its Second Half-Century.* Ford Foundation, 1995.

Rivers, Julian. "The New World Order?" *Cambridge Papers Towards a Biblical Mind vol.8*, no.4, 1999, pp. 1-4.

Rodriguez, Angel M. *Future Glory: The 8 Greatest End-time Prophecies in the Bible.* Review and Herald, 2002.

Rolland, Nadege. "China's Vision for a New World Order." *The National Bureau for Asian Research NBR Special Report*, no.83, 2020, 1-56.

Slaughter, Anne-Marie. "The Real New World Order." *The Council on Foreign Relations*, Sep./Oct. 1997, http://www.foreignaffirs.org.

Strand, Kenneth A. "Foundational Principles of Interpretation."

Symposium on Revelation-Book I. Edited by Frank B. Holbrook, DARCOM, vol. 3. Biblical Research Institute, 1992, pp. 3-34.

Thayer, Joseph Henry. *A Greek-English Lexicon of the New Testament. Being Grimm's Wilke's Clavis Novi Testamenti* (Trans. rev., and enl. ed.) IBT, 1998-2000.

Thirlwell, Mark P. "A New, New World Order? Challenges for International Economic Policy in the New Millennium." *Lowy Institute Perspectives*, March 2005, pp. 1-14.

Van Zyl, HC "Reading the New Testament from a Theological Perspective." *Acta Theologica vol.2*, 2008, pp. 133-145.

Yuan, Z. "Fighting Covid-19: Cooperation and the New World Order." *Tehran Times*, 3 Mar.   2020, pp. 1-3, https://www.tehrantimes.com/news/449524/Fighting -COVID-19-Cooperation-and-the-New-World-Order.

CHAPTER SIX- Marcelo E. C. Dias, PhD

"Building the peace of Christ in our divided and broken world: A Confession of Faith and a Call to Action, 2011." *The Lausanne Movement.* https://www.lausanne.org/content/ctc/ctcommitment#_ftn60 Accessed 12 October 2020.

"Disability and health." Fact Sheet. *World Health Organization,* 16 January 2018. https://www.who.int/news-room/fact-sheets/detail/disability-and-health Accessed 7 October 2020.

Ahmed, A. *IDA'AMUU (Medemer).* Los Angeles, CA: Tsehai Publishers, 2019.

Alvarenga, Darlan. "5,2 Milhões de Desempregados Procuram Trabalho há mais de 1 ano, Aponta IBGE." *G1 Economia,* https://g1.globo.com/economia/noticia/2019/05/16/52 -milhoes-de-desempregados-procuram-trabalho-ha-mais-de-1-ano-aponta-ibge.ghtml Accessed 7 October 2020.

Barakat, Bassel. "Divorce Rates Increase in Saudi Arabia Amid COVID-19." *Anadolu Agency,* 6 May 2020. https://www.aa.com.tr/en/middle-east/divorce-rates-increase-in-saudi-arabia-amid-covid-19/1866563#:~:text=Divorce%20rates%20in%20Saudi%20Arabia,the%20same%20period%20last%20year. Accessed 7 October 2020.

Bekele, Girma. *The In-Between People: A Reading of David Bosch through the Lens of Mission History and Contemporary Challenges in Ethiopia.* Eugene, OR: Wipf and Stock Publishers, 2011.

Bellizzi, Saverio, Nivoli, Alessandra, Lorettu, Liliana, Farina, Gabriele, Ramses, Merette, and Ronzoni, Anna R. "Violence Against Women in Italy During the COVID - 19 Pandemic." *Int J Gynecol Obstet,* vol.150, no.2, 2020, pp. 258-259.

Bond, Leticia. "SP: Violência contra Mulher Aumenta 44,9% Durante Pandemia." *Agência Brasil,* 20 April 2020. https://agenciabrasil.ebc.com.br/direitos-humanos/noticia/2020-04/sp-violencia-contra-mulher-aumenta-449-durante-pandemia Accessed 7 October 2020.

Carter, James E. and McLeod, Peter. "Isaiah." *The Teacher's Bible Commentary*, ed. H. Franklin Paschall & Herschel H. Hobbs. Nashville, TN: Broadman and Holman Publishers, 1972.

Chade, Jamil. "Pandemia Pode Levar 265 Milhões à Fome." *UOL Notícias,* 21 April 2020. https://noticias.uol.com.br/colunas/jamil-chade/2020/04/21/pandemia-pode-levar-265-milhoes-a-fome.htm Accessed 7 October 2020.

Evans, Robert A. and Parker, Thomas D. (eds). *Christian Theology: A Case Method Approach.* Eugene, OR: Wipf & Stock, 2001.

Gladstone, Rick. "First Famines of Coronavirus Era Are at World's Doorstep, U.N. Warns," 30 September 2020. *New York Times* https://www.nytimes.com/2020/09/05/world/africa/coronavirus-famine-warning-.html Accessed 7 October 2020.

Goldingay, John. *Isaiah for Everyone,* Old Testament for Everyone. Louisville, KY: Westminster John Knox Press, 2015.

Hodal, Kate. "One in 200 people is a slave. Why?" The Briefing. *The Guardian,* 25 February 2019. https://www.theguardian.com/news/2019/feb/25/modern-slavery-trafficking-persons-one-in-200 Accessed 7 October 2020.

Jeffery, Adam. "See Religions Around the World Adapt in the Age of Coronavirus." *CNBC,* 10 April 2020. https://cnb.cx/3j7Y4T5. Accessed 13 July 2020.

King Jr., Martin Luther. "Letter from a Birmingham Jail." African Studies Center. *University of Pennsylvania.* 16 April 1963. https://www.africa.upenn.edu/Articles_Gen/Letter_Birmingham.html Accessed 12 October 2020.

Krause, Gary. "Seeking the Shalom: Wholistic Adventist Urban Mission and Centers of Influence." *Journal of Adventist Mission Studies,* vol. 10, no. 2, 2014.

Livingston, J. Kevin. *A Missiology of the Road: Early Perspectives in David Bosch's Theology of Mission and Evangelism.* Cambridge: James Clark, 2013.

Love, Rick. "The Missing Peace of Evangelical Missiology: Peacemaking and Respectful Witness." Resources. *Rick Love,* 9-11 June 2008, https://www.ricklove.net/wp-content/uploads/2010/04/Peacemaking-and-Evangelism.pdf Accessed 7 October 2020.

Newbigin, Lesslie. *The Household of God: lectures on the nature of the church.* Eugene, OR: Wipf and Stock Publishers, 2008.

Nichol, Francis D. org. The Seventh-day Adventist Bible Commentary, vol. 4. Hagerstown, MD: Review and Herald Publishing Association, 1977.

Ott, C., et al. *Encountering Theology of Mission: Biblical Foundations, Historical Developments, and Contemporary Issues.* Grand Rapids, MI: Baker Publishing Group, 2010.

Pace, Aimee. "SA Divorce Rate Increased by 20% During

Lockdown." *CapeTownETC,* 2 July 2020. https://www.capetownetc.com/news/sa-divorce-rate-increased-by-20-during-lockdown/ Accessed 7 October 2020.

Polhill, John B. <u>Acts</u>, vol. 26, The New American Commentary. Nashville, TN: Broadman & Holman Publishers, 1992.

Prasso, Sheridan. "China's Divorce Spike Is a Warning to Rest of Locked-Down World." *Bloomberg BusinessWeek,* 31 March 2020. https://www.bloomberg.com/news/articles/2020-03-31/divorces-spike-in-china-after-coronavirus-quarantines Accessed 7 October 2020.

"What Lessons do Americans See for Humanity in the Pandemic?" Religion & Public Life. *Pew Research Center.* 8 October 2020 https://www.pewforum.org/essay/ what-lessons-do-americans-see-for-humanity-in-the-pandemic/ Accessed 12 October 2020.

Rosner, Elizabeth, "US divorce rates skyrocket amid COVID-19 pandemic." *NY Post,* 1 September 2020. https://nypost.com/2020/09/01/divorce-rates-skyrocket-in-u-s-amid-covid-19/ Accessed 12 October 2020.

Shapiro, Adam R. "Are Pandemic Protests the Newest Form of Science-Religion Conflict?" Religion & Politics. *Washington University Saint Louis,* 14 July 2020. https://religionandpolitics.org/2020/07/14/are-pandemic-protests-the-newest-form-of-science-religion-conflict/ Accessed 12 October 2020.

Smith, Gary V. *Isaiah 1–39,* ed. E. Ray Clendenen, The New American Commentary. Nashville, TN: B&H Publishing Group, 2007.

Stassen, Glen. *Just Peacemaking: Transforming Initiatives for Justice and Peace.* Louisville, KY: Westminster/John Knox Press, 1991.

Sunquist, Scott W. "A Historian's Hunches: Eight Future Trends in Mission, #3." *Fuller Blog on Patheos,* 1 Feb 2016.

https://www.patheos.com/blogs/fuller/2016/02/a-historians-hunches-eight-future-trends-in-mission-part-4/ Accessed 12 October 2020.

Vieira, André and Scaramuzzo, Monica. "XP vê desemprego atingir 40 milhões no Brasil sem 'Plano Marshall de verdade.'" Estadão Conteúdo. *UOL Economia,* 22 March 2020. https://economia.uol.com.br/noticias/estadao-conteudo/2020/03/22/xp-ve-desemprego-atingir-40-milhoes-no-brasil-sem-plano-marshall-de-verdade.htm Accessed 7. October 2020.

White, Ellen G. *A Call to Stand Apart.* Hagerstown, MD: Review and Herald Publishing Association, 2002.

White, Ellen G. *The Great Controversy.* Mountain View, CA: Pacific Press Publishing Association, 1911.

White, Ellen G. *Last Day Events.* Boise: ID: Pacific Press Publishing Association, 1992.

White, Ellen G. *Review and Herald.* 15 October 1908.

Widjaja, Paulus S. "Peace," in *Dictionary of Mission Theology*, ed. John Corrie. Downers Grove, IL: InterVarsity Press, 2007

Yee, Vivian. "In a Pandemic, Religion Can Be a Balm and a Risk." *New York Times,* 22 March 2020. https://www.nytimes.com/2020/03/22/world/middleeast/coronavirus-religion.html Accessed 12 October 2020.

CHAPTER SEVEN- Olayemi Adeoye, MBBS, PhD, MPH

Ainsworth, B. E. and F. Li. "Physical Activity During the Coronavirus Disease-2019 Global Pandemic." *J Sport Health Sci*, vol. 9, no. 4, 2020, pp. 291-292, doi: 10.1016/j.jshs.2020.06.004.

Badash, I. et al. "Redefining Health: The Evolution of Health Ideas from Antiquity to the Era of Value-Based Care." *Cureus*, vol. 9, no. 2, 2017, p. e1018, doi:10.7759/cureus.1018.

Boni, M. F. "Vaccination and Antigenic Drift in Influenza."
     Vaccine, vol. 26 Suppl 3, 2008, pp. C8-14, doi:
     10.1016/j.vaccine.2008.04.011.

Bourdeau, P. "The Man-Nature Relationship and Environmental
     Ethics." *J Environ Radioact*, vol. 72, no. 1-2, 2004, pp. 9-15,
     doi:10.1016/S0265-931X(03)00180-2.

Bramanti, B. et al. "The Third Plague Pandemic in Europe." *Proc
     Biol Sci*, vol. 286, no. 1901, 2019, p. 20182429,
     doi:10.1098/rspb.2018.2429.

Cock, K. M. and H. A. Weiss. "The Global Epidemiology of
     Hiv/Aids." *Trop Med Int Health*, vol. 5, no. 7, 2000, pp. A3-
     9, doi:10.1046/j.1365-3156.2000.00590. x.

Cohn, S. K. "Pandemics: Waves of Disease, Waves of Hate from
     the Plague of Athens to A.I.D.S." *Hist J*, vol. 85, no. 230,
     2012, pp. 535-555, doi:10.1111/j.1468-2281.2012.00603.
     x.

Coronaviridae Study Group of the International Committee on
     Taxonomy of, Viruses. "The Species Severe Acute
     Respiratory Syndrome-Related Coronavirus: Classifying
     2019-Ncov and Naming It Sars-Cov-2." *Nat Microbiol*, vol.
     5, no. 4, 2020, pp. 536-544, doi:10.1038/s41564-020-
     0695-z.

Demain, A. L. and S. Sanchez. "Microbial Drug Discovery: 80
     Years of Progress." *J Antibiot (Tokyo)*, vol. 62, no. 1, 2009,
     pp. 5-16, doi:10.1038/ja.2008.16.

DeWitte, S. N. "Mortality Risk and Survival in the Aftermath of
     the Medieval Black Death." *PLoS One*, vol. 9, no. 5, 2014,
     p. e96513, doi: 10.1371/journal.pone.0096513.

Dourmashkin, R. R. "What Caused the 1918-30 Epidemic of
     Encephalitis Lethargica?" *J R Soc Med*, vol. 90, no. 9, 1997,
     pp. 515-520, doi:10.1177/014107689709000916.

Faria, N. R. et al. "Hiv Epidemiology. The Early Spread and
     Epidemic Ignition of Hiv-1 in Human Populations."
     Science, vol. 346, no. 6205, 2014, pp. 56-61,

doi:10.1126/science.1256739.

Foley, P. B. "Encephalitis Lethargica and Influenza. I. The Role of the Influenza Virus in the Influenza Pandemic of 1918/1919." *J Neural Transm (Vienna)*, vol. 116, no. 2, 2009, pp. 143-150, doi:10.1007/s00702-008-0161-1.

Gayle, H. D. and G. L. Hill. "Global Impact of Human Immunodeficiency Virus and Aids." *Clin Microbiol Rev*, vol. 14, no. 2, 2001, pp. 327-335, doi:10.1128/CMR.14.2.327-335.2001.

Ghanemi, A. et al. "Will an Obesity Pandemic Replace the Coronavirus Disease-2019 (Covid-19) Pandemic?" *Med Hypotheses*, vol. 144, 2020, p. 110042, doi: 10.1016/j.mehy.2020.110042.

Greene, W. C. "A History of Aids: Looking Back to See Ahead." *Eur J Immunol*, vol. 37 Suppl 1, 2007, pp. S94-102, doi:10.1002/eji.200737441.

Haas, C. "[the Antonine Plague]." *Bull Acad Natl Med*, vol. 190, no. 4-5, 2006, pp. 1093-1098, https://www.ncbi.nlm.nih.gov/pubmed/17195627.

Henry, J. et al. "Parkinsonism and Neurological Manifestations of Influenza Throughout the 20th and 21st Centuries." *Parkinsonism Relat Disord*, vol. 16, no. 9, 2010, pp. 566-571, doi: 10.1016/j.parkreldis.2010.06.012.

Hoffman, L. A. and J. A. Vilensky. "Encephalitis Lethargica: 100 Years after the Epidemic." *Brain*, vol. 140, no. 8, 2017, pp. 2246-2251, doi:10.1093/brain/awx177.

Hoffman, W. W. "The Patient as Covid: The Destructive Bias of Politicized Science - Flashpoints, Obligations and the Burden of Coming Together." *S D Med*, vol. 73, no. 8, 2020, pp. 372-374, https://www.ncbi.nlm.nih.gov/pubmed/32809297.

Javed, B. et al. "Impact of Sars-Cov-2 (Coronavirus) Pandemic on Public Mental Health." *Front Public Health*, vol. 8, 2020, p. 292, doi:10.3389/fpubh.2020.00292.

Kamel Boulos, M. N. and E. M. Geraghty. "Geographical Tracking and Mapping of Coronavirus Disease Covid-19/Severe Acute Respiratory Syndrome Coronavirus 2 (Sars-Cov-2) Epidemic and Associated Events around the World: How 21st Century Gis Technologies Are Supporting the Global Fight against Outbreaks and Epidemics." *Int J Health Geogr*, vol. 19, no. 1, 2020, p. 8, doi:10.1186/s12942-020-00202-8.

Kim, H. et al. "Influenza Virus: Dealing with a Drifting and Shifting Pathogen." *Viral Immunol*, vol. 31, no. 2, 2018, pp. 174-183, doi:10.1089/vim.2017.0141.

Kuszewski, K. and L. Brydak. "The Epidemiology and History of Influenza." *Biomed Pharmacother*, vol. 54, no. 4, 2000, pp. 188-195, doi:10.1016/S0753-3322(00)89025-3.

Ligon, B. L. "Plague: A Review of Its History and Potential as a Biological Weapon." *Semin Pediatr Infect Dis*, vol. 17, no. 3, 2006, pp. 161-170, doi: 10.1053/j.spid.2006.07.002.

Limaye, R. J. et al. "Building Trust While Influencing Online Covid-19 Content in the Social Media World." *Lancet Digit Health*, vol. 2, no. 6, 2020, pp. e277-e278, doi:10.1016/S2589-7500(20)30084-4.

Littman, R. J. "The Plague of Athens: Epidemiology and Paleopathology." *Mt Sinai J Med*, vol. 76, no. 5, 2009, pp. 456-467, doi:10.1002/msj.20137.

Littman, R. J. and M. L. Littman. "Galen and the Antonine Plague." *Am J Philol*, vol. 94, 1973, pp. 243-255, https://www.ncbi.nlm.nih.gov/pubmed/11616517.

Madhav, N. et al. "Pandemics: Risks, Impacts, and Mitigation." *Disease Control Priorities: Improving Health and Reducing Poverty*, edited by rd et al., 2017, https://www.ncbi.nlm.nih.gov/pubmed/30212163.

Mamun, M. A. and M. D. Griffiths. "First Covid-19 Suicide Case in Bangladesh Due to Fear of Covid-19 and Xenophobia: Possible Suicide Prevention Strategies." *Asian J Psychiatr*, vol. 51, 2020, p. 102073, doi: 10.1016/j.ajp.2020.102073.

Marc, L. G. et al. "Hiv among Haitian-Born Persons in the United States, 1985-2007." *Aids*, vol. 24, no. 13, 2010, pp. 2089-2097, doi: 10.1097/QAD.0b013e32833bedff.

Martin, P. M. and E. Martin-Granel. "2,500-Year Evolution of the Term Epidemic." *Emerg Infect Dis*, vol. 12, no. 6, 2006, pp. 976-980, doi:10.3201/eid1206.051263.

McFarlane, R. A. et al. "Land-Use Change and Emerging Infectious Disease on an Island Continent." *Int J Environ Res Public Health*, vol. 10, no. 7, 2013, pp. 2699-2719, doi:10.3390/ijerph10072699.

Meltzer, M. I. et al. "The Economic Impact of Pandemic Influenza in the United States: Priorities for Intervention." *Emerg Infect Dis*, vol. 5, no. 5, 1999, pp. 659-671, doi:10.3201/eid0505.990507.

Morowitz, M. J. et al. "Contributions of Intestinal Bacteria to Nutrition and Metabolism in the Critically Ill." *Surg Clin North Am*, vol. 91, no. 4, 2011, pp. 771-785, viii, doi: 10.1016/j.suc.2011.05.001.

Mouritz, A. A. St M. *The Flu: A Brief History of Influenza in U.S. America, Europe, Hawaii.* Advertiser Publishing Co., 1921.

Nelkin, D. and S. L. Gilman. "Placing Blame for Devastating Disease." *Soc Res (New York)*, vol. 55, no. 3, 1988, pp. 361-378, https://www.ncbi.nlm.nih.gov/pubmed/11650267.

Pike, B. L. et al. "The Origin and Prevention of Pandemics." *Clin Infect Dis*, vol. 50, no. 12, 2010, pp. 1636-1640, doi:10.1086/652860.

Potter, C. W. "A History of Influenza." *J Appl Microbiol*, vol. 91, no. 4, 2001, pp. 572-579, doi:10.1046/j.1365-2672.2001.01492. x.

Riedel, S. "Edward Jenner and the History of Smallpox and Vaccination." *Proc (Bayl Univ Med Cent)*, vol. 18, no. 1, 2005, pp. 21-25, doi:10.1080/08998280.2005.11928028.

--------"Plague: From Natural Disease to Bioterrorism." *Proc (Bayl*

Univ Med Cent), vol. 18, no. 2, 2005, pp. 116-124, doi:10.1080/08998280.2005.11928049.

Riva, M. A. et al. "Pandemic Fear and Literature: Observations from Jack London's the Scarlet Plague." *Emerg Infect Dis*, vol. 20, no. 10, 2014, pp. 1753-1757, doi:10.3201/eid2010.130278.

Ross, A. G. et al. "Planning for the Next Global Pandemic." *Int J Infect Dis*, vol. 38, 2015, pp. 89-94, doi: 10.1016/j.ijid.2015.07.016.

Saunders-Hastings, P. R. and D. Krewski. "Reviewing the History of Pandemic Influenza: Understanding Patterns of Emergence and Transmission." *Pathogens*, vol. 5, no. 4, 2016, doi:10.3390/pathogens5040066.

Sharp, P. M. and B. H. Hahn. "Origins of Hiv and the Aids Pandemic." *Cold Spring Harb Perspect Med*, vol. 1, no. 1, 2011, p. a006841, doi:10.1101/cshperspect. a006841.

Shope, R. "Global Climate Change and Infectious Diseases." *Environ Health Perspect*, vol. 96, 1991, pp. 171-174, doi:10.1289/ehp.9196171.

Spyrou, M. A. et al. "Ancient Pathogen Genomics as An emerging Tool for Infectious Disease research." *Nat Rev Genet*, vol. 20, no. 6, 2019, pp. 323-340, doi:10.1038/s41576-019-0119-1.

Szucs, T. D. "Economic and Social Impact of Epidemic and Pandemic Influenza." *Vaccine*, vol. 24, no. 44-46, 2006, pp. 6776-6778, doi: 10.1016/j.vaccine.2006.06.072.

Taubenberger, J. K. and J. C. Kash. "Influenza Virus Evolution, Host Adaptation, and Pandemic Formation." *Cell Host Microbe*, vol. 7, no. 6, 2010, pp. 440-451, doi: 10.1016/j.chom.2010.05.009.

Thucydides. "The Plague in Athens. Thucydides. The History of the Peloponnesian War. Translated by Thomas Hobbes." *N C Med J*, vol. 41, no. 4, 1980, pp. 230-232, https://www.ncbi.nlm.nih.gov/pubmed/6991956.

Tognotti, E. "Lessons from the History of Quarantine, from Plague to Influenza A." *Emerg Infect Dis*, vol. 19, no. 2, 2013, pp. 254-259, doi:10.3201/eid1902.120312.

Tountas, Y. "The Historical Origins of the Basic Concepts of Health Promotion and Education: The Role of Ancient Greek Philosophy and Medicine." *Health Promot Int*, vol. 24, no. 2, 2009, pp. 185-192, doi:10.1093/heapro/dap006.

Tsiompanou, E. and S. G. Marketos. "Hippocrates: Timeless Still." *J R Soc Med*, vol. 106, no. 7, 2013, pp. 288-292, doi:10.1177/0141076813492945.

Wiederhold, B. K. "Using Social Media to Our Advantage: Alleviating Anxiety During a Pandemic." *Cyberpsychol Behav Soc Netw*, vol. 23, no. 4, 2020, pp. 197-198, doi: 10.1089/cyber.2020.29180.bkw.

Williams, K. C. and T. H. Burdo. "Hiv and Siv Infection: The Role of Cellular Restriction and Immune Responses in Viral Replication and Pathogenesis." *APMIS*, vol. 117, no. 5-6, 2009, pp. 400-412, doi:10.1111/j.1600-0463.2009.02450. x.

Wu, H. J. and E. Wu. "The Role of Gut Microbiota in Immune Homeostasis and Autoimmunity." *Gut Microbes*, vol. 3, no. 1, 2012, pp. 4-14, doi:10.4161/gmic.19320.

Xiang, M. et al. "Impact of Covid-19 Pandemic on Children and Adolescents' Lifestyle Behavior Larger Than Expected." *Prog Cardiovasc Dis*, 2020, doi: 10.1016/j.pcad.2020.04.013.

Zhu, N. et al. "A Novel Coronavirus from Patients with Pneumonia in China, 2019." *N Engl J Med*, vol. 382, no. 8, 2020, pp. 727-733, doi:10.1056/NEJMoa2001017.

CHAPTER EIGHT -Robert Osei-Bonsu, PhD, M Ed. & Samson D. Dakio, M.A

Balz, Horst. "synteleia." *Exegetical Dictionary of the New Testament*. Edited by Horst Balz and Gerhard Schneider. Eerdmans, 1993. 3: 309-312.

Bauer, G. "*tiktō*." *The New International Dictionary of the New Testament.* Edited by Colin Brown. Zondervan, 1986. 1:186-187.

Bertram, Georg. "*ōdin*." *Theological Dictionary of the New Testament.* Edited by Gerhard Friedrich. Translated by Geoffrey W. Bromiley. Eerdmans, 1974. 9: 667-674.

Bloomberg, Craig L. *Matthew. The New American Commentary.* Vol. 22. Broadman Press, 1992.

Brecha, Bob. "Why the Pope's Encyclical Laudato Si' Is Important for Non-Catholics." September 21, 2015. www.wyso.org/commentary/2015-09-21/why-the-popes-encyclical-laudato-si-is-important-for-non-catholics. Accessed August 10, 2020.

Brown, Jeannine K. *Matthew: Teach the Text Commentaries Series.* Baker Books, 2015.

Ceballos, Gerardo. IV. "Pope Francis' Encyclical Letter Laudato Si', Global Environmental Risks, and the Future of Humanity." *The Quarterly Review of Biology*, September 2016, (91:3): 285-295.

Change your Life, Biblically, vol. II. Jesus Christ Prison Ministry, 1997 -2001.
"Christianity and Peace." http://unitingforpeace.com/wp-content/uploads/2019/04/Christianity_and_Peace.pdf. 2011. Accessed July 28, 2020.

Coenen, L. "*archē*." *The New International Dictionary of New Testament Theology.* Edited by Colin Brown. Zondervan, 1986. 1: 164-165.

Delling, G. "*archē*." *Theological Dictionary of the New Testament: Abridged in One Volume.* Edited by Gerhard Kittel and Gerhard Friedrich. Translated by Geoffrey W. Bromiley Eerdmans, 1985. 81-83.

__________. "*synteleia*." *Theological Dictionary of the New Testament.* Edited by Gerhard Kittel and Gerhard Friedrich. Translated by Geoffrey W. Bromiley Eerdmans, 1985. 8: 64-66.

__________. *"telos." Theological Dictionary of the New Testament.* Edited by Gerhard Friedrich. Translated by Geoffrey W. Bromiley. Eerdmans, 1972. 8: 49-57.

Ferrell, Vance. *A Biblical Defense: Defending Our Historic Beliefs about the Sanctuary in Daniel and Hebrews.* Harvestime Books, 2003.

"General Secretariat United States Conferences of Catholic Bishops." *Laudato Si': On Care for Our Common Home.* www.usccb.org/offices/general-secretariat/laudato-si-care-our-common-home. Accessed August 10, 2020.

Hick, John. "Ecumenism since the start of the 20th century." www.britannica.com/topic/Christianity/Christianity-and-world-religions. Accessed August 6, 2020.

"History and Structure: The Role of the WCC in International Affairs." Revised edition (August 1999). www.wcc-coe.org/wcc/what/international/ia-booklet.html. Accessed August 6, 2020.

Kennedy, John F. *Remarks of Senator John F. Kennedy at the Democratic city Committee Annual Pre-Election Dinner in Easton, Pennsylvania, October 30, 1957.* www.jfklibrary.org/archives/other-resources/john-f-kennedy-speeches/easton-pa-19571030. Accessed August 10, 2020.

Kumar, Satish. *Slow Sunday: The Simple Solution to Global Warming,* September 2009. www.theguardian.com/environment/cif-green/2009/sep/17/low-carbon-sunday. Accessed August 10, 2020.

Küng, Hans. "Religion, Violence, and Holy Wars." *International Review of the Red Cross,* (87: 858), 2005. 253-268.

Maxwell, C. Mervyn. *God Cares, vol 2: The Message of Revelation for You and Your Family.* Vol. 1. Oshawa, Ontario: Pacific Press, 1985.

"Ministerial Association General Conference of Seventh-day Adventists." *Seventh-day Adventist Minister's Handbook.* Ministerial Association General Conference of Seventh-day Adventists. 2009.

Morgan, Barbara J, ed. *The Bible through the Ages*. Reader's Digest, 1996.

Mounce, Robert H. *Matthew: Understanding the Bible Commentary Series*. Ada, MI: Baker Publishing Group, 1990.

Müller, D. "*archē*." *The New International Dictionary of New Testament Theology*. Edited by Colin Brown. Zondervan, 1986. 1: 164.

Nichol, Francis, ed. *The Seventh-day Adventist Bible Commentary*. Review and Herald,1955, 1977. 4:775; 5: 495-498.

"Peace Agreement Ceremony, the Highlight of the World Alliance of Religions' Peace Summit." *The Christian Journal: The Leading Christian Newspaper*, September 2014. http://tcjonline.org/peace-agreement-ceremony-the-highlight-of-the-world-alliance-of-religions-peace-summit/. Accessed August 11, 2020.

Pullella, Philip. *Pope urges politicians to take 'drastic measures' on climate change*. September 1, 2019. www.reuters.com/article/us-environment-pope/pope-urges-politicians-to-take-drastic-measures-on-climate-change-idUSKCN1VM161. Accessed August 10, 2020.

Stefanovic, Zdravko. *Daniel: Wisdom to the Wise: Commentary on the book of Daniel*. Pacific Press, 2007

Strong, James. *Strong's Exhaustive Concordance of the Bible: Updated and Expanded Edition*. Hendrickson Publishers, 2007. S.v. "*ōdin*."

Weiss, K. "*archē*." *Exegetical Dictionary of the New Testament*. Edited by Horst Balz and Gerhard Schneider. Eerdmans, 1990. 1:161-163.

Winks, Robin W. et al. *A History of Civilization*, 8th ed., *Prehistory to 1715*, vol. 1. Prentice-Hall, 1992.

Zodhiates, Spiros. "*ōdin*." *The Complete Word Study Dictionary of the New Testament*. AMG Publishers, 1992. 1497-1498.

CHAPTER NINE- Nsengumuremyi Ananie, M.A, MBA

Alder, Cora & Schaublin. "US Evangelicals: From Prophecy to Policy". *Policy Perspective*, Vol.8/11, September 2020, https://css.ethz.ch/content/dam/ethz/special-interest/gess/cis/center-for-securities-studies/pdfs/PP8-11_2020-EN.pdf.

Bwire J (2020). Museveni orders closure of schools, suspends religious gatherings over coronavirus. Daily Monitor. https://www.monitor.co.ug/News/National/Museveni-closes-schools-religiousgatherings-coronavirus/688334-5495888-srauuwz/index.html.

Dusengimana, Theogene. Interview. Conducted by Nsengumuremyi Ananie, 21st September 2020

Gatsinzi, Patrick. Interview. Conducted by Nsengumuremyi Ananie, 21st September 2020.

Hagee, J. "Coronavirus: Dress Rehearsal for the new world order". YouTube video, 2020, https://www.youtube.com/watch?v=H_vNWmqWmZc

Hasel, Frank M. "No war has ever done this to us". In *Reflections* 70, April 2020.Biblical Research Institute.

IMF F&D. "How will the world be different after Covid-19? Six Prominent thinkers reflect on how the pandemic has changed the world". *Finance and Development.* June 2020.

Isiko, A.P. "Religious construction of disease: An exploratory appraisal of religious responses to the COVID-19 pandemic in Uganda". *Journal of African Studies and Development,* Vol12 (3), July-September 2020, DOI: 10.5897/JASD2020.0573

Jannace, Tiffany. A New World Order: The Rule of Law, or the Law of Rulers? *Fordham International Law Journal*, 42(5), 2019, https://ir.lawnet.fordham.edu/ilj.

Kang'entu, Mark. Interview. Conducted by Nsengumuremyi Ananie, 21st September 2020.

Ministerial Association /General Conference of the Seventh-day Adventist. *Seventh-day Adventists believe*. Ministerial Association, Silver Spring, 2005.

Muthuri, Wilson. Interview. Conducted by Nsengumuremyi Ananie, 21st September 2020.

Motaharnia, Salehi. The New World Order in the Twenty-First Century. *Journal of History Culture and Art Research, 6(1), 2017,* doi: http://dx.doi.org/10.7596/taksad.v6i1.775.

New World Order (conspiracy theory).https://en.wikipedia.org/wiki/New_World_Order_(conspiracy_theory). Accessed October 2020.

New World Order (Politics). https://en.wikipedia.org/wiki/New_world_order_(politics). Accessed October 2020.

Niyigena, Timothee. Interview. Conducted by Nsengumuremyi Ananie, 21st September 2020.

Ntakirutimana, Emmanuel. Interview. Conducted by Nsengumuremyi Ananie, 21st September 2020.

Parker Martin. "Secret Societies: Intimations of Organization. Organization Studies". *SAGE Journals*, August 2015, DOI: 10.1177/0170840615593593.

Ruzindana, Dieudonne. Interview. Conducted by Nsengumuremyi Ananie, 21st September 2020

White, Ellen G. *Manuscript Releases, vol.8*. Trustees of Ellen G. White Publications, 1978.

White, Ellen G. *Evangelism*. Review and Herald Pushing Association, 1946.

White, Ellen G. *Last day events*. Pacific Press Publishing Association, 1992.

White, Ellen G. *The Great Controversy*. Pacific Press Publishing Association, 1911.

White, Ellen G. *Selected message*. Trustees of Ellen G. White Publications, 1980.

White, Ellen G. Testimonies for the Church, Vol.1. Pacific Press Publishing Association, 1855.

White, Ellen G. Testimonies for the Church, Vol.8. Pacific Press
Publishing Association, 1904.
White, Ellen G. The Desire of Ages. Pacific Press Publishing
Association, 1898.
White, Ellen G. *Early Writings*. Review and Herald Pushing
Association, 1945.
Wieland, Robert J. *Revelation of the things to come*. Stanborough Press
Ltd, 2014

CHAPTER TEN- Nehemiah M. Nyaundi, PhD

*A Dictionary of the Bible Dealing with Its Language, Literature, And
Contexts Including The*
Biblical Theology, vol. III. Edited by James Hastings. New York:
Charles Scriber's Sons.
Adeyemi, Babatunde. 'A Historical Review of the Influence of
Perestroika and Glasnost on Africa's Socio-Political and Economic
Development' in Akporobaro, F.B.O. ed. *Studies in The
African Human Condition and Development Issues in the Post
-Colonial Era:* Ilisan Remo: School of Education and
Humanities, Babcock University, 2015:119-136.
Berle, Mulugeta G. 'The Norms and Structures for African Peace
Efforts: The Africa and
Security Architecture', *International Peacekeeping*, 2017
.24:4, 661-685, DOI.1080/13533312.2017.1346475
Chambaliss, Barbe. *Women Peace-makers: What We Can Learn from
Them*. Paonia, Colorado:
Red Truck Enterprises, 2020.
Chege, Sam. *Life is God's Best Gift: Wisdom from the Ancestors on Finding
Peace and Joy in the World Today,* 2017
Constitution of Kenya, In Chapter Four Bill of Rights, Article
32, 2010.
Di Marzio, Raffaela. 'Freeedom of Religion and its Role in
the Promotion of Peace.' (Centre for udies on Freedom of
Religion, Belief and Conscience, Italy)

REFERENCES

Eregare, Emmanuel O. 'A Historical Analysis of Church Politics and Politicking in the 21st Century' in Emmanuel Orihentare Eregare, ed. *A Survey of Church Politics in the Twenty- Century: Re-Examining Religion-State Governance, Leadership and Laities.* Babcock University Press, 2018.

From Violence to Peace: A Challenge for African Christianity, edited by Mary N. Getui and Peter Kanyandago. Nairobi: Acton Publishers, 1999.

Katz, Yuval. Interacting for Peace: Rethinking Peace Through Interactive Digital Platforms. Social Media + Society April-June 2020: I-II

Kenya Bureau of Statistics, Population Census 2019.

Malcom X and Alex Haley. *The Autobiography of Malcom X: As Told to Alex Haley.* Ballantine Books (Paperback edition), 1992.

Manchala, Deenabandhu, ed., *Nurturing Peace: Theological Reflections on Overcoming Violence.* Geneva: WCC Publications, 2005.

McIntosh, Alastair. 'Peace in the Tiger's Mouth' in Fernando Enns, Scott Holland and Ann K. Riggs eds., *Seeking Cultures of Peace: A Peace Church Conversation.* Telford, Pennsylvania, 2004.

Mugambi, Jesse. 'The Christian Ideal of Peace and Political Reality in Africa' in Mary N. Getui and Peter Kanyandago, eds. *From Violence to Peace: A Challenge for African Christianity*: Nairobi: Acton Publishers, 1999:70-96.

Newman, Barclay M. and Eugene A. Nida. *A Translator's Handbook on The Gospel of John.* London: United Bible Societies, 1980.

Nyaundi, Nehemiah M. *Rethinking God. Exploring the Interface Between Religion and Social Reality,* Shapf Chancery Publishers, 2015.

Nyaundi, Nehemiah M. 'Violence and Relative Deprivation in Kenya' in Mary N. Getui and Peter Kanyandago, eds. *From Violence to Peace: A Challenge for African Christianity*: Nairobi: Acton Publishers, 1999:41-56.

Omeje, Kenneth. *Peace-Building in Contemporary Africa*. (Routledge
     Studies in African Development), 2019

Oxford Advanced Learner's Dictionary of Current English. A.S Hornby,
     ed. Oxford University
     Press, 2001.

Sandole, Denis J.D. Peace and Security in the Postmodern World.
     London: Routledge Studies in
     Peace and Conflict Resolution, 2007.

The Analytical Greek Lexicon Revised (1978 Edition). Grand Rapids
     Michigan: Zondervan
     Publishing House, 1978.

The NIV Exhaustive Concordance. Edward W. Goodrick and John R.
     Kohlenberger III, eds.
     Grand Rapids, Michigan: Zondervan Publishing House,
     1990,

The New York Times (Online Edition).

Tutu, Bishop Desmond. *No Future Without Forgiveness*, (Paperback),
     2000. Bishop Tutu is a
     Nobel Peace Prize laureate for 1984.

UN Universal Declaration of Human Rights, 1948.
          van Lersel, F. *Humanitarian Intervention and the Pursuit for
          Justice. A Pax Christi Contribution
          to a Contemporary Debate*. Peeters Publishers, 1995.
          Wengst, Claus. *Pax Romana and the Peace of Jesus Christ*.
          Fortress Press, 1987.

Online Sources
1. Israel, United Arab Emirates and Bahrain peace deal:
   https://nytimes.com/2020/09/15/us/politics/trump-
   israel
2. Malcom X Speech (Prospects for freedom, 1965)
   www.malcomx.com>quotes
3. Egypt – Ethiopia Nile water conflict
4. John Lennon: Give Peace a Chance Song.
   alphahistory.com>Vietnam war>john-Lennon-give-peace.

CHAPTER ELEVEN- Emmanuel Orihentare Eregare, PhD.

"Amnesty International", *Freedom of Expression*. Retrieved from https://www.amnesty.org/en/what-we-do/freedom-of-expression/ on the 9th of March, 2021.

A Global Government is Waiting in the Wings. Accessed from https://nymag.com/news/features/conspiracy-theories/new-world-order/ on Nov 15, 2013.

Barry Fell, *America B. C.* New York: Pocket Books, 1976

Christopher Columbus. Accessed on 19th May, 2021 on

Cusack, M.F. *Converted Nun of Kenmare, 'The Black Pope'*. London: Marshall, Rusell & Co.,1896.

Encyclical letter, in the Great Encyclical Letters of Pope Leo X111, (June 20, 1894).

Epperson, A. R. *The New World Order*. USA: Amazon,2016.

Eregare, E.O. "Live and Let Live Mind-set: A Modernistic and Post-modernistic Approach to Ecumenism". *Asia-Africa Journal of Mission and Ministry*, Vol. 21, 2020, pp. 114-126.

Eregare, E.O. *An African Christian Church History: Seventh-day Adventist Cosmology in Edo/Delta States: 148-2021 & Ecumenical initiatives*. Lagos: Christ Coming Books, 2013.

Eregare, E.O. Ekpendu, I.C. & Adesina. "Ecumenism and the Church in the Post-Modern Era: Historical, Biblio-Theological and Missiological Appraisal". *Asia-Africa Journal of Mission and Ministry*, Vol.15, pp.51-69, Feb. 2016.

Faragher, J.H. Out of Many: A History of American People, New York, 2000.

Ferguson, E. *Church History (Vol.1): From Christ to the Pre-Reformation*. Michigan. Zondervan, 2015.

Finley, M.A. *The Next Superpower: Ancient Prophecies, Global Events, and Your Future*. Hagerstown, Md.: Review and Herald Publishing Association, 2005, chapter 13

Griffith, S.H. *The Church in the Shadow of the Mosque: Christians and Muslims in the World of Islam*. Princeton University Press, p.14.

Hector, M. *The Jesuits on History. Springfield.* Missouri: Ozark Book Publisher, 1900.

Hitchcock, M. *After the Empire: Bible Prophecy in Light of the Fall of the Soviet Union.* Wheaton, IL: Tyndale House Publishers, 1994.

Ice, T. D. "*Is America in Bible Prophecy?*". *Article Archives.* 69. Retrieved from https://digitalcommons.liberty.edu/pretrib_arch/69 on the 28 February, 2021.

John Cabot and the first English Expedition to America. Accessed from www.historic.uk.com>historyUK

Kamran, M. *9/11 and the New World Order.* Lahore: University of Punjab, 2014.

Keely, B.L. "Conspiracy Theory". *The Journal of Philosophy*, Vol. 96, No 3, March, 1999, pp.109126.

Knight, G.R. *Turn Your Eyes upon Jesus.* Hagerstown: Review and Herald Publishing Association, 2013.

Lumen, G. Report. https//www.vatican.va/archive/hist_councils/ii_vatican_council/documents/vatii_const19641121_lumen-gentium_en.html, 2014.

McBirnie, S. *Antichrist.* Dallas :P Acclaimed Books, 1978.

Motaharnia, M., & Salehi, E. (2017). "The New World Order in the Twenty-First Century". *Journal of History Culture and Art Research*, 6(1), 852-862.

Nash, G.B. et al. *The American People: Creating a Nation and a Society*, USA: Harper Collins, 1996.

New World Order (Politics). Accessed fromhttps://en.wikipedia.org/wiki/New_world_order_(politics) on the 2nd May, 2021.

Our Lady of Fatimah. https//www.washingtonpost.com/news/retropolis/wp/2017/10/13/our-lady-of Fatima-the-v, 2021.

Reformation. Retrieved fromhttps://www.britannica.com/event/ on 21st of March, 2021.

Riplinger, G.A. *New Age Bible Versions*. USA. Virginia: AV Publication Cooperation, n.d

Robbins, J, W.' *Ecclessiastical Megalomania'-The Economic and Political Thought of the Roman Catholic Church*. USA: The Trinity Foundation, 2016.

Scruggs, T.M. *The World of Music*, Vol. 47, No. 1, Musical Reverberation from the Encounter of Local and Global Belief Systems (2005), pp. 91-123 (33 pages)

Sherwood, H. *Catholic and Protestant Leaders Unite to mark start of Reconciliation.* Retrieved fromhttps://www.theguardian.com/world/2017/oct/31/catholic-and-protestant-leaders-unite-mark-start-reformation-archbishop-canterbury-service on the 5th of April, 2017.

Smith, U. *The United States in the Light of Prophecy*. Retrieved from http://www.gutenberg.org/files/12364/12364-h/12364-h.htm, 1874, accesses on the 28th February, 2021.

Stefanovic, R. *The Book of Revelation: Guidelines for responsible and meaningful preaching.* Retrieved from www.ministrymagazine.org/archive/2017/07/09/ on the 12th March, 2021.

Sumner, C. "*Prophetic Voices about America.*" published in the Atlantic Monthly of September, 1807.

Sunstein, C.R. & Vermeule, A. "Conspiracy Theories", John M. Olin *Program in Law and Economics Working Paper* No. 387, 2008.

The Church of God International, Who Changed the Sabbath to Sunday? Retrieved fromhttps://www.cgi.org/who-changed-the-sabbath-to-Sunday on the 12th of March, 2021.

The Club of Rome. Retrieved from https://www.clubofrome.org/impact-hubs/climate-emergency/crafting-the-post-covid-world/ on the 11th of March, 2021.

The New World Order. Retrieved from https://dictionary.cambridge.org/dictionary/english/new-world-order on the 2nd of May, 2021.

The Political Organizations of the 1850s (2021: n.p). Retrieved from https://mappinghistory.uoregon.edu/english/US/US21 -00.html.s

White, E.G. *The Great Controversy*. Pacific Press Publishing Association, 1911.

White, E.G. *World crises Foretold*. USA: Shelter Rock Books, 2002.

Wright, N.T. *God and the Pandemics: A Christian Reflection on the Coronavirus and its Aftermaths*. Grand Rapids, MI: Zondervan Reflective, 2020